ballistic missile defense

Policy Sciences Book Series

A Series of Studies, Textbooks, and Reference Works

Edited by YEHEZKEL DROR

Hebrew University of Jerusalem

PUBLISHED

Benson D. Adams
Ballistic Missile Defense, 1971

Yehezkel Dror
Design for Policy Sciences, 1971

Yehezkel Dror
Ventures in Policy Sciences, 1971

Harold D. Lasswell
A Pre-View of Policy Sciences, 1971

Beatrice K. Rome and Sydney C. Rome
Organizational Growth through Decisionmaking, 1971

Walter Williams
Social Policy Research and Analysis, 1971

IN PREPARATION

Joseph P. Martino
Technological Forecasting for Decisionmaking

ballistic missile defense

benson d. adams

american elsevier
publishing company, inc.
NEW YORK · 1971

AMERICAN ELSEVIER PUBLISHING COMPANY, INC.
52 Vanderbilt Avenue, New York, N.Y. 10017

ELSEVIER PUBLISHING COMPANY, LTD.
Barking, Essex, England

ELSEVIER PUBLISHING COMPANY
335 Jan Van Galenstraat, P.O. Box 211
Amsterdam, The Netherlands

International Standard Book Number 0-444-00111-5

Library of Congress Card Number 74-165800

Copyright © 1971 by American Elsevier Publishing Company, Inc.

All rights reserved.
No part of this publication may be reproduced,
stored in a retrieval system, or transmitted
in any form or by any means, electronic,
mechanical, photocopying, recording,
or otherwise, without the prior
written permission of the publisher,
American Elsevier Publishing Company, Inc.,
52 Vanderbilt Avenue, New York, N.Y. 10017.

Manufactured in the United States of America

To JEAN R. BROWNLEE,
to whom I owe more than I can ever repay
and
to the memory of my cousin HANNON
and the happy years we spent together.

Contents

Series Editor's Introductory Note ix
Preface xi
Acknowledgments xiii
Introduction 1

Part I: Nike-Zeus

Chapter 1. The Origin of Missile Defense Efforts in America to 1955   17
Chapter 2. Nike-Zeus—1956 to 1958 22
Chapter 3. Nike-Zeus—1959 to the Kennedy Administration . 32
Chapter 4. The Death of Zeus—1961 to 1963 44

Part II: Nike-X

Chapter 5. Zeus Plus Sprint Equals X—1963 63
Chapter 6. Missile Defense and the Partial Nuclear Test Ban Treaty   76
Chapter 7. Nike-X and Damage Limitation—1964 84
Chapter 8. Opposition to Missile Defense Begins—1964 . . 92
Chapter 9. Missile Defense—The Modular Approach—1965 . 108
Chapter 10. The Year of Surprises—1966 125

Part III: Sentinel

Chapter 11. Sentinel—The Chinese System Decision . . . 145
Chapter 12. The Sentinel Decision—The End of the
            No-Deployment Policy 165

Part IV: Safeguard

Chapter 13. From Sentinel to Safeguard 177
Chapter 14. Safeguard 198

Part V: Analysis and Conclusions

Chapter 15. U.S. Missile Defense Policy in Retrospect . . . 239
Bibliography 250
Index 270

Series Editor's Introductory Note

Despite the critical significance of policymaking for human destiny, very little is known about it. Especially in respect to complex issues on which policy evolves over a long time without single and easily identifiable critical decision events—our understanding approximates zero. Consequently, efforts to improve such policymaking processes lack a reliable empiric basis and are of doubtful validity. Thorough study of complex policy-evolution processes is, therefore, an essential requisite for significant progress in policy sciences.

The book *Ballistic Missile Defense* by Benson D. Adams is such a study of the most complex weapons decision ever faced by the United States. Based on exhaustive study of all available unclassified sources, this book presents an in depth case study of policy evolution. Thus, it constitutes an important brick in the empiric foundations necessary for policy sciences.

Policymaking and its improvement are the main subject and mission of policy sciences. This implies main concern with metapolicies and megapolicies. But direct contributions to better policies on concrete issues are also an essential output of policy sciences. By this criterion too, this book is a valuable volume in the *Policy Sciences Book Series,* because of its significant saliency to better policymaking.

YEHEZKEL DROR

Preface

The central subject of this book is the evolution and formulation of American missile defense policy, the controversy it has engendered, and the factors which have influenced it. Little of the voluminous existing material relating to missile defense deals with policy.

The labyrinth of technical, strategic, and political considerations surrounding the missile defense program is bared here, along with the policy decisions affecting it. The origin, nature, and issues involved in the ballistic-missile defense (BMD) controversy are also delineated. It should be remembered that the primary policy issue concerning missile defense, once the feasibility of developing a missile defense system was established, was whether to deploy it.

The U.S. missile defense policy is important and significant because it is unique. Unlike other post-World War II weapon policy decisions and debates—such as, whether an H-bomb could or should be developed, whether an air defense system of the United States was desirable or feasible (the BMD affair resembles the air defense debate in many respects), or the ICBM/IRBM controversy—the BMD affair is unprecedented in its openness and duration, the public's awareness of it, the role of nongovernmental participants and their influence on the decisionmakers, and the role Congress played. This is in direct contrast to the weapons debates of the late 1940s and 1950s which were resolved relatively quickly and secretly within the Government.

This book should be useful to those engaged in the study of policy analyses and formulation, of the decisionmaking process, and of the interaction of science, military affairs, and public policy. As a case study, it is a complement to a text for a course in policy analysis, science and public policy, or national security affairs.

The author has relied on primary source material, including congressional hearings, speeches, and articles. The writings of the military editors and correspondents of *The New York Times* and *Washington Post* were used extensively.

The author is a firm believer in the strategic defense of the United States as a complement to strategic offensive forces and as an alternative to a strategic offensive arms race. He defines strategic defense as:

> All the operations, actions, preventive measures, precautions, and weapon systems integrated into *a system of defense* to blunt or reduce

the consequences of enemy attack or counterattack to the United States.

A system of defense includes: anti-submarine forces; counterforce attacks; missile, air, and space defense; early warning, surveillance, and intelligence; passive defense; and civil defense.

While the author has undertaken a critical look at policy, he has tried to present the pros and cons of the technical characteristics of the ballistic-missile defense (BMD) systems discussed here and the arguments for and against deployment. He makes no attempt to judge the merits of either the systems or the arguments.

The views, judgments, and opinions contained in this work are solely those of the author and are not to be construed as those of the author's present or past employers.

BENSON D. ADAMS

Washington, D. C.

Acknowledgments

For her understanding, encouragement, patience with my work habits, and help in compiling the bibliography with our son Harris, I want to say "thanks" to my wife, Natalie.

To my son Harris who was always asking, "Do you have to work on your book?" when he wanted to play, I can finally answer, "No."

I owe much to the invaluable editorial assistance and advice of Micci Pope, who saw this manuscript through "n" drafts.

To Jan Baker, Barbara Combs, Iris Gilbert, Elizabeth Hutton, Stephanie Low, Alyce Pink, Zolma Nathanson, Ellen Sapp, Phyllis Smith, and Virginia Veeder I owe many thanks for their collective typing and proofreading efforts.

I wish to acknowledge permission to quote from the following:

> Freeman J. Dyson, "Defense Against Ballistic Missiles," *Bulletin of the Atomic Scientists,* June 1964.

> N. Talensky, "Antimissile Systems and Disarmament," *Bulletin of the Atomic Scientists,* February 1965.

> Senator Strom Thurmond, "The Gap in Ballistic Missile Defense," *Data on Defense and Civil Systems,* June 1963.

Introduction

Ballistic-missile defense (BMD) involves the most costly, complex, and controversial weapon system ever developed by the United States. Presented here is certain background information—on deterrence, the technical aspects of BMD, and strategic weapons development after World War II—which is necessary for understanding how American missile defense policy evolved.[1]

The policy and subsequent controversy which characterized the American BMD effort derived from whether such a system was technically and economically feasible. And, if it were, was it politically and strategically desirable to deploy it?

Deterrence—prevention of attack—depends for its success on psychological factors such as perception, intentions, and behavior. American missile defense policy and the controversy over it stem from differing perceptions and evaluations of Soviet intentions and behavior by American policymakers, their advisers, and the strategic/military community.

Deterrence and American Nuclear Strategy

The cornerstone of U.S. national security policy since the late 1940s has been deterrence or, more precisely, an invulnerable second-strike deterrent strategy. Deterrence is the prevention of action by fear of the consequences. It is a state of mind brought about by the existence of a credible threat of unacceptable counteraction communicated to the enemy by a variety of means—policy statements, statements of intent, diplomatic notes, and

---

[1] A variety of terms and acronyms is used in conjunction with missile defense, including ABM (anti-ballistic missile), which technically refers only to the missile components of a ballistic-missile defense (BMD) system. BMD is used to refer to the complete system, the radars, computers, command, control, communications, and interceptors. Because of the public nature of the missile defense controversy, ABM has become synonymous with BMD and has largely replaced it in public writing. In this study the distinction between BMD and ABM is maintained. Other terms and acronyms used are: AICBM (anti-intercontinental ballistic missile); anti-missile missile; missile defense, meaning against ballistic-missile attack; and the numerous names and acronyms given to particular BMD systems like BAMBI, ARPAT, SABMIS, or ABMIS.

actions. Deterrence is designed to prevent some action inimical to the interests of the deterrer. What that action is must be defined clearly and communicated to the enemy. While deterrence is concerned with influencing the enemy's behavior, his intentions, and his actions, it also must be concerned with the enemy's military capability. Considerations of enemy capability enter into the deterrence equation because a credible threat and the means for carrying it out can be affected if the enemy reduces his fear of the consequences or threatens the survival of the deterrer's retaliatory force by developing and deploying certain kinds of military capability. Deterrence can fail by design or miscalculation.

The United States has adopted a strategy of deterrence to prevent the launching of a nuclear attack against either the United States or its allies by China or the Soviet Union. The means for communicating and carrying out, if necessary, the nuclear threat (of wreaking unacceptable damage to the attacker's cities and population) are embodied in the American strategic offensive retaliatory forces. These forces consist of a triad of weapons: land-based intercontinental ballistic missiles (ICBMs), submarine-launched ballistic missiles (SLBMs), and Strategic Air Command (SAC) bombers.

Since the United States is committed to a second strike—i.e., accepting an attack before retaliating—the deterrent forces must be made invulnerable to nuclear attack so that under any circumstance a portion will survive. Whatever portion survives must be capable of wreaking unacceptable damage to the aggressor's cities and population (countervalue targets). It is this credible threat, to strike against the cities and population of a country and to destroy it as a viable society, that makes deterrence work and the enemy fear the consequences. For the present, both the United States and the Soviet Union have this capability, no matter who strikes first (mutual deterrence).

Mutual deterrence is reasonable, as long as the deterrent equation remains symmetrical. The deterrent balance can be altered in a number of ways: add more offense, provide the offense with a counterforce capability, or add strategic defense. At present, the deterrent equation has been altered unfavorably for the United States by the Soviet Union. The Soviets possess an extensive air defense system and civil defense program and have embarked on the deployment of a missile defense system around Moscow. They are increasing the size of their land-based ICBM force and adding a counterforce capability in the form of a multiple-warhead ICBM, the SS-9. The United States with no missile defense, limited civil and air defense, still relies primarily on offensive retaliation to deter the Soviets. This asymmetrical alteration to the mutual deterrence equation has had two consequences: (1) by deploying and possessing defense, the Soviets may come to fear the consequences less; and (2) by providing a counterforce

Introduction 3

capability, they increase the vulnerability—i.e., reduce the survivability—of the U.S. retaliatory force. In the event of an attack, the vulnerability of the retaliatory force may preclude sufficient numbers of surviving missiles and/or bombers for a credible second strike. In either case, the credibility of the U.S. deterrent threat has been reduced by the introduction of Soviet defense or by the U.S. need to defend against the Soviet's counterforce capability. Central to the missile defense controversy and missile defense policy have been how much and what kind of effect the introduction of defense will have on deterrence. For example, some argue that defense destabilizes in a deterrent environment; others contend that it depends on the enemy's strategy and on the targets being protected.

While the question of defense compatibility with deterrence has formed one part of the missile defense issue, the question of whether such a system could be built and the technical problems solved formed the other. In this country, technological developments for BMD policy have been inseparable from political, strategic, and economic considerations and have proceeded along several lines. To understand the effect of each new technological development on missile defense policy, it is important to understand some of the technical aspects of missile defense and the countermeasures the offense might employ to overcome the defense.

Ballistic-Missile Defense Systems and Concepts [1]

A missile defense system is designed to protect a target system from ICBM attack by intercepting the reentry vehicle(s)—RV—of an incoming enemy ICBM or a shorter range SLBM. Missile defense's contribution to deterrence is to make a missile attack unattractive to a potential enemy.

A BMD system consists of: (1) radars to detect, track, and find the RV; (2) computers that take the radar data and predict trajectories and track objects, distinguish the real RV from decoys, eliminate false targets, and allocate and guide the interceptors to the real target; (3) missile interceptors that carry the weapons used to destroy the incoming RV; and (4) an internetted command, control, and communication system necessary for operating the missile defense.

A BMD system could be ground, air, sea, or space based. Most systems have been ground based, although both a sea-based system (Seaborne Anti-Ballistic Missile Intercept System—SABMIS) and an air-based system (Airborne Ballistic-Missile Intercept System—ABMIS) are being proposed by the Navy and Air Force, respectively. Space-based BMD systems that use satellites have been under consideration intermittently

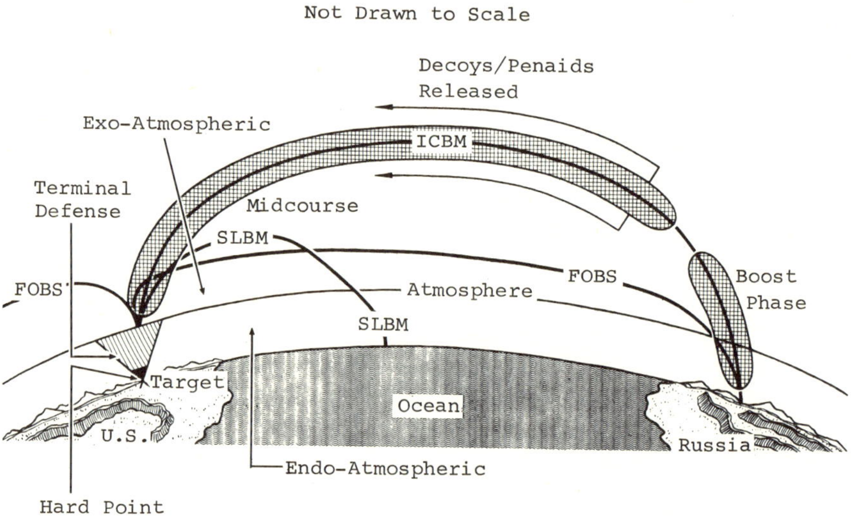

FIGURE 1. Missile Defense Concepts.

for at least a decade since the BAMBI (Ballistic-Missile Boost Intercept) system was proposed.

Any ballistic missile passes through three phases during its flight: the boost phase, the midcourse phase, and the terminal phase. The time of flight, the reentry angle, the altitude reached, and the warning time available to the defense will vary according to the type of missile; i.e., ICBM or SLBM, the point of launch, and the missile's trajectory. Accordingly, a missile defense system can be classified as a boost-phase, midcourse, or terminal defense system. The boost-phase of a ballistic missile lasts between 3 and 5 minutes, during which time the missile motors boost an ICBM to an altitude of 100 miles and an SLBM to 25 miles, and to a speed of about 5.5 miles per second. A boost-phase BMD, then, would have to be positioned near or above the launch site to intercept the offensive missile. This is why most boost-phase missile defense systems now contemplated are space based.

The midcourse phase begins after the missile's motors have cut off and the missile is properly aligned on its trajectory to the target. This is the longest phase of the flight, lasting about 20 to 25 minutes for an ICBM and about 5 to 20 minutes for, an SLBM, depending on the distance at which the missile is launched from the target. During this phase, the missile may coast upward to an altitude of 800 to 900 miles (around 600 miles or less for SLBM) at about 5.5 miles per second; then it starts to fall back toward earth on a ballistic trajectory, as gravity slows it down, and it begins

Introduction

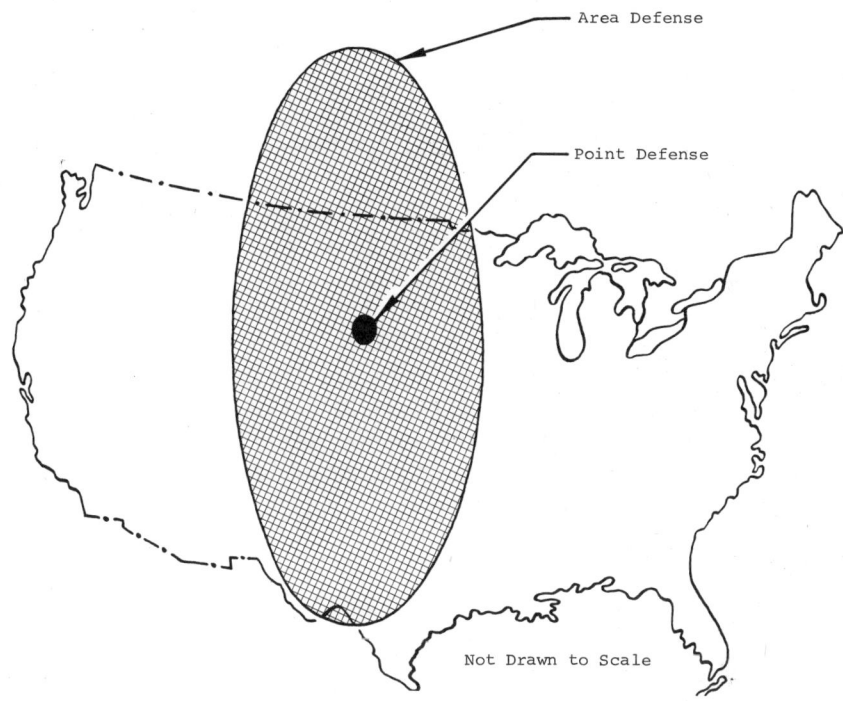

FIGURE 2. Comparison of Area and Point Defense.

its descent into the earth's atmosphere. During the midcourse phase the decoys, chaff, penetration aids (penaids), and multiple independent reentry vehicles (MIRVs) begin to deploy in order to confuse and/or saturate the defense. A midcourse defense is designed to intercept RVs along the midcourse trajectory phase of flight. A characteristic of a midcourse interceptor is its long range; with this capability it is possible to build a few defense sites capable of defending a large area. All midcourse intercept systems are then, in effect, area defenses. The area covered, however, will depend on the flyout time and range of the interceptor and the tactics employed by the offense. A long-range intercept system might conceivably destroy the enemy RV before the decoys, chaff, and penaids deploy.

A terminal defense system engages the enemy RV during its last stage of flight, which lasts about 2 minutes, or less, as the RV is slowing down and reentering the earth's atmosphere (beginning at 400,000 feet down to 150,000 feet). This wide range is due to the effects the RV and the reentry cloud experience as they enter the atmosphere. At about 400,000 feet, the atmosphere spreads and flattens the chaff; at lower altitudes the chaff and lighter decoys are stripped away, dispersed, or slowed at a faster rate than that of the RV, making discrimination possible. At 150,000 feet, the RV has heated up from reentry and its wake is susceptible to radar detection. Allowing the RV cloud to enter the atmosphere and have the atmosphere filter the debris, chaff, decoys, and penaids so that the RV becomes distinguishable is called atmospheric filtering. A terminal interceptor might actually intercept at altitudes of 140,000 feet, or less—the more likely altitude being between 25,000 and 75,000 feet.

A terminal interceptor has a high acceleration rate, a range of tens of miles, and uses a small nuclear warhead to kill the RV. The system requires a high acceleration rate to get out to the RV as quickly as possible in order to use the largest possible warhead that would not affect the target below. Because the system carries a smaller warhead than an exo-atmospheric system, its miss distance must be less—i.e., accuracy must be higher—than systems using large warheads. There would be little direct radiation, fallout, blast, or heat from a terminal interceptor using a small nuclear warhead, because the intercept would take place high enough above the target (5 to 15 miles) to prevent those effects. The short time of the terminal phase and the need to intercept as high as possible to avoid nuclear effects compel a terminal defense to have high acceleration interceptors. Close-in, hard point missile defense is also a terminal defense system, but because the target it is protecting—i.e., an ICBM silo—is hardened, intercept may take place at altitudes as low as several miles. The systems which have forced the U.S. missile defense development effort have been terminal urban defense systems. Only recently, with the advent of the improved SPARTAN (ABM), has an area intercept system been possible. Table 1 outlines the evolution of the NIKE/BMD system. A description of the missile defense problem follows.

Detection—every BMD system must have a detection and surveillance sensor system associated with it in order to search, acquire, and track an object. Most sensor systems use ground-based radars which are limited to line-of-sight detection. Several spaceborne sensor systems using multi-sensor surveillance capabilities, such as infrared, optical, and radar, are deployed to provide additional warning time in the event of attack. The detection and track data are fed into the BMD system's computer.

Discrimination—is the process of screening and sorting all the tankage, booster debris and fragments, decoys, chaff, and penaids from the MIRVs or RVs. The offense could employ electronic jammers or nuclear blackout effects on the radars to aid penetration. A variety of means for discrimination involves both the sensor and computer. These techniques include:

TABLE 1

EVOLUTION OF THE NIKE BMD SYSTEMS—ALL URBAN DEFENSES

Name of System	NIKE-ZEUS	Revised NIKE-ZEUS		NIKE-X	Modular NIKE-X	Building Block NIKE-X	SENTINEL	SAFEGUARD	
Year	1957-1959	1960-1961	1962	1963-1964	1965-1966	1967	1967	1969	1970
Principal Systems and Defense Type — Radars	FAR				VHF Radar (Later UHF PAR)	PAR Early Acquisition	PAR	PAR	PAR
	LAR	ZAR		MAR	MAR	MAR Development Stopped 1969			
	MTR	MTR			TACMAR	TACMAR			
	TTR	TTR	MSR	MSR	MSR	MSR	MSR	MSR	MSR
		DDR							
Interceptors	ZEUS Terminal	ZEUS Terminal	SPRINT Terminal	ZEUS SPRINT	New ZEUS Area SPRINT	Exo-atmospheric Intercept SPARTAN Area SPRINT	SPARTAN SPRINT	SPARTAN SPRINT	Improved SPARTAN SPRINT
Postulated Threat	Unsophisticated	Limited Decoys		Multiple Objects	Same as Nth Country	Multiple Objects Unsophisticated— No Decoys Soviet Chinese Nth Country	Potential for ICBM Defense Light Area Defense Later To Be Expanded to Heavy Area and Terminal City Defense Soviet Chinese Unsophisticated— No Decoys	Soviet Multiple Objects Hard Point Defense of MINUTEMAN Sites Expandable to Light Area Defense Against China SPARTAN SPRINT	Same as 1969 but More and Heavier HPD and Start Site Development for Light Area Defense (5 Out of 12 Sites) Against China
Discrimination Technique						Atmospheric Separation			

Key:

FAR   Forward Acquisition Radar
LAR   Local Acquisition Radar
MTR   Missile Tracking Radar
TTR   Target Tracking Radar
ZAR   ZEUS Acquisition Radar
DDR   Decoy Discrimination Radar

MSR   Missile Site Radar
MAR   Multifaced Phased-Array Radar
VHF   Early Acquisition Phased-Array Radar (VHF)
TACMAR Tactical Multifaced Phased-Array Radar
PAR   Perimeter Acquisition Radar (UHF)
HPD   Hard Point Defense

radar imagery of nose-cone ablation due to heating, atmospheric sorting and filtering, differences in closing speeds, and differences in radar signatures. The computer receives and interprets the sensor data; identifies likely targets; discriminates between warheads and decoys by comparing or matching speeds, radar cross sections, radar imagery and radar signatures produced by various materials, shapes, and masses. In addition, the computer keeps track of objects, eliminates false targets, rejects blackout signals, predicts trajectories and possible aim points, and allocates and guides the interceptors upward toward the RV.

Destruction—for exo-atmospheric kill, destruction is accomplished by X rays and, to a lesser degree, by the electromagnetic pulse (EMP) produced by detonation of a nuclear weapon. For endo-atmospheric kill, nuclear weapons are used, also, but they must be much smaller if they are to avoid destroying the defended target. They depend on neutron kill or blast shock to kill or disable the RV. Nonnuclear kill techniques—for example, hyper-velocity impact methods for missile defense—have been proposed and are being investigated, but they require very high accuracies for sure kill and these are not yet obtainable. For the present, sure kill is still best obtained with nuclear weapons.

The offense can employ a variety of means for penetrating defenses. By using depressed or lofted trajectories rather than optimum-payload, minimum-energy trajectories, the offense can increase the chance of surprise, reduce warning time and probabilities of detection by the defense. The enemy could choose to use SLBMs fired close to the targets, because of their shorter flight times, rather than the ICBM with its longer flight time. The offense can use other means for defeating the defense, such as saturating a target with more RVs than interceptors to exhaust the missile interceptors. The MIRV makes this tactic possible and economical, although MIRV has other purposes than defense saturation. The offense can neutralize the defense by attacking or blinding missile defense radars. It can harden the RVs against the nuclear effects of the defensive missiles. Radars can be deceived by a number of methods. These include dispensing chaff, light decoys, balloons, cones, and heat-resistant decoys; using active electronic countermeasures; and destroying the RV booster in order to create debris and fragments which will return radar echoes. Each of these countermeasures will affect or increase the cost to the defense by: reducing warning and track time; forcing the employment of radars of several frequencies, shifts in radar frequencies, or use of higher power radars; forcing the defense to wait longer than it would like before firing; deploying more interceptors and radars; or developing longer range interceptor systems with forward-based radars which would have to be defended. While the defense would be forced to pay a price, the offense would also pay. It would pay in the form of reduced payloads, lower accuracies, and higher costs to make sure that decoys and penaids were put on credible trajectories, and to provide multiple and maneuverable RVs. As in any other period of weapon development, the dialectic between offense and defense continues in the era of the ballistic missile.

American Strategic Weapon Development since World War II

Even with the experience of German and Allied World War II rocket development still fresh in their minds, several prominent American scientists, called upon in 1945 to advise the fledgling U.S. Air Force on future technological developments, expressed doubt as to the feasibility of intercontinental ballistic missiles and recommended, instead, greater emphasis on jet propulsion.[2] As a result, the United States decided to build an intercontinental jet bomber fleet as the mainstay of its deterrent force. Similarly, it was believed in the United States that the Soviets would also take the bomber route to a nuclear delivery force.

The conclusion in the von Kármán report concerning ICBM feasibility was reached despite Germany's success with its A-4 (V-2) missile and the additional scientific evidence, gathered during the late stages of the war, that Germany had plans for an even longer range A-4; an ICBM to be launched both from land and by submarine, the A-10; and a 3-stage rocket for space exploration [2].

In 1947 a document entitled *Operational Requirements for Guided Missiles* relegated ICBM research to a priority below the development of missiles for air defense, jet fighters, and bombers. In 1947, on the strength of this report's recommendations—which were based on the large size of the A-bomb at that time, the limited research and development

---

[2] This emphasis on jet propulsion was the major finding of a committee headed by the late Dr. Theodore von Kármán in a report published in August 1945 entitled *Where We Stand*. The recommendations of this report were published in December 1945 under the title *Toward New Horizons*, the introductory volume of which was entitled *Science: The Key to Air Supremacy*. The von Kármán Committee was convened by the Chief of the Army Air Force, General H. H. Arnold, who in his "Third War Report to the Secretary of War" foresaw many of the technological developments which were to occur in the 1940s and 1950s. Pages 73–75 of *Science: The Key to Air Supremacy* discussed missile defense. See *The War Reports of General Marshall, General Arnold and Admiral King*, J. B. Lippincott Co., pp. 452–459 and 462–467. It is interesting to note that the eminent director of the Office of Scientific Research and Development, Dr. Vannevar Bush, also doubted the technical feasibility of an ICBM; see his *Modern Arms and Free Men*, Simon and Schuster, 1949, Chapter 8, p. 71, and, in particular, pp. 83–87.

(R&D) funds available, and the von Kármán survey—the ICBM project (MX-774), which was later to be revived as the ATLAS, the first U.S. ICBM, was canceled [3]. Subsequent research on ICBM development was continued privately by the Convair Aircraft Division of General Dynamics, on whose initiative the effort was carried forward until it was revived in 1951 by the Air Force as part of the National Security Council Paper 68 (NSC 68) recommendations [4].

The NSC 68 analysis of American security played a central role in the American rearmament program commencing in late 1949 and is relevant to the BMD affair. This National Security Council analysis was initiated as a result of the fall of China and the Soviet detonation of an atomic bomb. The latter raised the question and precipitated a debate over whether an H-bomb should be developed and whether it was technically feasible to do so. NSC 68 concluded that by 1954 the Soviets would be capable of launching a devastating nuclear attack by bomber on the United States. As a result of this assessment of the Soviet threat, the analysis recommended that *certain* measures be undertaken to strengthen the size and survivability of the U.S. strategic retaliatory forces; i.e., the SAC bomber force. One of the recommendations was to build an active air defense to protect the bombers, provide warning of an attack, and provide a means for defeating a bomber attack without resorting initially to nuclear retaliation. The system was to include: a successive line of trans-Canadian radar early warning systems, dispersed fighter-interceptor groups, deployment of anti-aircraft missile batteries, an airborne alert of a portion of the bomber force, and a hardened and sheltered command and control system to ensure reliable communications in the event of nuclear war.

This commitment to strategic defense eventually precipitated a heated debate (the forerunner of the BMD controversy of the 1960s) among some of the nation's most eminent physicists and scientists, many of whom not only worked on the A-bomb and H-bomb programs but also previously participated in the debate over the feasibility and desirability of developing the H-bomb. The debate over air defense contained most of the same arguments later to be found in the debate over missile defense. The air defense controversy was concerned with whether the money spent on defense might not be better spent on offense to strengthen the credibility of the deterrent, whether a defense was economically and technically feasible, whether offensive countervalue retaliation was the best alternative, and whether countervalue retaliation was morally and ethically acceptable, now that H-bombs existed.[3]

---

[3] A discussion with additional references to the air defense controversy can be found in Samuel Huntington, *The Common Defense,* Columbia University Press, 1961, pp. 326–41, and in Robert Gilpin, *American Scientists and Nuclear Weapons Policy,* Princeton University Press, 1962, *passim.*

Introduction

The thinking, then, in the United States after the war was: until nuclear weapons were refined and reduced in size, an ICBM would be impractical. Although definite progress had been made in the refinement of the Hiroshima and Nagasaki bombs, a light enough warhead which would provide a distinct advantage in destructive capability over aircraft-delivered nuclear weapons was not yet available. The solution to this problem, unknown then, was the later development of the H-bomb. Besides its being relatively inexpensive, the advantage of a thermonuclear weapon was its tremendous energy and destructive capability compared to an atomic bomb. In November 1952 the "Mike" test at Eniwetok confirmed the fact that a thermonuclear device was feasible. The "Shrimp" shot of March 1954 completely revolutionized ICBM design, for it showed that the warhead could be married to the ICBM without the necessity of designing the missile and its huge propulsion system around a large unsophisticated warhead.[4]

While additional problems were to be solved—nose-cone reentry, propulsion systems, accuracy, and reliability—the breakthrough in warhead size and yield radically altered the whole ICBM prospect. The possibility of delivering nuclear weapons over intercontinental distances appeared feasible from both a technical and an economic standpoint.

The Air Force accelerated its own program because of these technical developments, the reports by German rocket engineers and technicians repatriated from Russia that the Soviets were developing ballistic missiles,[5]

---

[4] The reverse procedure was followed by the Soviets, who built their missiles around their large warheads. Consequently, their huge booster rockets were a distinct advantage to them in lofting heavy orbital payloads into space. Additional advantage was to accrue from these large boosters in that they could incorporate extremely high-yield weapon payloads (20 to 40 megatons) or allocate space to penetration aids or decoys in order to fool a BMD system without sacrificing an appreciable proportion of their warhead.

[5] Intelligence had been accumulating since the early 1950s about the Soviet strategic weapons program. See Charles J. V. Murphy, "Krushchev's Paper Bear," *Fortune*, Vol. LXX., No. 6., December 1964, p. 114. According to Marshall Shulman, the Soviet Union decided "to concentrate its resources upon research and development of nuclear weapons, rocket delivery systems, and jet aircraft. . . . The expectation was that this accelerated development of new weapon systems and the continued emphasis in the Soviet economy upon heavy industry would yield a shift in the balance of power favorable to the Soviet Union." Marshall D. Shulman, *Stalin's Foreign Policy Reappraised*, Atheneum Publishing Company, 1965, p. 25. Note that Shulman is writing here of conditions in Moscow in the spring of 1949. The decisions taken about weapons and delivery systems must have been made some time earlier, given lead times. Shulman, Murphy, and other analysts indicate that the Soviets intended all along to develop an ICBM force and deliberately tricked the United States into intensified production of bombers. Another interpretation is that the Soviets started both heavy bomber and ICBM development but thought ICBMs more promising and tried to convince the United States they were building bombers when in fact their whole program had shifted to ICBMs.

and the "certain measures" recommended in NSC 68. In 1953 Trevor Gardner was appointed Special Assistant for Research and Development to Harold Talbott, then Secretary of the Air Force. Gardner established a committee known as the "Teapot Committee"— actually the Strategic Missiles Evaluation Committee—headed by Dr. John von Neumann. It met for the first time on November 7, 1953. The conclusions of this committee were based on a reevaluation of the Millikan Committee's Report of December 1952, which recommended a relaxation of the technical requirements for an ICBM, although it did not recommend an acceleration of the ICBM program. The "Teapot Committee," taking into consideration the technical problems that had been solved since the Millikan Committee Report, foresaw the practicality of having an ICBM operational before 1960. It emphasized that if this nation were to avoid being placed in mortal danger, a new ICBM program would have to be instituted immediately with top national priority (as it was in September 1955 by the President), since "only a quantum jump could avoid catastrophe in the 1959–1960 period." [5] In December 1957, four months after the Soviet test flight, the ATLAS ICBM was successfully fired and met all test objectives.[6]

Soviet Military-Technological Efforts

The Soviet acquisition of an A-bomb by 1949, an H-bomb by 1953, their test launch of an ICBM in August 1957 (before that of the United States), the orbiting of Sputnik in October 1957, and the Soviet testing and deployment of a BMD in 1960 (later suspended) cast into doubt the universal belief that the United States possessed and could hold the technological leadership of the world.[7] While the original Soviet ICBM was very inaccurate,

---

[6] Not the lack of economic resources nor the lack of scientific and technological knowledge, but the failure of the United States to understand weapon technology's potential for political power caused the United States to lose the ICBM, space satellite, and now possibly the missile defense race. The ICBM race revealed a new factor in the cold war: The rapidly changing nature and acceleration of weapon technology had led to a technological conflict between the two superpowers. The cruciality of this conflict is evident when it is realized that any product of military technology which makes possible an advantage for one side over the other may alter the balance of power between the two nations.

[7] The Soviet technological triumphs were the results of espionage; the ruthless shortening of lead times; an extremely early commitment (1921) to mass education as the basic necessity for building a modern, technologically advanced state; extensive pre-World War II basic and applied research on the atomic nuclei and rocketry; a large technical manpower base applied to a massive R&D effort to solve the particular problem; luck; some shrewd decisions; astute, farsighted observations; and a concentrated, centrally managed R&D establishment.

Introduction

nevertheless it could strike the United States directly. It was predicted that in a few years, by 1960–1962, the Soviets would have enough ICBM's to destroy SAC and whatever U.S. ICBMs then existed. Overnight the U.S. superiority in manned-bomber deliverable nuclear weapons was challenged by a radically new means of delivery. The Soviet development and deployment of an ICBM radically altered the strategic balance. The race to develop and deploy an ICBM force began, with the Soviets ahead—if not technically and numerically, then at least psychologically and politically. With the successful development of an ICBM, the search for a defense started.

References

Note: In Chapters 1–15 periodical reference notation can be interpreted as follows: title of periodical, issue number, year in brackets, page(s). At no time is the number immediately preceding the year of publication to be mistaken for the volume number.

[1] Numerous open and unclassified sources deal with the technical aspects of missile defense and the means for defeating it. Some of the best are:

G. W. Rathjens and G. B. Kistiakowsky, "The Limitation of Strategic Arms," *Scientific American*, 1[1970]19.

Herbert F. York, "Military Technology and National Security," *Scientific American*, 2[1969]17.

G. W. Rathjens, "The Dynamics of the Arms Race," *Scientific American*, 4[1969]15.

Hans A. Bethe and Richard L. Garwin, "Anti-Ballistic-Missile Systems," *Scientific American*, 3[1968]21.

Jerome Wiesner and Herbert F. York, "National Security and the Nuclear-Test Ban," *Scientific American*, 4[1964]27.

Leon Dulberger, "Strategic Missile and Air Defense," *Space/Aeronautics*, 4[1966]62.

Michael P. London, "Advanced Strategic Missiles," *Space/Aeronautics*, 6[1968]58.

"Sentinel and Beyond," *Space/Aeronautics*, 4[1968]42.

Michael Getler, "Arms Control and the SS-9," *Space/Aeronautics*, 6[1969]38.

Michael P. London, "Safeguard: Is There a Choice?" *Space/Aeronautics*, 6[1969]48.

Herman Lowenhar, "ABM Radars: Myth vs. Reality," *Space/Aeronautics*, 6[1969]65.

Charles Johnson, "Ballistic Missile Defense Radars," *IEEE Spectrum*, 7[1970]32.

Daniel J. Fink, "Strategic Warfare," *Science and Technology*, 32 [October 1968] 54–68.

Barry Miller, "Studies of Penetration Aids Broadening," *Aviation Week and Space Technology*, 17[1967]90; this whole issue is a "Special Report on Ballistic Missile Defense."

The October 1960 issue of *Astronautics* is devoted to the technical problems of missile defense. See also: Ian Smart, *Advanced Strategic Missiles: A Short Guide*, Adelphi Paper No. 63, December 1969, published by the Institute for Strategic Studies (London); the best single nontechnical discussion of the technical problems of missile defense and offensive missiles.

The United States Air Force Report on the Ballistic Missile, Kenneth F. Gantz, ed., Doubleday, 1958, has some good technical material on ICBMs, pp. 199–270, and on missile defense, pp. 139–150.

Johan Holst and William Schneider, Jr., *Why ABM: Policy Issues in the Missile Defense Controversy*, Pergamon Press, 1969, Part I.

Abram Chayes and Jerome Wiesner, *ABM: An Evaluation of the Decision to Deploy an Antiballistic Missile System*, Signet, 1969, *passim*.

[2] James McGovern, *Crossbow and Overcast*, Paperback Library, 1964, *passim*.

David Irving, *The Mare's Nest*, Little Brown and Co. 1964, *passim*.

Alfred J. Zaehringer, *Soviet Space Technology*, Harper, 1961, pp. 14–30.

Ernst Klee and Otto Meck, *The Birth of the Missile: The Secrets of Peenemünde*, E. P. Dutton, 1965.

[3] Dr. Ernest G. Schwiebert, "USAF's Ballistic Missiles 1954–64," Chapter 2: "Scientists, Too, Are Fallible," *Air Force and Space Digest*, 3[1964]52. See also, U.S. House of Representatives, Eleventh Report by the Committee on Government Operations, *Organization and Management of Missile Programs*, 86th Cong., 1st Sess., 1959, H. R. 1121, pp. 8–14, 69, hereafter cited as *Missile Management Programs*.

[4] Samuel Huntington, *The Common Defense*, Columbia University Press, 1961, pp. 47–53; a discussion of the NSC 68 Paper.

[5] Schwiebert, p. 83.

PART I
Nike-Zeus

CHAPTER 1

The Origin of Missile Defense Efforts in America to 1955

The Precursors of ZEUS

The search for a defense against missiles began on September 8, 1944, when the first German A-4 (V-2) rocket landed in a Paris suburb. In 1945 the General Electric Company's Project Thumper studied possible defense against the V-2. The report concluded that defense was beyond the scope of contemporary technology; the only adequate defense was to prevent the launching of the rocket by destroying or capturing the launch site [1]. Missile defense science also traces its origins to German efforts begun during the war to develop surface-to-air antiaircraft rockets designed to defend against the Allied bomber offensive.

With German wartime work as a basis, an American surface-to-air missile (SAM) was developed. From this effort grew the nation's first BMD system [2].

In 1944 the Army contracted with the General Electric Company for research and development on a long-range surface-to-surface missile and a high-altitude antiaircraft missile. The antiaircraft missile program was Project Thumper. The surface-to-surface program, Project Hermes, began in November 1944 as technical intelligence teams ranged through Germany following American infantry, collecting parts, documents, personnel, rockets, photographs, blueprints, notes, and correspondence from the German rocket program. All this material was shipped to the United States. With the aid of the Dornberger-von Braun team of about 130 rocket scientists brought to this country from Europe under contract (Project Paperclip), 100 V-2 missiles were eventually assembled and fired by General Electric [3]. The Hermes project provided a wealth of scientific and technical data used later for U.S. ICBM and BMD development programs. A consequence of this program was the initiation of high-altitude and upper-atmospheric research programs. Such programs are essential to missile defense and to the understanding of offensive warhead reentry phenomena [4].

Another Army project, initiated in 1945 as Project NIKE, which was to have a profound impact on the BMD program, was the result of the development contract with the Bell Telephone Laboratories and Western Electric Company. This led to the development and engineering of a whole family of antiaircraft missiles from which the ABM eventually emerged [5].

Two other missile projects, which later emerged as rivals to the Army's BMD project during the chaotic years following the first Soviet space and missile firings, were initiated in early 1945 by the Army Air Force (later the U.S. Air Force) and the Navy. The Navy's project was the problem of defending carrier task forces from kamikaze and high speed aerial threats. This project, conducted at the Johns Hopkins Applied Physics Laboratory, was known as Bumblebee. From this research a family of surface-to-air missiles—TALOS, TERRIER, and TARTAR—was developed for shipboard use. The Navy recommended TALOS in 1959 as an ABM rivaling ZEUS.

The Air Force, like the Army and Navy, gained a great deal of knowledge from the Hermes project and the V-2 firings. In 1945 the Air Force and Boeing Aircraft Company initiated the GAPA (ground-to-air pilotless aircraft) project. GAPA was a supersonic research vehicle using both rocket and ramjet propulsion. Later it was merged with G.E.'s Thumper program to develop the "collision intercept" method for destroying a ballistic missile. These were merged later with the University of Michigan's Aeronautical Research Center WIZARD program [6]. WIZARD, like TALOS, was to compete in later years with the Army's BMD system for the missile defense mission. Out of the GAPA project grew the Air Force's BOMARC area air defense missile. The existence of the BOMARC program and the Army's NIKE program triggered a conflict later in the 1950s between the two services over responsibility for U.S. air defense. The resolution of this conflict had significant bearing on the BMD program.

Antimissile design technology grew out of (1) the antiaircraft missile projects; (2) the high-altitude rocket research carried out at White Sands; and (3) the Teak, Orange, Starfish, Bluegill Triple Prime, and three Argus upper-atmosphere U.S. nuclear tests carried out between August 1958 and September 1962. Even before actual development of a BMD began in 1956,[1] scientists and far-sighted individuals pondered the problem of

---

[1] There is some interesting evidence that missile defense work and development were occurring before 1956. For example, it was revealed in 1953 that Sylvania Electric Company had begun work on a mobile field army BMD system called PLATO, which was once considered for use with the NIKE-ZEUS. The project, at first a competitive study between Sylvania and Cornell Aeronautical Laboratories, came under the purview of Sylvania when the Cornell study was terminated in September 1957. The entire project was canceled in 1958. (See *Anti-Missile Defense,* published

Origin of Missile Defense Efforts

defending against long-range ballistic missiles. Much of this conceptualization showed considerable clarity, technical sophistication, and remarkable foresight into the problems later encountered in BMD development.

In 1945 a report entitled *Atomic Explosives for Defensive and Offensive Purposes*, by R. G. Sachs, discussed the problems of defense against bomber formations and missiles of the V-2 type carrying nuclear bombs and/or dummy warheads (decoys) [7]. He wrote of the advantage of using defensive weapons equipped with nuclear bombs to destroy large formations of delivery vehicles. Sachs elaborated on the problem of protecting both the offensive and defensive warhead from radiation effects and the problem of civilian exposure to the atmospheric blasts of defensive nuclear weapons. He concluded:

> . . . it is necessary to recognize that if even a very small percentage of the attacking missiles get through, they will do tremendous damage unless cities and industries have been greatly decentralized. The defense will probably be carried out, in part, with guided AA missiles. It is very likely that at least some of these guided missiles should be provided with atomic warheads from the point of view of economy and of efficiency in action. [8]

This report, though speculative, was highly accurate in predicting the shape of things to come for ballistic-missile defense. In his last war report, also written in 1945, General of the Army H. H. Arnold Commanding General of the U.S. Army Air Forces in World War II predicted the need for an ABM:

> . . . although there now appear to be insurmountable difficulties in an active defense against future atomic projectiles similar to the V-2 but armed with atomic explosives, this condition should only intensify our efforts to discover an effective means of defense. [9]

Bernard Brodie, in *The Absolute Weapon,* published in 1946, discussed the possibility of long-range intercontinental missiles that would carry nuclear weapons. Brodie thought that there was no immediate defense against such

---

by Government Data Publications, Washington, D. C., 1965, p. 59). It was reported that Columbia University in 1951 had set up an electronics research laboratory largely for anti-ballistic-missile studies. Peter Binzen, "Colleges and War: Can Secret Research Be Justified in the National Interest?" *Philadelphia Sunday Bulletin,* May 28, 1967, Sections 2, p. 1. *The New York Times* of November 20, 1957, reported a conversation in which David Greenglass, convicted atomic spy, said that he remembered Julius Rosenberg's telling of passing antimissile secrets to the Soviet Union before his (Rosenberg's) arrest in 1950.

weapons as the V-2.[2] In 1952 Kenneth Gatland, a noted rocket expert, published a book describing among other things a possible missile interceptor rocket, a missile defense system, and the ICBM-ABM duel [10].

Speculation as to what configuration a BMD system might assume was altered drastically in 1953 to 1955, as evidence of major Soviet activity in ICBM development accelerated the U.S. ICBM program and led to the initiation of a BMD program. In November 1955 serious efforts at developing a missile defense system began when the Bell Telephone Laboratories (BTL) undertook a feasibility study for the Army (even before the first ICBM ever flew) on the problems and practicality of missile defense [3] [11]. The Western Electric Company and the Douglas Aircraft Company supported BTL in this effort.

In 1956 the Bell Telephone study was completed under the direction of the Army Rocket and Guided Missile Agency (ARGMA). During the same year, ARGMA issued R&D contracts to Bell Telephone, Western Electric, and Douglas for basic research on a BMD system. In 1957 the NIKE-ZEUS Guided Missile Defense System Project was established by the Ordnance Technical Committee, Headquarters U.S. Army. In 1958 the Committee authorized ZEUS as a full-scale development program.

References

[1] *Toward New Horizons.* A report submitted to General of the Army H. H. Arnold on behalf of the Army Air Force Scientific Advisory Group by Th. von Kármán, December 1945.

[2] Thirteen years later in his classic book *Strategy in the Missile Age,* Brodie wrote "the old adage that every new offensive development inevitably provokes the development of a suitable defense is hard to justify historically, and it is certainly excessively optimistic for the nuclear era. One should hesitate especially to apply it to the ballistic missile. That is not to say that effective active defenses against the missile are technically impossible, or their development should not be pursued; it is only to point out that one must have extraordinary faith in technology, or a despair of alternatives, to depend mainly on active defenses. The relevant problems are political and social as well as technological." p. 221.

[3] BTL was selected for the ABM study effort because of its long experience in developing surface-to-air missiles, dating to 1944, when it undertook Project NIKE. From this project evolved the Army antiaircraft missiles NIKE-AJAX and HERCULES. The third-generation member of this family of antiaircraft missiles, ZEUS, was to become an ABM. It was revealed in the May 20, 1970, *Washington Post,* p. A1, that Bell Laboratories would not be accepting any new missile defense business after 1972, but that they would complete work on the SAFEGUARD BMD program. The reasons given were to devote resources to other technical problems and to avoid antiwar protests.

[2] *Missile Management Programs,* p. 8.

[3] For more information on the U.S. technical intelligence effort see:

Michael Bar-Zohar, *The Hunt for German Scientists,* Hawthorne, 1967.

Samuel Goudsmit, *Alsos,* Henry Schuman, Inc., 1947.

Clarence G. Lasby, "Operation Paperclip: German Scientists Come to America," *The Virginia Quarterly Review,* 3[1966]366, Summer 1966, pp. 366–377.

[4] "G.E. Reveals Hermes Missile Milestones," *Aviation Week and Space Technology,* 10[1954]26.

[5] U.S. Senate, Preparedness Investigating Subcommittee of the Committee on Armed Services, *The United States Guided Missile Program,* prepared by Charles Donnelly, 86th Cong., 1st Sess., 1959, p. 4, hereafter cited as *U.S. Guided Missile Program.*

[6] Schwiebert, p. 152.

[7] R. G. Sachs, *Atomic Explosives for Defensive and Offensive Purposes,* deleted copy, Ballistic Research Laboratory Report No. 590, 1945, declassified with deletions by the Atomic Energy Commission, August 19, 1958.

[8] Sachs, pp. 11–12.

[9] *The Third War Report of General H. H. Arnold,* p. 464, in *The War Reports of General Marshall, General Arnold and Admiral King.*

[10] Kenneth Gatland, *Development of the Guided Missile,* Philosophical Library, 1952.

[11] *Missile Management Programs,* p. 125.

CHAPTER 2

Nike-Zeus—1956 to 1958

Conflict and Organization

Before research on ZEUS began, a political conflict arose between the Army and Air Force. The dispute concerned jurisdiction over (1) tactical air support, (2) continental air defense, (3) intermediate and intercontinental ballistic-missile development, and (4) military airlift. To help ease the confusion and controversy associated with the decade-old American missile program, Secretary of Defense Charles Wilson issued a directive on November 26, 1956, to the members of the Armed Forces Policy Council, entitled *Clarification of Roles and Missions to Improve the Effectiveness of Operation of the Department of Defense*.[1] This directive attempted to clarify the responsibilities of and limitations on each service with regard to several matters, including guided missiles.

This directive gave the Army responsibility for developing, procuring, and manning land-based, surface-to-air missiles for point defense. The Air Force was assigned responsibility and control over land-based, surface-to-air missiles for area defense.[2]

Unfortunately, this directive did not specify the threat—i.e., air or missile threat—to which each type of defense was to be addressed. Moreover, until the systems were ready for development and testing, it was not known whether area or point defenses would be more effective. The directive did not indicate which service was to have operational control over a defense system, once it was developed and deployed. Despite the directive, the conflict over the air and missile defense systems of the Army

---

[1] The text of the directive can be found in *U.S. Guided Missile Programs*, p. 114.
[2] The directive delineated the point from area defense as follows: "Area and point defense systems cannot be defined with precision. Area defense involves the concept of locating defense units . . . remote from and without reference to vital installations, industrial complexes, or population centers." Several paragraphs later, the directive states: "One distinguishing feature of point defense missiles is that their guidance information is received from radars located near the launching sites. The present state of the art justifies development of point defense surface-to-air missile systems for use against air targets at expected altitudes out to a horizontal range of 100 nautical miles."

(NIKE-HERCULES and ZEUS) and those of the Air Force (BOMARC and WIZARD) continued.

Early in 1956, with missiles assuming a greater role in U.S. defense policy, Secretary Wilson reestablished the Office of the Director of Guided Missiles (it had been dissolved in 1953), but renamed it Office of the Special Assistant for Guided Missiles. By 1957 the BMD program was a joint Army–Air Force effort which was monitored by the Anti-Ballistic Missile Committee of the Department of Defense. Each service was working on its own solution to the problem. Despite additional reorganizations and reconstituted advisory and coordinating committees between 1956 and 1958, it was never clear whether coordination and ultimate responsibility for BMD were to be with the Defense Department or with a particular military service, and whether this military service would be given responsibility for coordinating all R&D projects of a joint or interdepartmental nature [1].

On November 15, 1957, Secretary Wilson's successor, Neil H. McElroy, changed the name of the Office of the Special Assistant for Guided Missiles to the Director of Guided Missiles. The function of the director, unlike the special assistant, was to guide "all activities in the Department of Defense relating to research, development, engineering, production, and procurement of guided missiles." [3] [2] More confusion resulted when the Department of Defense Reorganization Act of 1958 created the post of Director of Defense Research and Engineering (DDR&E). Dr. Herbert York, Chief Scientist for the Advanced Research Projects Agency (ARPA), was appointed Director of DDR&E. Early in December 1957 it was reported that the Air Force was to establish the Directorate of Astronautics to deal with BMD, satellites, and futuristic weapons. The directive was suspended two weeks later, when it was learned that the President was to announce the creation of ARPA in his State of the Union Address in January 1958. ARPA, a part of DDR&E, was created to direct all BMD and satellite development efforts. Until recently, ARPA exerted considerable influence on the BMD development program through its Project Defender.[4] Project Defender was transferred to the

---

[3] The Director's Office was dissolved again in 1959.
[4] The Project's formal task called for research, experimentation, and systems feasibility studies to determine the technological possibilities of advanced defenses against exoatmospheric offensive vehicles (i.e., to find something better than ZEUS). Its aim was to explore fundamental phenomena, develop new concepts, and apply new techniques. Project Defender was divided into five working parts: (1) general research and development (lasers, atomic and nuclear physics), (2) techniques and devices (radar, optical, infrared), (3) missile phenomenology (launch, midcourse, terminal), (4) systems and concepts (BAMBI, GLIPAR, ARPAT), and (5) penetration aids.

Army in March 1968 and is now known as the Advanced Ballistic Missile Defense Agency.

ARPA had a mandate to issue instructions to the military; to eliminate duplicate or unpromising programs; and to approve, modify, or disapprove programs and projects in the military.

As one of its functions, ARPA was delegated to oversee the BMD program and to investigate all possible defenses against space vehicles and ballistic missiles. ARPA was a new kind of agency—a small management team concerned with advanced research in weaponry projects of potential military significance. Having its own budget and being administratively above the three services, the Agency could concentrate on advanced research without involvement in immediate service requirements and interservice rivalries.

The ZEUS Program Begins

The NIKE-ZEUS feasibility study, completed in October 1956 by Bell Telephone Laboratories, looked promising enough to warrant spending an additional $30 million for additional studies and initiating a development program [3].

The principal system elements of NIKE-ZEUS consisted of various radars and the ZEUS rocket. Radar components were the forward acquisition (FAR) and local acquisition (LAR) radars. The former was designed as a surveillance radar capable of scanning the entire visible sky within a 1,000-mile range. The system was designed to operate as follows: The FAR would acquire the ICBM and maintain continuous surveillance at a range of about 600 miles; then it would give information on the incoming target to the LAR. LAR would track the target, acquire trajectory data, and assign these data to target track radars (TTR). TTR would then take over automatically from LAR and furnish continuous and precise trajectory information to the computers, which would determine the intercept point. ZEUS was a command guidance system like all the NIKE missiles (i.e., it required two radars: one for target acquisition and one to track, guide, and command the missile to intercept). In NIKE-ZEUS, the latter function was performed by the missile-track radar (MTR).

Coordinating the flow of information from all these detection devices and directing it to the ZEUS was the Target Intercept Computer (TIC). Its role was to solve guidance and control problems by integrating TTR and MTR data as soon as possible. The entire TIC operation had to be automatic and continuous to cope with the high speed of the RV and the short time available for missile flyout and intercept.

The NIKE-ZEUS rocket was originally designed as a third-generation SAM to counter supersonic bomber threats. The Bell Laboratories feasibility study indicated its potential as a missile interceptor. However, in keeping with the arbitrarily assigned range limitation of Secretary Wilson's November 1956 memorandum assigning point defense to the Army, the ZEUS originally had only a 100-mile range[4]. This would not be the first time that arbitrarily set range limitations would hinder ABM interceptors. ZEUS consisted of a booster and two stages. The first missile interceptor version of ZEUS was designed to counter only the single warhead RV of an ICBM. This version could not discriminate decoys and penaids from RVs.[5] But decoys and penaids then were only a concept; in fact the United States was only beginning to understand reentry phenomena.[6] Decoys and other aids were not yet available to U.S. ICBMs in the late 1950s and certainly not to the Soviets. Yet the fact that ZEUS could not discriminate figured heavily in the arguments not to deploy it, even though the need for discrimination in the late 1950s was virtually nonexistent. Even if the booster and tankage were deliberately fragmented to hide the RV, there would have been time for atmospheric filtering of the debris because of the limited range of the ZEUS interceptor. In the late 1950s, RV technology—shapes and materials—was in its infancy and the RVs were big blunt objects with large radar images, not the slim conical systems of today.

By September 1957, the ZEUS program was moving into the component development stage after a year's experimental work. Component development was a necessary preliminary to full-system development, according to the testimony of Secretary of the Army Wilber M. Brucker before the Senate Subcommittee on Preparedness in December 1957 [5]. At this time an intensive interservice fight was shaping up over the feasibility of BMD and its operational jurisdiction. The Air Force's area defense BMD (WIZARD), while still being designed, was promoted by the Air Force as this country's chief BMD system (even though ZEUS was two years ahead of it). The Army appeared very optimistic about ZEUS. Testifying before

---

[5] It should be noted that the U.S. penaid/decoy program did not start until 1961.
[6] In July 1958, Dr. Ernest Stuhlinger, Director of the Research Laboratory at the Army Ballistic Missile Agency, said during an interview concerning the results of Operation Gaslight: "One of the most important things we learned during Operation Gaslight was how to discern a warhead from a missile body as it reenters the atmosphere. This is extremely important from an anti-missile standpoint." In light of this statement and the absence of any decoys or penaids deployed on U.S. missiles in 1958, the argument offered by ZEUS opponents that ZEUS could not discriminate seems ill-founded. Operation Gaslight was a series of photographic, spectrographic, and radiometric studies made of the U.S. JUPITER intermediate-range ballistic missile (IRBM) reentry on May 18, 1958. See "Operation Gaslight: Anti-Missile Breakthrough," *Missiles and Rockets,* July 14, 1958, p. 14.

the same Senate committee as Brucker, Army Chief of Staff General Maxwell Taylor stated: ". . . I am quite confident of our ability to move forward into the anti-missile-missiles field . . . ." [6] Earlier, Taylor had said that the United States could not only have a missile defense but it could have it at a reasonable cost [7]. Others in the Defense Department did not share the Army's enthusiasm; usually they felt the weapon to be prohibitively costly or technically infeasible.

When asked about ZEUS by Senator Stuart Symington (D-Mo.), Defense Secretary McElroy said: "The problem is not a fiscal problem, but is a technical problem," and although there might have been a fiscal constraint placed on the ZEUS program, it was not the "limiting factor in the progress of the anti-missile-missile program." [8]

On November 7, 1957, the Gaither Committee submitted its report to President Dwight Eisenhower. The report of this committee has never been released or made public, but over the years participants, or those with access to participants, have revealed various aspects of the committee's report. Among the several assignments given this committee was "to study the deterrent value of our retaliatory forces and the economic and political consequences of any significant shift of emphasis or direction in defense programs." [7] As a result of this charge the committee undertook an examination of active and passive defenses as they contributed to deterrence and what protection they afforded the country in the event deterrence failed.[8] One of the recommendations of this committee, to be given the highest priority, was BMD protection of SAC bases against a possible future Russian missile attack.

While the Air Force was engaged in developing an area BMD system (WIZARD) of its own and vying for operational control of the BMD program if and when it were deployed, it opposed the Army's BMD concept, arguing that offensive retaliation (an Air Force mission) was the best defense. The Air Force was also urging the Joint Chiefs of Staff (JCS) not to deploy the Army's ZEUS because: (1) it could be deceived; (2) the Air Force would lose some of its area defense responsibilities; (3) it

---

[7] This section is based on the testimony of Dr. Robert C. Sprague before the Senate Armed Services Committee, June 23, 1969. Sprague came to head the Gaither Committee upon the illness of Rowan Gaither, its original head. See *U.S. Congressional Record*, 91st Cong., 1st Sess., June 25, 1969, pp. S7166–7169. The quotation is found on p. S7167; the BMD recommendation on p. S7168.

[8] It is interesting to note that another member of the Gaither Committee, Dr. Jerome Wiesner, later President Kennedy's science advisor and a leading BMD opponent, wrote in his book, *Where Science and Politics Meet,* McGraw-Hill, 1965, pp. 44–45, that the Gaither Report stressed the futility of trying to provide security through a combination of active and passive defense.

Nike-Zeus—1956 to 1958

was good only against an unsophisticated RV; (4) it would cost as much as the whole ICBM program; (5) a deterrent to war must be based on offensive capability; (6) the Army's missile was technically infeasible; (7) it could not be deployed before 1961, the period of the anticipated "missile gap"; (8) it would lead to the creation of a Maginot Line complex;[9] and (9) the Soviets would probably not remain idle in creating offensive capabilities if a defense against the ICBM were found [9]. With few exceptions, any time BMD deployment seemed likely, these same arguments would reappear. In fact, many of these same decade-old arguments were used in the great BMD debate of 1969, despite the tremendous improvements in missile defense since ZEUS.

On January 16, 1958, as a result of this interservice rivalry, Secretary McElroy sent directives to the Army and Air Force delineating responsibilities for continuing the development of an anti-missile system. The Air Force was told:

> ... to continue as a matter of urgency that portion of its current development effort in the WIZARD program that pertains to early warning radars, tracking and acquisition radars, communication links between early warning radars and the active defense system, SAGE [semi-automatic ground environment, an air defense control center], and the data processing components required to form an integrated system. These above elements are to be compatible with a missile system having design and performance characteristics as described for the NIKE-ZEUS weapon system. The Air Force program will be limited at this time to the work in the above areas.

To the Army went orders:

> ... to continue development effort in the NIKE-ZEUS program as a matter of urgency, concentrating on system development, that will

---

[9] The Maginot Line was not an ill-conceived concept. The concept envisioned a heavily fortified line designed to halt a German offense between Montmedy and Switzerland. Its size and strength gave it an aura of impenetrability. A fatal weakness of the Line was that it could be turned and enveloped from the rear. To compensate for this weakness several farsighted proponents of armor warfare suggested that the Line be *backed* by numerous highly mobile and independent French armored task forces to fill any breech in the Line. Unfortunately, the conservative, cautious, and defense-minded French High Command, supported by the Defense Ministry, never understood how armor might be employed except in direct support of the infantry. Consequently, despite the superiority of their armor compared to Germany's, their inability to comprehend the use of armor as an independent striking force doomed the Line. People not understanding this came to see in the Line's failure a monument to the stupidity of the military and its ill-conceived expensive ideas. In the author's opinion, the real significance of the Maginot Line is the failure of those in power to heed new ideas.

demonstrate the feasibility of achieving an effective, active AICBM system in an electronic counter-measure and decoy environment.

The program will be limited at this time to work on the missile and launch system, and those acquisition, tracking, and computer components required for an integrated missile system [10].

This directive failed to specify which service was to have operational control of the system except that the Army was to develop it.[10] At House hearings on the matter of operational control of the BMD, Deputy Secretary of Defense Donald Quarles indicated that no decision had been made. The Chairman of the House Armed Services Committee, Carl Vinson, was not satisfied by this answer, fearing a repetition of the earlier U.S. Army-Air Force feud over THOR-JUPITER IRBM development and control, wrote a letter to Secretary of Defense McElroy stating that total responsibility for developing and operating the BMD should be assigned to the Army. Several months later, in Senate Defense Appropriations hearings, Quarles said that the Army was in complete charge of BMD development and operation. The directive also appeared to be giving ARPA overall authority and control for developing both the missile defense and the detection system network. The Army was directed to transfer $57 million of its budget to ARPA for work on ZEUS. However, because of the urgent need for missile defense, both services were to continue without any unwarranted duplication but under ARPA's direction. The rapid progress made by the Army resulted in the $57 million's being restored. Until the dissolution of the Office of the Director of Guided Missiles in 1959, the BMD program was left under that office's direct supervision, while ARPA was responsible for advanced research in the field.

Secretary McElroy, resuming his testimony before the Senate Preparedness Subcommittee on January 22, 1958, reported that the BMD project was given top priority and that $195 million was earmarked for the program:

> . . . these funds will accelerate development of this system's readiness for production, and will be devoted primarily to research and engineering aspects instead of actual production and development which, in our judgment, would at this time be premature. Funds will be used for a variety of associated purposes including test sites, range instrumentation, facilities, etc. This project also includes a broad approach to fundamental problems involved in the advancement of the state of the art in radar, guidance, radiation phenomena, etc. [11].

---

[10] In 1970 no decision had been made as to who would control SAFEGUARD, except that the Army would develop it.

This was the first of the eight successive and almost identical pronouncements by Secretaries of Defense which, while development activities would continue, would consider production and deployment of an ABM as being premature.

Later hearings by the subcommittee revealed the Air Force's unhappiness with the split jurisdiction between area and point defense; also, doubt as to the feasibility of shooting down an ICBM.

Two months after McElroy's January 1958 directive halting the WIZARD program, the Air Force appealed the Defense Secretary's decision, claiming that the Army's ZEUS did not have the growth potential to handle possible enemy evasion, decoy, and countermeasure tactics. In addition, the Air Force agreed with the Senate Preparedness Committee's resolution to "put more effort into developing anti-missile missiles." [12] The Air Force, therefore, urged that it be allowed to continue the WIZARD program. It reasoned that WIZARD would be a competitive and back-up BMD system to the ZEUS.

Dr. Richard C. Raymond of General Electric TEMPO (Technical Military Planning Operation), speaking at the Third Annual Air Power Symposium in Salt Lake City in March 1958, predicted that *both* a long-range area defense ABM and a short-range system, the latter corresponding to the Army's ZEUS, would be developed. Dr. Raymond argued that the present ZEUS system would become obsolete before it became operational because of ICBM improvements [11] and new detection methods. His dual concept of anti-missile defense included the Air Force WIZARD program. Dr. Raymond agreed that for point defense of hard targets using the atmosphere to filter warheads was adequate, especially if the protected points were missile sites where the defended missile could be launched before the attacking warheads detonated. With soft targets, such as cities, an area defense was absolutely necessary. An area defense would require the ability to discriminate warheads from decoys beyond the atmosphere [13]. Dr. Raymond's speech was highly prophetic of the NIKE-X BMD system of 1963–1967 and the present SAFEGUARD system.

As a result of Secretary McElroy's earlier testimony regarding the prematurity of producing ZEUS, the Defense Department cut $507 million from the Army's request for production funds. The Army felt the system should be deployed immediately because the risk in not doing so was be-

---

[11] In 1958 the Office of the Secretary of Defense convened a committee to investigate the hypothetical penaids which could be available to the offense. The committee reported on the feasibility of the offense's employing decoys, chaff, tank fragments, reduced radar reflectivity, nuclear blackout, and multiple warheads. See Herbert F. York, "ABM, MIRV, and the Arms Race," *Science*, 3942[1970]257, July 17, 1970, pp. 257–260.

coming greater. Because of delay in the appropriations, ZEUS production would be delayed at least a year. Secretary McElroy, relying on his advisers (principally those at ARPA), favored postponing the decision until the missile system was more fully developed. ARPA scientists advised the Secretary that too many unknowns were associated with intercepting an ICBM. In particular, ARPA's Chief Scientist, Dr. Herbert York, wanted to investigate the various phenomena associated with reentry before making any commitment to deployment [14].

In November 1958, Dr. Richard Holbrook, a scientist in ARPA's missile defense group, said during a speech at the Atlanta Chapter of Sigma Delta Chi (the honorary journalistic fraternity) that the then currently envisaged version of ZEUS would not provide an effective defense against multiple RVs, decoys, penaids, and radar jammers unless many interceptors were bought [15]. Holbrook's speech prophesied the offensive situation at the end of the 1960s rather than at the end of the 1950s.

At the Geneva Surprise Attack Conference [12] convened in November 1958, Western arms control experts drafted a proposal for deploying a BMD system with its attendant sensors to warn and cope with a surprise ICBM attack. The conference ended in December 1958 as the Soviets and Western Allies could not agree on an agenda and differed over whether the conference was to be technical or political [16].

At year's end there was every indication, too, that the Army-Air Force feud about roles and missions would be revived over BMD development and control.

References

[1] *Missile Management Programs,* pp. 16–17.

[2] *U.S. Guided Missile Program,* p. 43.

[3] *Missile Management Programs,* pp. 134–136.

[4] U.S. Senate, Preparedness Subcommittee of the Committee on Armed Services, *Inquiry into Satellite and Missile Programs,* Part I, 1957, 85th Cong., 2nd Sess., p. 581, hereafter cited as *Satellite and Missile Programs.*

[5] *Satellite and Missile Programs,* p. 476.

---

[12] This was one of several arms control and disarmament conferences of the post-World War II period. See *United States Defense Policies Since World War II* prepared by Charles H. Donnelly of the Legislative Reference Service of the Library of Congress, House Document No. 100, 85th Cong., 1st Sess., GPO, 1957, pp. 56-58, for a brief review of these conferences and proposals.

[6] U.S. Department of Defense News Release No. 1053–57, October 28, 1957, p. 5.

[7] Both quotations from *Satellite and Missile Programs,* p. 253.

[8] Jack Raymond, "Air Force Urges Joint Chiefs Bar Army Missile Bid." *The New York Times,* November 21, 1957, p. 1.

[9] U.S. House of Representatives, Committee on Armed Services, *Hearings on Investigation of National Defense Missiles, Pursuant to House Resolution 67,* 85th Cong., 2nd Sess., 1958, p. 4196.

[10] *Satellite and Missile Programs,* Part 3, pp. 2359–60.

[11] *Satellite and Missile Programs,* Part 2, p. 2017.

[12] *Satellite and Missile Programs,* Part 2, p. 2315.

[13] "Dual Missile Defense Predicted," *Aviation Week and Space Technology,* 13[1958]27.

[14] "Army Unhappy on Nike-Zeus Cut," *Missiles and Rockets,* 3[1958]32.

[15] "Nike-Zeus May Be Inadequate, Top Defense Scientist Warns," *Aviation Week and Space Technology,* 19[1958]33.

[16] U.S. Library of Congress, Legislative Reference Service, *United States Defense Policies in 1958,* prepared by Charles H. Donnelly, House Document No. 227, 86th Cong., 1st Sess., 1959, hereafter referred to as *U.S. Defense Policies in 1958.*

CHAPTER 3

Nike-Zeus—1959 to the Kennedy Administration

As a result of (1) Secretary McElroy's January 1958 directive giving the Army responsibility for ZEUS development and the Air Force responsibility for the BMD surveillance system, and halting the WIZARD program of the Air Force; (2) the creation of ARPA to direct all other BMD research; and (3) a major reorganization of the Department of Defense; the earlier Army-Air Force conflict over BMD development appeared to be resolved. However, a new controversy was developing between the proponents of ZEUS (i.e., the Army) and its opponents in ARPA, the Air Force, and the Department of Defense. This controversy revolved around BMD's technical feasibility.

In 1959 Army-Air Force competition for missile defense funds got under way at its usual brisk pace. The Air Force was engaged in developing the Ballistic-Missile Early Warning Systems (BMEWS) and doing additional BMD work under ARPA. The Army, continuing its work on ZEUS, requested additional production funds (there was sufficient R&D money) to speed the program toward a 1962 operational date. General Taylor, Chief of Staff, stated the Army's position in congressional testimony:

> My reservation in this area arises from the unopposed ICBM threat and my conviction that the importance of obtaining this unique anti-missile weapon at the earliest possible date out-weighs the possible financial risks inherent in initiating selective production [1].

The Air Force and Navy contended, however, that additional funds for production were premature, claiming that some of the new approaches to missile defense would make ZEUS obsolete. Roy W. Johnson, Director of ARPA, presented that agency's program for advanced studies in missile defense. One of the primary areas of exploration was the flight dynamics of missiles and their reentry into the atmosphere. Johnson said that a BMD system should be: (1) technically feasible, (2) capable of reacting to all missile threats in all types of environments, (3) economical, and (4) operational at the earliest possible date. The criteria, as stated, did not apply to ZEUS; whether this was deliberate, because of ARPA's opposition to ZEUS, or whether a better approach to BMD appeared feasible, is unknown. However, Johnson said that present advanced BMD efforts were designed to "leapfrog" the weaknesses of ZEUS, which were the inability to identify the enemy warhead from other objects and decoys and lack of a satisfactory positive mechanism for destroying the RV [2].

By 1959 the Air Force clarified its position on missile defense. Air Force Assistant Secretary of Defense for R&D Richard E. Horner told the House Appropriations Committee that a careful analysis of the WIZARD system had demonstrated that it would cost more than it was worth. The Air Force, Horner said, also felt this way about ZEUS, arguing that ZEUS could easily be overwhelmed by attacking RVs. The Air Force believed that missile defense money might better be spent for increased offensive capability [3]. This is an important point and is elaborated in the following paragraphs.

Emphasis on offensive capabilities has been the dominant theme of the Air Force in the post-World War II period when it was given the mission of delivering nuclear weapons. The creation of the Strategic Air Command (SAC) to deliver these weapons, the pervasive influence of SAC in the Air Force, and its fascination with bombers have been obstacles to deploying and maintaining strategic defense forces, both air and missile defense. The Air Force's position is based on a belief in the supremacy of the offense, the guarding of its roles and missions, and a belief once held that only it should possess the bomb and its means of delivery, subordinating everything else to that mission. The nuclear weapon and its means of delivery were the penultimate for carrying out Douhet's theory of strategic air warfare—destroy the enemy's will to resist by destroying his cities and population.

At the heart of the nuclear deterrent strategy of the United States is the ability to destroy an aggressor's cities and population. Once the Soviet Union achieved this capability, vis-à-vis the United States, it was felt that a certain amount of security would prevail in the world because of mutual deterrence. If the only purpose of the U.S. nuclear war forces, as most Americans believe, is to deter war, then any change by the Soviets in the deterrent equation can be met by increasing the number or type of U.S. offensive deterrent forces. Defense, then, is viewed as a waste of money which could best be spent on offensive retaliatory forces to maintain a credible deterrent. While this strategic argument has been used by opponents of BMD, it also supports the Air Force view which favors emphasis on offensive weapons.

While the Army wanted to continue the ZEUS development program, it also wanted to produce and deploy it, but the Administration was against producing ZEUS. For fiscal 1960, beginning July 1, 1959, the Army recommended $1.3 billion for the ZEUS program. This figure included $300 million for research and development and $700 million for tooling, production facilities, and some ZEUS bases. Later this figure was reduced to $620 million. By the time it reached Congress, the budget-minded Administration had pared the total request to $300 million. In the end, the $300 million was approved and Congress voted an additional $137 million to begin production of ZEUS [4]. However, the Administration refused to allow the Army to spend the $137 million, feeling that the system was not ready for deployment and questioning whether a workable defense was possible. A committee (the Skifter Committee) was appointed to evaluate the technical feasibility of ZEUS by February 1960 in order to determine whether it should be produced.

The policy of funding missile defense research and development, but not approving deployment and production, was a consistent pattern of U.S. missile defense policy until September 1967. This "dual" policy points up the policymaker's dilemma.

Given the Soviet "believed" ICBM threat: Should money be spent to procure a weapon whose ability to destroy ICBM RVs is questioned? With this dual policy—money for R&D and none for production—the threat is of secondary importance to the budgetary considerations. For, if the system proves workable, then its operational deployment probably would be delayed beyond the time it was required. Conversely, if the system proves unworkable, then significant amounts of money will have been saved by not producing it. In either case, a calculated risk had to be taken, since no defense would exist when it was needed.

These attacks on the ZEUS compelled the Army to defend its position. The Army contended that ZEUS could provide adequate point defense of vital targets and prevent U.S. retaliatory forces from being destroyed on the ground. The existence of ZEUS would increase the cost of a Soviet attack and raise doubt whether the attack would even succeed. Its real advantage was in the system's growth potential and capability to counter Soviet decoys, which, it was asserted, the system was then capable of detecting in limited numbers. The system's greatest weaknesses were that it could be easily saturated;[1] it was less than perfect, and the detonation of a defensive warhead at too low an altitude could just as effectively destroy the target ZEUS was protecting as it could an enemy warhead.

While the arguments for and the limitations of ZEUS which the Army advanced were concurred in by many other experts trying to view the problem objectively, the Army asked: If ZEUS were canceled and the money put into more offensive missiles as the Air Force argued, how much

---

[1] This was at the time of the supposed "missile gap."

better off would the United States be as the Soviet ICBM threat continued or it developed a BMD of its own? Over the next several years, these arguments were to become crucial in the BMD controversy.

Aside from the Administration's doubt about the weapon's technical feasibility, the projected and anticipated cost of ZEUS was a prime consideration in ruling against the system's deployment. With a presidential election year approaching, the Administration was preoccupied with balancing the budget and maintaining defense spending at no more than $40 billion. Given these circumstances, it would be difficult to expect the Administration to go along with the Army's estimated $2 billion fiscal 1961 budget request for ZEUS deployment. Because any money for production would have to come from the $40 billion defense budget, any decision to produce and deploy ZEUS around American cities had to be made by the White House.

A major difficulty of ZEUS deployment was its great cost. Since the services had no additional funds, the Administration would have to raise the defense budget. While this would upset the budget and the plans for a tax cut, a decision not to deploy ZEUS could provide a real campaign issue. By 1959 it was apparent that the BMD issue was far "more involved with dollars, strategy, and politics than with technology." [5]

Phillip J. Klass, a senior editor of *Aviation Week and Space Technology,* reported that the Skifter Committee, headed by President Eisenhower's scientific advisors, Dr. George Kistiakowsky and Dr. H. R. Skifter, recommended continuing the ZEUS project at least through the scheduled 1962 full-scale Pacific tests [6].

Klass argued that it was militarily and psychologically unsound for a country not having a first-strike strategy to depend solely on offensive deterrence without providing some defense. Since ZEUS is the only ABM available, why not take a calculated risk and deploy it? The critics argued that the huge Soviet ICBM boosters allowed the Soviets to carry a variety of decoys and warhead packages. And it is in this very capability to sort decoys from warheads that ZEUS is ineffective. There was no evidence, however, that the Soviets had any decoys. Moreover, the Army contended that by the time the Soviets had acquired them, ZEUS would have a discrimination capability. Until the discrimination problem was solved, contended the ZEUS opponents, the practicality of missile defense was limited. As ARPA scientists on the Down-range Anti-missile Measurement Project (DAMP)[2] pointed out, it was the inability to discriminate warheads from tankage,

---

[2] The Army and ARPA had earlier begun the DAMP Project to gain data on missile detection and tracking phenomena during the terminal phase of all U.S. missile tests.

boosters, ionization, and whatever else showed upon radar signal returns (and not what an ABM could or could not protect) which affected the feasibility and desirability of ZEUS.

By the end of 1959, the ABM was no nearer deployment than it was in 1957–58. However, considerable research and development funds had been and were being expended on missile defense, both by the Army and ARPA. The continued reluctance of the Administration to deploy and produce the system appeared to be based more on political and economic than technical considerations. Yet, according to official testimony, it was the technical uncertainties which determined whether ZEUS would be produced, not the political or economic (see below). The Army stood alone in its insistence that ZEUS was effective and had growth potential, but the reservations and doubts of higher authorities prevented the Army from going ahead with production. As 1960 began, the controversy over the missile defense program focused on whether to produce and deploy the system before results of the research and development tests were known.

Secretary of Defense Gates, responding to questions by Chairman George Mahon (D-Tex.) of the House Appropriations Committee, said that only time would tell if a credible solution to ballistic-missile defense were possible.

Secretary Gates said that the program:

> . . . was given an enormous amount of consideration by the President's Scientific Advisory Committee, by our Director of Research, by the Joint Chiefs of Staff. It was a very important decision from the standpoint of the defense of the United States and, second, financially. The first one is much more important than the financial because an antimissile defense is vital—if it can be successfully developed. [7]

He said that the ZEUS program was being pushed as a developmental effort and that ARPA was spending more than $100 million annually for missile defense exploratory efforts.

The Army's position was best expressed by General Arthur G. Trudeau, Chief of Army Research and Development:

> Since my last appearance before this committee there have been continuing demonstrations of the growth potential of the NIKE-ZEUS system. Design changes, resulting in significant improvement in system performance, have already included increases in power, sensitivity of radars, and improvements in the design and effectiveness of the missile itself. On the basis of progress to date, I am confident that the ZEUS system will achieve its design objective, that its growth potential is dynamic, and that it can and will be successfully developed to meet and master the ballistic missile threat of the Soviet Union . . . . [8]

Dr. Herbert F. York, Director of DDR&E, said in his presentation before the committee:

> After the most painstaking review it was decided to press forward as rapidly as practicable with the research, development, test, and evaluation of this system, but not to place it into production. The funds required for fiscal 1961 will provide the necessary radars, computers, target missiles, defense missiles, test range facilities, and other equipment required to carry out a full scale realistic test program to determine the operational feasibility of the complete NIKE-ZEUS system. It is expected that these tests will provide the basis for a final decision . . . . [9]

Dr. York, in testimony at times vague and contradictory, argued that the objectives of BMD were: (1) to protect the deterrent force and (2) to protect the population. Both of these objectives, he suggested, could be accomplished by means other than ZEUS, which was vulnerable to saturation and was unable to discriminate. These means included: passive defense; air and ground alerts; hardening, mobility, and dispersing the deterrent force; and building shelters for the population. While it was necessary to create an effective missile defense, and he urged continued efforts to develop an ABM, Dr. York thought ZEUS was not the answer because of its susceptibility to saturation and vulnerability to attack [10]. But Dr. York did not believe that the money being spent on ZEUS was being wasted. Since "the area of ballistic missile defense is probably the most important research and development area in which the Department of Defense is operating," he felt the expenditures for ZEUS were providing the knowledge and experience on which some future BMD system might be based [11]. Dr. J. P. Ruina, Assistant Director for Air Defense in DDR&E, said that the Joint Chiefs concurred in fiscal 1961 with the decision not to deploy ZEUS.[3]

According to General Austin Betts, Director of ARPA, the heart of the problem was whether or not decoys could downgrade the system. Another question, he said, was whether the Soviets would ever waste rockets just to carry decoys (this testimony was given before the advent of multiple warheads) and whether decoys were practical and efficient. Betts also asked whether, given lead-time considerations, the defense deployed then (1960) or in 4 or 10 years was going to match the offensive threat. While advocates of ZEUS claimed the system had growth potential and would be able to discriminate decoys effectively, this did not change the fact that "our knowledge today of the over-all re-entry physics and

---

[3] Both Dr. York and Dr. Ruina were to oppose SAFEGUARD.

related decoy problem is inadequate." The technical uncertainties and high cost of this questionable system pervaded the entire issue, Betts felt, and had to be resolved in order to meet the arguments of those opposed to missile defense [12].[4]

By March 1960, it was clear that a decision to produce and deploy ZEUS would not be forthcoming because of political and economic considerations. A temporary freeze on fiscal 1961 spending for ZEUS was announced in February while the Administration reexamined the program's research and development requirements.

The likelihood for deploying ZEUS was set back in early 1960 by the results of Project Defender's GLIPAR program. GLIPAR involved the investigation and testing of all novel and extreme ideas for missile defense. Some of the suggested schemes included: fields, plasmas, "death ray" beams, solid material impact, cold gases, use of H-bombs to release X rays, and use of large nuclear weapons outside the atmosphere to destroy everything (warheads, tankage, decoys, etc.). While several ideas were proved infeasible, many could not be tested at all. Therefore, the GLIPAR program concluded that no promising solution to the ICBM defense problem within the bounds of available scientific knowledge appeared possible in the 1970–80 period [13].

By August the Army indicated that ZEUS was now ahead of schedule because (1) the radar range had been increased to 1,000 miles, (2) radar power had been doubled, and (3) an increased ability to discriminate and track reentry vehicles now existed. It was also revealed that full-scale test firings at Kwajalein atoll in the Pacific would start in early 1962.

In October *The New York Times* reported that the Soviets were working on an ABM similar to ZEUS. This was the start of the aborted (1962) Leningrad BMD deployment [14].

ARPA revealed during the same month that, under the aegis of Project Defender, a series of feasibility studies had been initiated with Boeing, Convair, TRW (Thompson-Ramo-Woolridge, Inc.), and the Lockheed Aircraft Company to investigate a satellite-borne anti-ICBM defense system. This project was designed to kill ICBMs in the boost phase of their flight. Earlier, TRW completed a study called RBS (Random Barrage System) which projected the employment of a multitude of armed satellites to detect and destroy ICBMs before burnout. Convair worked on a competing design called SPAD (Satellite Protection for Area Defense), which

---

[4] Betts pointed out, for a nonaggressor nation (i.e., one committed to a second strike), a strong active defense is the best hope of destroying the enemy's offensive capability. In effect, an active defense is a counterforce capability. It suggests the intention of restraint and nonaggressiveness. Later, as Chief of Army Research and Development, Betts was to become a staunch supporter of the Army's BMD program.

Nike-Zeus—1959 to the Kennedy Administration

used a polar orbit pattern rather than the TRW random orbit approach [15]. These systems had a number of drawbacks, tremendous cost to maintain large numbers of satellites in orbit, international political objections to having armed satellites in orbit, and the long development time associated with obtaining an operational capability (probably not before 1975).

In November 1960, after the Democrats had won the Presidential election, the Army began a major campaign to accelerate the ZEUS program in the upcoming legislative battles of 1961.[5] The Army's strategy was to argue that it had made such rapid developmental progress and technical advances that ZEUS was six months ahead of schedule. The Army decided to ask for enough money to begin full-scale production (which would commit the Defense Department to spend between $5 billion and $15 billion over the next 9 years). In an attempt to win its campaign, the Army formed a committee headed by Richard S. Morse, Assistant Secretary of the Army for Research and Development, to survey the ZEUS program to see if it was far enough along to warrant committing funds for production and site development. The committee consisted of Defense and White House representatives. Additional support for the Army's position came from Representative Overton Brooks (D-La.), Chairman of the House Committee on Science and Astronautics, who wanted the Defense Department to release the extra $137 million voted by Congress the year before.

As in the previous six years, the Army stood alone in its convictions that the system would work. It continued to oppose Air Force allegations that ZEUS was ineffective and that BAMBI was better—although BAMBI would not be ready until 1975. It had to answer the Administration's technical questions if it were to forestall the political decision not to produce the system.

By 1960 NIKE-ZEUS entered its second phase. The major difference between the revised NIKE-ZEUS system and its predecessor was in the combining of the FAR and LAR acquisition radars into a single ZEUS Acquisition Radar (ZAR). The ZAR was composed of two units: a transmitter with a huge triangular antenna and a receiver. Under operating conditions, the ZAR was to pinpoint an incoming target and place it under

---

[5] When (in 1961) it was decided to postpone deployment of NIKE-ZEUS, *Army Magazine* (the official magazine of the Association of the United States Army) for February 1961 appeared with a special issue promoting ZEUS. In it there were several advertisements by the prime contractors and their subcontractors depicting the role of each in the ZEUS program. Most fascinating was a two-page map showing the distribution and allocation of the $410 million ZEUS contracts in each of 37 states, with California and New Jersey getting the largest shares. Within two weeks after this issue appeared, a number of representatives and senators urged the immediate production of ZEUS.

the surveillance of a Decoy Discrimination Radar (DDR), an addition to the original ZEUS system. The Army, feeling that earlier criticism directed against the discrimination capability of ZEUS was valid, added the DDR to the missile system. The DDR supplied the information required to separate the real warhead from the decoys and penaids. Once the target was identified, the TTR (Target Tracking Radar) took over, as in the original system.

In the first six years of its development, the BMD system had remained on schedule throughout its various research, development, testing, and evaluation phases. At the same time, components were added in order to counter the more sophisticated threats which seemed to be developing. Yet the story of these first six years is one of technical advancement and political frustration; on two occasions during the Eisenhower Administration the decision was made to withhold production and deployment of ZEUS. In 1960 the Army predicted that it could begin deploying ABMs around key cities by 1963 if it were given funds to initiate production. Again, despite continuing congressional support, the Administration withheld permission for production, ordering instead that all tests be completed and evaluated before a decision on production was made. The Joint Chiefs of Staff supported the Administration's position, and recommended that research and development on the NIKE-ZEUS system continue, thus delaying still further the earliest date of deployment. Under different circumstances, this would not necessarily have been important but, with evidence being gathered of a Soviet effort to develop and deploy a BMD, time became crucial, and the effort to develop and deploy a BMD became a technological, political, and military race between the Soviet Union and the United States.

Opposition to BMD

Within the American scientific community, opposition to ZEUS was mounting. Dr. Edward Teller, one of the key developers of the U.S. H-bomb skeptical of ZEUS's ability to shoot down an ICBM, felt that, while one missile might be able to shoot down another, the enemy's means of baffling a BMD were relatively cheap compared to the cost of shooting down the ICBM [16].

In December 1960 one of the first clear-cut statements against deploying even an effective missile defense system was made by Dr. Jerome Wiesner, soon to be President Kennedy's science advisor and a prominent figure in the opposition to missile defense. At the Sixth Pugwash [6] [17]

---

[6] Pugwash is an informal meeting of East-West scientists to deal with a variety of scientific problems affecting international relations, especially the question of

Conference held in Moscow at the end of 1960, Dr. Wiesner presented a number of specific proposals aimed at achieving mutual deterrence and maintaining strategic parity between the United States and the Soviet Union. He said:

> It is important to note that a missile deterent system would be unbalanced by the development of a highly effective anti-missile defense system and if it appears possible to develop one, the agreements should explicitly prohibit the development and deployment of such a system. [18]

As early as 1960, the impact of advancing weapons technology was making it clear to some individuals that economic and technical resources were being expended on weapons but that no additional security was being attained for either the Soviet Union or the United States. At the same time, technology was not yet capable, so it was thought, of developing a defense against the ICBM. ICBMs (made invulnerable) properly deployed by both sides, it was believed, could bring about a stable international environment. The most important task confronting the world was to slow down the arms race, allow both sides to acquire equalized invulnerable strategic deterrents based primarily on hardened or submarine-launched ballistic missiles and then eliminate the danger of nuclear war by de-emphasizing advanced technology which might upset the stable situation [19].

References

[1] U.S. Senate, Joint Hearings Before the Preparedness Investigating Subcommittee of the Committee on Armed Services and the Committee on Aeronautical and Space Sciences, *Missile and Space Activities*, 86th Cong., 1st Sess., 1959, p. 23.

---

disarmament. The initiative for the conference came from Bertrand Russell English mathematician, philosopher, and disarmament advocate and it was financed by Cyrus Eaton, an industrialist sympathetic to the Communists. The name derives from Eaton's estate in Nova Scotia, where the first conference was held. In the early 1960s, as arms control literature increased, it became apparent that measures of arms control might be accomplished through informal rather than formal political talks. Pugwash was an example of these informal talks. At the Sixth Pugwash Conference, the scientists felt that building mutual confidence between the Soviet Union and America was essential to ending the arms race. A number of individuals associated with BMD and some who opposed it attended the Pugwash Conferences on arms control, some later becoming U.S. Government officials, advisers, and consultants. See J. Rotblat, *Pugwash—The First Ten Years: History of the Conferences of Science and World Affairs* (New York: Humanities Press, 1969) for a complete list of the attendees through the 16th Conference, September 1966.

[2] U.S. House of Representatives, Committee on Appropriations, *Department of Defense Appropriations for Fiscal Year 1960,* Part 6, 86th Cong., 1st Sess., 1959, pp. 108–110, hereafter referred to as *House Appropriations for FY 1960.*

[3] *House Appropriations for FY 1960,* pp. 164–174.

[4] U.S. Library of Congress, Legislative Reference Service, *United States Defense Policies in 1959,* House Document No. 432, 86th Cong., 2nd Sess., 1960, p. 24, hereafter cited as *U.S. Defense Policies in 1959.*

[5] James Baar, "Painful Nike-Zeus Choice Draws Near," *Missiles and Rockets,* 44[1959]18.

[6] Phillip J. Klass, "Defense Group Evaluates ZEUS Potential," *Aviation Week and Space Technology,* 18[1959]31.

[7] U.S. Congress, House, Hearing Before the Subcommittee of the Committee on Appropriations, *Department of Defense Appropriations for 1961,* Part 1, 86th Cong., 2nd Sess., 1960, pp. 30–31, hereafter cited as *House Defense Appropriations FY 1961.*

[8] *House Defense Appropriations FY 1961,* Part 6, pp. 117–118.

[9] *House Defense Appropriations FY 1961,* Part 6, p. 14.

[10] *House Defense Appropriations FY 1961,* Part 6, pp. 42–44, 105.

[11] *Missile Management Programs,* pp. 43, 58.

[12] Brigadier General A. W. Betts, Director of ARPA, "Stop that Missile," *Ordnance,* 243[1960]345, November-December 1960, p. 345.

[13] James A. Fusca, "Future ICBMs Look Unstoppable," *Missiles and Rockets,* 6[1960]12, March 7, 1960, p. 12, and *Anti-Missile Defense,* Government Data Publications, Washington, D.C., 1965, p. 16, hereafter cited as *Anti-Missile Defense.*

[14] Jack Raymond, "U.S. Says Russians Plan Anti-Missile," *The New York Times,* October 15, 1960, p. 3.

[15] *Anti-Missile Defense,* pp. 37, 46, and "ARPA Studies Satellite-Borne Anti-ICBM Defense System," *Aviation Week and Space Technology,* 18[1960]33.

[16] U.S. Library of Congress, Legislative Reference Service, *United States Defense Policies in 1960,* prepared by Charles Donnelly, House Document No. 207, 87th Cong., 1st Sess., 1961, p. 57, hereafter cited as *U.S. Defense Policies in 1960.*

[17] Additional source material on Pugwash can be found in: Department of State, Foreign Service Institute, *Bibliography on Science and World Affairs,* November 1964, pp. 152-157. For a comprehensive study of the role and impact of Pugwash and of Soviet influence at the first five Pugwash Conferences, see U.S. Congress, Senate, Subcommittee to Investigate the Administration of the Internal Security Laws of the Committee on the Judiciary, *The Pugwash Conferences,* 87th Cong., 1st Sess., 1961. See also: Duane Thorin, *The Pugwash*

Movement and U.S. Arms Policy (New York: Monte Cristo Press, 1965) and *Proceedings from Pugwash to the World of Disarmament,* Sabrepen Syndicate, McLean, Virginia, 1964.

[18] Jerome Wiesner, *Comprehensive Arms Limitation Systems,* text of a paper prepared for and delivered to the Sixth Pugwash Conference, Moscow, November 29, 1960; p. 247 of the *Conference Proceedings.* An edited version of Wiesner's paper can be found in his book *Where Science and Politics Meet* (New York: McGraw-Hill, 1965).

[19] From the Foreword by Dr. Wiesner in the Special Arms Control Issue of *Daedalus,* 4[1960]678.

CHAPTER 4

The Death of Zeus—1961 to 1963

The inauguration of a Democratic President in January 1961 gave impetus to a thorough-going examination of U.S. defense policies. NIKE-ZEUS, a center of controversy from its inception, was one of the items considered. The Kennedy Administration had two major questions about ZEUS: (1) was it technologically feasible and (2) would its costs be commensurate with its capabilities?

The New York Times of February 18, 1961, carried an interview with the chiefs of Army research and development (military and civilian) [1]. The chiefs felt that a large-scale Soviet BMD and other strategic missile efforts would lead to an alteration in the balance of power. Richard Morse, Assistant Secretary of the Army (R&D), asserted that Soviet efforts had been going on for a long time and that the NIKE-ZEUS should be committed to production if the United States was to avoid losing the BMD race. The Joint Chiefs, in a reversal of their 1960 position against ZEUS production, agreed with this assessment. For the first time, the military publicly confirmed the existence of a Soviet BMD effort. Until then detailed reports of the Soviet effort had been almost nonexistent, although *The New York Times* had reported it in October 1960.

The Army renewed its efforts for beginning long leadtime component production for ZEUS, arguing that a BMD system was necessary for enforcing a disarmament agreement (it would provide security against cheating) and for hedging against the accidental firing of an ICBM. However, resistance was building up in DDR&E against any production decision until questions about the system's technical feasibility were answered.

Meanwhile, the Air Force in conjunction with the Aerospace Corporation was pursuing its boost intercept (BAMBI) program and various concepts for intercepting ICBMs using satellites. BAMBI was still years from completion. Unlike previous Army-Air Force differences over air and missile defense jurisdiction and responsibility, the Army had no objection to the Air Force program which was funded by ARPA, except to argue that ZEUS could be in operation long before BAMBI at considerably less cost than the likely $10 billion for BAMBI.

The Death of Zeus—1961 to 1963

On April 4, 1961, while outlining the need for a defense against ICBMs to the Senate Armed Services Committee, Defense Secretary Robert S. McNamara [1] discussed ZEUS progress:

> . . . tests of components, ground radar and the first and second stages of the missile are now in progress at the White Sands and Point Mugu missile ranges. Late this year the complete missile will be fired, and next year the first tests against single ATLAS-boosted target missiles will begin. Formal system demonstration is scheduled to begin in the summer of 1962. [2]

The advantages of ZEUS, he said, mean that:

> Successful development may force an aggressor to expend additional resources to increase his ICBM force. It would also make accurate estimates of our defensive capabilities more difficult for a potential enemy and complicate the achievement of a successful attack. Furthermore, the protection that it would provide, even if for only a portion of our population, would be better than none at all. [3]

These points, McNamara said, are used by proponents of the system to justify production of certain long leadtime ZEUS components. He questioned the validity of beginning production, since:

> There is still considerable uncertainty as to its technical feasibility and, even if successfully developed, there are many serious operating problems yet to be solved. The system, itself, is vulnerable to ballistic-missile attack, and its effectiveness could be degraded by the use of more sophisticated ICBM's screened by multiple decoys. Saturation of the target is another possibility, as ICBM's become easier and cheaper to produce in coming years. Finally, it is a very expensive system in relation to the degree of protection that it can furnish. [4]

Therefore, he and the President recommended:

> . . . that we not undertake ZEUS production at this time, but that we proceed to develop ZEUS as rapidly as money will permit it to be developed and we are recommending, as you have seen, $270 million for that purpose in fiscal year 1962. [5]

---

[1] Considerable insight about the direction, goals, and assumptions of U.S. defense policy can be gained from a study of the BMD issue as discussed in the Annual Posture Statements of Secretary of Defense Robert S. McNamara. McNamara was the chief architect of the nation's BMD policy for over seven years. It was during this period that U.S. missile defense policy shifted from a technical issue and military problem to a political issue.

In the congressional testimony which followed, McNamara revealed how he made his decision. McNamara said he listened "to proponents and opponents, both of whom were advancing the national interest, both of whom were specialized in certain aspects of the problem." [6] Furthermore:

> In the case of ZEUS, I asked the five senior Bell Laboratory executives working on the problems to come down to my office and meet with me and the Deputy Secretary for 2 or 3 hours to discuss the ZEUS system in great detail. [7]

He discussed ZEUS with the JCS, Service Secretaries, and the scientific community. The scientific community, McNamara pointed out, did not act with one mind when dealing with highly controversial matters. On the question of ZEUS, many of its members had opposing views. McNamara said:

> The decisions were made by the President, based on recommendations which I made, based on long and exhaustive personal analysis and discussions with the parties concerned. [8]

In his decision not to order deployment as the Army wanted before ZEUS was fully developed, McNamara pointed out that the expenditure of funds for the procurement of facilities and production of materials would be wasted if subsequent changes were made in later stages of design and development. To hedge against the technical-military uncertainty associated with ZEUS, including its vulnerability to attack, ARPA, in Project Defender, was studying other BMD systems [9].[2]

Congressman Phil Weaver (R-Neb.) asked McNamara whether evidence of the Soviet deployment of BMD would affect his decision. McNamara replied:

> I do not believe it would affect my recommendations in any way because I have assumed that we must take account of the possibility that they will have such a system. [10]

Secretary of the Army Elvis Stahr, testifying on the Army budget, advocated limited production for ZEUS, since it was the free world's only BMD and therefore worth the investment. An additional reason for be-

---

[2] One such system was called ARPA Terminal Defense (ARPAT). ARPAT was automatically to detect and identify hostile ICBMs after their launching, then guide a dart-shaped platform into the atmosphere (20,000 to 100,000 feet) where it would dispense a multiplicity of hypersonic projectiles in random patterns against incoming warheads. The ARPAT concept was a step beyond ZEUS because of its ability to fire large numbers of defensive missiles from one launch vehicle, whereas ZEUS required one launch vehicle for each defensive warhead launched.

ginning production, said Stahr, was the evidence of Soviet BMD activity. Stahr felt the investment in BMD would not be wasted, since the scientific fallout in the form of new radar and propellant technology and reentry information for ICBM development would present returns equally as valuable as the original investment in ZEUS. Stahr voiced confidence in the system and in its ability to discriminate decoys from warheads, although he had no proof that it could discriminate. In keeping with Secretary McNamara's decision, Stahr suggested a continuing review of the entire BMD program [11].

The effect of these decisions was once again to deny ZEUS production funds, although the system continued to meet all technical deadlines.

Indicative of the controversy over ZEUS, General Lyman Lemnitzer, Chairman of the Joint Chiefs of Staff, pointed out:

> There are differences of opinion in the Joint Chiefs of Staff, but in my own experience, the differences are not nearly as great on the military aspects of NIKE-ZEUS as they are within the scientific community on the technical aspects of the NIKE-ZEUS. I do not see why there should be a great hue and cry made about differences of military opinion on NIKE-ZEUS, and no reference whatsoever made to the wide variety of differences in scientific and technical circles on the same weapon systems.[3] [12]

Chief of Staff for the Army, General George Decker, testified:

> ... due to the serious military, political, and psychological disadvantages which would ensue if the Soviets were to deploy an anti-missile system before we do—the Army will continue to press forward with the NIKE-ZEUS development, in order to ensure its earliest possible availability. [13]

Several members of Congress in 1961 were quite active in promoting the NIKE-ZEUS. The leading spokesman in the Senate for deploying BMD has been and still is Strom Thurmond (R-S.C.) who has since been joined by several others, including Senator Henry Jackson (D-Wash.). As early as 1961 Thurmond (then a Democrat) argued the Army's case for going into production of NIKE-ZEUS because this system "can provide the defense this Nation needs to meet and master the intercontinental ballistic missile threat." The early deployment of ZEUS, he said, will "reduce lead

---

[3] It was later brought out that the Joint Chiefs did recommend beginning limited production on NIKE-ZEUS, but the decision was not unanimous. Lemnitzer explained that even though a majority of the Joint Chiefs of Staff concurred on a given issue, this did not always become the view of the corporate body. The dissenters have a right to carry their views to the Secretary or even the President.

time to an irreducible minimum; keep the Army-industry team and facilities together, and reduce the time the United States is without adequate defense." [14] Senators Everett Jordan (D-N.C.), Frank Carlson (R-Kan.), and later, Karl Mundt (R-S.D.) associated themselves with Thurmond's position.

Later, Representative George P. Miller (D-Calif.) urged:

... the time has come for the Administration, Congress, the press, and our people to face the fact that the United States will struggle in a straitjacket if it does not parallel its retaliatory ICBM with an antimissile-missile defensive weapon system against the ballistic blackmail of the Soviet Union.[4]

... Unless we have such a defense in being within the next 2 or 3 years, the United States will be wide open for another Pearl Harbor disaster— a disaster indescribable in terms of liberty, lives, and treasure. [15]

On February 13 Representative Daniel Flood (D-Pa.) argued for producing NIKE-ZEUS: "... a defensive capability assumes the same importance as the ability to retaliate, if we are to survive." [5] Flood continued:

The nation that first develops and deploys an adequate defense against intercontinental or submarine-launched ballistic missiles will enjoy a strategic advantage. If such a defense is first developed by Russia, we can expect extensive offensive military action or ballistic blackmail. The Soviets will no longer depend upon economic, political, psychological, or limited war offensives to attain their goals. [16]

On March 13, 1961, Representative Flood read the reply he received from the White House acknowledging receipt of his letter to President Kennedy. The reply said: "The Secretary of Defense is fully aware of the urgency attached to this matter and is taking every reasonable action to develop and deploy an effective anti-ballistic missile weapons system at the earliest practical date." [17]

---

[4] Miller had read into the *Congressional Record* the lead editorial of the February 1961 *Army,* which was devoted entirely to the NIKE-ZEUS.

[5] Flood sent his statement and a copy of the January 31, 1961, issue of *Missiles and Rockets* (a special series of articles devoted to NIKE-ZEUS) to President Kennedy. Flood thought so much of this issue that he sent a copy to each member of the House with the comment, "this series, in my experience, represents the most thorough and comprehensive analysis of a major weapons system presented in public print during these recent years of revolutional [sic] progress in science and technology." Senator Thurmond sent a copy of the same issue to every member of the Senate.

The Death of Zeus—1961 to 1963

While the question whether the United States *should* deploy NIKE-ZEUS was being debated, the United States, by virtue of its Declaration to the United Nations General Assembly on a Program for General and Complete Disarmament, committed itself on September 25, 1961, to a reduction in the number and levels of strategic vehicles, including BMD. This proposal for general and complete disarmament (GCD) based the reduction of arms on a number of stages, each of which involved inspection and verification [18].

The Soviets shattered the 34-month-old unofficial nuclear test moratorium on September 1, 1961, by testing a nuclear weapon in the atmosphere. This Soviet program continued through October 30, 1961.

On November 2, 1961, President Kennedy ordered preparations made for resuming U.S. atmospheric testing, pending an evaluation of the Soviet tests.

There were conflicting opinions as to the purpose of the 1961 Soviet test series. Some of the Soviet tests involved large-yield weapons (5 megatons or over) which were thought to be much too big for defensive missile warheads. However, the authoritative British technical journal *The Aeroplane and Astronautics* described in detail a method for destroying ICBMs using electromagnetic pulse and particle radiation; both are emitted during the explosion of nuclear and thermonuclear weapons [19].[6] Part of the purpose of the Soviet test series then could have been devoted to developing a kill mechanism for a missile defense system. Hanson Baldwin, former military editor of *The New York Times,* reported a number of years later that two Soviet ICBMs simultaneously were destroyed in 1961–62 during one of the Soviet atmospheric nuclear tests [20].

The implications of the Soviet tests for the perfection of BMD, more than anything else, compelled the United States to resume its own atmospheric nuclear testing program in order not to fall behind the Soviets in BMD [21].[7] There were indications that the Soviets had been developing

---

[6] These methods were known in theory, but determination of whether they would work demanded test data. Publicly, little was revealed about how an ABM might kill an ICBM, although methods had been alluded to in the press. L. Kraar writing in the March 20, 1959, *Wall Street Journal* ("Missile Defenses," p. 13) reported that nuclear blasts in space could cause defensive radar blackouts and present the possibility of using some form of radiation effect to destroy ICBM warheads. Probably Kraar was basing his statement on some of the upper atmosphere tests of the previous year (1958) carried out in the South Atlantic and Pacific Oceans.

[7] As a result of the Soviet test and announcements about their gains in missile defense, ARPA announced the HELMET Project. Designed to avoid saturation and discrimination problems, HELMET destroyed everything that was reentering the atmosphere in front of, behind, under, above, or alongside the warhead reentry vehicle. HELMET was eventually terminated because the nonnuclear kill mechanism

missile defenses as far back as the the late 1940s. In October 1961, Marshal R. Malinovskii Soviet Minister of Defense stated, at the 22nd Party Congress, "The problem of destroying rockets in flight has been successfully solved." [22] Not only was there a race between the Soviet Union and the United States to find a defense against ICBMs, but there was a race to deploy it first.

At his November 8, 1961, news conference, before the analysis of data about the Soviet tests, President Kennedy said that the United States must maintain its lead and superiority in nuclear weapon development. Should the data reveal that the Soviets had made advances in their knowledge of high-altitude nuclear phenomena, then commensurate action to ensure U.S. security must be taken [23].

In the meantime, President Kennedy had appointed a panel to evaluate the Soviet tests and make recommendations concerning resumption of the U.S. testing program. The Chairman, Dr. Hans Bethe, a Nobel Prize winner in physics, professor of physics at Cornell and director of the theoretical physics division at Los Almos during World War II, became a spokesman against resumption of testing, arguing that the low yield of the Soviet weapon tests (1 to 5 megatons) indicated that the Soviets were actually developing a MINUTEMAN type of missile (i.e., a hardened U.S. solid-fuel ICBM with small warheads for counterforce attacks rather than the large warheads then on Soviet missiles) for "city busting." Dr. Bethe believed that Soviet testing lessened the danger of war, because it indicated a Soviet intention to build an invulnerable deterrent which, when complete, and in conjunction with the U.S. invulnerable deterrent, would lead to stability. This argument for each side's possessing an invulnerable deterrent was the forerunner of the mutual-deterrence concept. Dr. Bethe dismissed the contention that a Soviet BMD would upset the balance of power, because a BMD is "virtually impossible" to develop [24]. This was in sharp contrast to President Kennedy's position both before and after March 2, 1962, when he announced the resumption of U.S. atmospheric nuclear testing.

On February 7, 1962, President Kennedy stated that a new situation had been created by the Soviet testing. First, the preparations had been conducted in secret, while the United States was negotiating a test-ban treaty. Second, it had ended the unofficial nuclear test moratorium. This presented grave questions "as to the long-range safety of avoiding all

---

and low cost rocket booster, both of which were essential for the feasibility and practicality of the project, were unavailable and could not be developed at the time. See J. Holahan, "What Have We Got to Counter the ICBM Threat," *Space Aeronautics,* November 1961, p. 1.

atmospheric tests, while the U.S.S.R. remained able to prepare in secret, and then test at will." Regarding the Soviet tests he said:

> They have been in preparation for many months, and we could see a period go by, possibly of another year or year and a half, of secret preparations being made, and suddenly a new series of tests, with extrapolations from those tests, particularly on matters involving, maybe, an antimissile missile. [25]

When the decision to resume nuclear testing was made, the President announced on national television specifically why this resumption was necessary:

> The fact of the matter is that we cannot make similar studies without testing in the atmosphere as well as underground. For in many areas of nuclear weapons research we have reached the point where our progress is stifled without experiments in every environment. The information from our last series of atmospheric tests in 1958 has all been analyzed and re-analyzed. It cannot tell us more without new data, and it is in these very areas of research—missiles penetration and missile defense, for example—that further major Soviet tests, in the absence of further Western tests, might endanger our deterrent. [26]

Such tests were the only way of gaining knowledge about BMD warhead design and kill radius, of exploring high-altitude effects, and of redressing the advantage the Soviets may have gained from their test series for BMD development.

Despite several successful ZEUS tests, two of which were simulated (i.e., programming an actual ICBM flight on computer tape and allowing ZEUS computers to carry out radar and fire control intercept), and the Soviet BMD program, the Defense Department's policy on producing ZEUS did not change. The Army's unequivocal faith in the system with its potential antisatellite capability, its investment of over $1 billion in the project, and the existence of two ZEUS prototype testing installations at White Sands, New Mexico, and Kwajalein Island did not change the Defense Department's opinion that too many technical problems remained to be solved before the system could become operational.

By the end of 1961 the future of ZEUS was very much in doubt. For the second consecutive year over $120 million intended for production was held back. It seemed inevitable in the upcoming Authorization and Appropriations Hearings a conflict would develop between the Army and the Defense Department over ZEUS. Meanwhile, most of the research studies sponsored by ARPA indicated no possibility of a breakthrough in missile defense in the near future. The research activities centered around plasmas and little-understood electromagnetic phenomena, areas in which intelligence information indicated the Soviets were also interested. These efforts in BMD research, collectively known as "x-weapons," indicated that any new solution to the missile defense problem was 5 to 10 years away. On December 21, 1961, the Army disclosed that ZEUS for the first time had intercepted another missile in flight [27].

In 1962 Secretary of Defense McNamara identified the ABM problem in the broader context of strategic defense. Of the six defense tasks he foresaw, four required top priority and were related to missile defense. They were: (1) improve the certainty and timeliness of the ICBM attack warning system; (2) provide an active defense against ICBMs; (3) improve defenses against submarine-launched missiles; and (4) provide, to the extent possible, fallout protection for U.S. population [28].

Here for the first time McNamara identified the civil defense program (fallout shelters) with BMD. In the 1961 Posture Statement no mention of shelters in relation to ZEUS had been made; now, deployment of ZEUS was made contingent on a shelter program.

In his 1962 House budget testimony, Defense Secretary McNamara reiterated his earlier position:

> . . . we must also do whatever is possible to develop, produce, and deploy an effective system of active defense against ICBM attack. We have extensive development programs on NIKE-ZEUS and on more advanced versions of terminal defense systems, as well as on other ideas involving underdeveloped technology. [29]

According to Secretary McNamara, providing a defense is paramount, but there are significant and serious questions as to the practicality of the NIKE-ZEUS system:

> . . . we are not recommending funds for its procurement and deployment at this time, but we are requesting the maximum amount of funds which can be effectively used in 1963 in the research and development program to continue development and testing on a top priority basis. [30]

In his testimony to the Senate, McNamara pointed out:

> A 100-percent-effective system of military defense against ICBM's and submarine launched missiles is technically impossible. At least during the period 1963 through 1967 we will have to rely for our survival on a combination of military and civil defense measures. [31]

In 1962 testimony revealed that a difference of opinion existed between the Defense Department and the Army over ZEUS capabilities and

The Death of Zeus—1961 to 1963

feasibility and t he Army's desire to begin procurement [32]. Illustrative of this continuing difference of opinion was the Army's request for $401.2 million for ZEUS in fiscal 1963, while the Defense Department requested only $235 million. The final figure was for $272.1 million [33].

When Representative Gerald Ford (R-Mich.) attempted to find out how the upcoming tests would affect a possible production date decision for NIKE-ZEUS, Secretary McNamara said ". . . the tests by themselves will have little effect on the decision as to whether we will or will not proceed into production." [34] His rationale for this statement was based on certain (off the record) technical problems which the upcoming test would not solve and the fact that the long-awaited ZEUS tests would not be carried out under combat conditions (no degraded environment, decoys, or use of a defensive nuclear warhead to kill the RV). The Secretary pointed out there were still gaps in our knowledge about missile defense kill mechanisms. Answers to these questions would not be revealed until the upcoming atmospheric nuclear test data were analyzed.[8]

The prohibitive cost of a ZEUS deployment around 25 cities (about $10 billion to $14 billion) along with these other considerations combined to make ZEUS deployment farther from reality.

Dr. Harold Brown, Director of DDR&E, shed additional technical light on the decision not to produce ZEUS. Congressman Robert Sikes (D-Fla.) asked Brown how DDR&E evaluated ZEUS. Brown replied that testing was proceeding satisfactorily, but there were many questions about the ultimate value of ZEUS as a weapon system. However, he stated that once one is in the BMD business, one does not get out of it, even if it is difficult to find a satisfactory solution. In fact, ". . . even if we think it will never be satisfactory we should continue. We have to go ahead with such a program." The logic of developing one system, testing it, and incorporating the new improvements gives ". . . us data, whether or not NIKE-ZEUS is ever used, as to possible deployment and possible deployments of other systems." The major obstacle to the NIKE–ZEUS, Brown said, was the decoy discrimination problem [35].

Major General Dwight Beach, Army Deputy Chief of Research and Development, told the House Appropriations Committee ZEUS had passed the point of hitting "one bullet with another bullet" and was capable of selecting out of "debris, garbage, and decoys . . . the warhead." [36] On the basis of this statement, ZEUS had fulfilled its original objective set forth

---

[8] These questions would still not be answered completely as no attempt to intercept a live ICBM with a live ABM was being made. The suggestion for such tests had been turned down earlier by President Kennedy.

in 1956 when the program was initiated. As in the previous year, the Army's position on production was: [9]

> . . . that certain items take . . . to develop on a production basis; and if we ever wanted to reduce the time and start to deploy, we could make progress at this time by allocating certain money to preproduction efforts which would then reduce the ...... lead time which exists at this time before ZEUS could go into production. [37]

General Decker said, before this same Committee, that any kind of defense can be saturated if enough means are applied against it. The problem with this argument, he felt, was that ". . . the opponents of ZEUS were giving a lot more credit to the . . . ." [38] Elaborating, General Trudeau said:

> . . . the obvious deterrent effect of forcing them to multiply by a factor of ...... the number of missiles they need to do a job is a very, very important aspect of this ...... the cost, the diversion of effort from other things where they are trying to compete with us economically. [39]

By April 1962, even before tests began in the Pacific, it was quite evident that ZEUS was finished as a weapon system, although R&D on it would likely continue. Its major function in the test series was to gather data on warhead and decoy signatures and to produce information that would be valuable to future anti-missile systems. The Army did not fight this decision. Instead, it decided to look at the missile defense problem with the goal in mind of developing a weapon system rather than merely providing a test bed for missile defense research, a function which it now felt was ARPA's responsibility.

Although the Army remained relatively silent over the Administration's decision regarding ZEUS, General Arthur Trudeau, the Army's Chief of Research and Development, did not. General Trudeau expressed considerable confidence in the system and continued arguing for its production. He revealed that the Army was working on several improvements to the present system [40]. One involved a high-acceleration, quick-reaction missile; the other, a multifaced phased-array radar. Both these improvements were to result in a new BMD system in the 1963–1964 period. Both components, he said, were adequately funded for fiscal 1963, but the Army's request for $133.7 million for pre-production funds again was turned down [41].

On April 18, 1962, the United States submitted an outline of *Basic*

---

[9] Deletions in this and following excerpts are due to censoring in the orginal congressional document.

Provisions of a Treaty on General and Complete Disarmament in a Peaceful World to the Eighteen Nation Disarmament Committee (ENDC). Again, this draft treaty provided for three stages of arms reduction, but unlike the General Assembly proposal, it specifically mentioned in Stage I "antimissile missile systems, together with related fixed launching pads. (The parties would declare their armaments by types within the category,)" [42]

One of the earliest opponents of BMD, Dr. Hans Bethe, felt it was a good thing BMD was infeasible, since a BMD system deployed by either the Soviet Union or the United States would precipitate an arms race and destabilize the existing nuclear balance. The Army maintained that no deterrent had ever remained stable, nor had any weapon ever remained ascendant over a counter weapon. Dr. Bethe's argument was part of the reason for his opposition to the resumption of nuclear testing and was echoed by the Federation of American Scientists statement, which said, ". . . in the present advanced state of nuclear weapons, no step comparable in terms of weapon yield to the thermonuclear breakthrough is feasible." These arguments against BMD—the existence of a weapon plateau and the destabilizing effect of BMD—were to appear more frequently as BMD feasibility increased [43].

On July 20, 1962, a ZEUS missile at Kwajalein Island intercepted an ATLAS ICBM fired from Vandenberg Air Force Base, California [44]. The United States continued its ABM tests independently of the nuclear tests (a new series was begun in October 1962) and intercepted two more ICBMs (including one with decoys) before the end of 1962.

Still there remained many skeptical and unconvinced people, including Defense Secretary McNamara, who predicted such successes but still would not sanction production and deployment. Commenting on this test, Secretary McNamara said that U.S. ICBMs could still penetrate any ABM defense, but the test did show the extensive and continuing interest the United States had in missile defense. These tests also did not convince Administration officials that the configured system could cope with the advanced ICBM threats expected in the late 1960s. These officials concluded that four major improvements were needed in the ZEUS system: (1) develop a new radar simultaneously to acquire, evaluate, and track large numbers of targets; (2) increase the altitude at which interception could take place; (3) develop a high-acceleration missile; and (4) use the discrimination radar as a target track radar [45]. Since the effort to develop a BMD was not being abandoned, the problem was to determine which of several alternatives was most feasible. Three were considered:

1. Continued development and testing of the present **NIKE-ZEUS** system, and the separate development of an advanced radar

2. Development of the four major improvements listed above an̲_____
   ployment of a system which would initially incorporate part of
   proposed improvements

3. Development of a more advanced system, to be known as NIKE-X,
   incorporating the SPRINT missile and advanced radars; and a
   deferred decision as to ABM deployment [46]

The alternative chosen was to reorient the ZEUS program, to ask for $450 million for NIKE-X development, and meanwhile to continue ZEUS testing and Project Defender.

The fact that an alternative approach to ZEUS looked feasible and was being considered indicated the shift in thinking in the Defense Department regarding missile defense. In no small way did the Defender program and the 1962 Pacific tests contribute to this change, since both these programs helped to clarify the missile defense problem to the extent that a new operational BMD concept emerged. This new concept—an urban defense system (UDS)[10] combined with a hard point defense system (HPDS) for the protection of ICBM sites and command control posts—was to influence greatly the technical direction, appearance, and configuration of the missile defense systems which emerged from the NIKE-X program in the late 1960s as SENTINEL and later as SAFEGUARD.

Any decision to deploy BMD involves a number of political, technical, and economic considerations. A prime consideration is the economic and

---

[10] The only missile defense systems this country has ever carried far enough along to produce prototypes for testing have been for city protection. Component research has been carried out for other types of defenses but rarely beyond the conceptual or developmental engineering stage. At present several schemes for close-in hard point terminal missile defense are being studied. A hard point defense system (HPDS) is less costly and complex than an urban defense system because the target is smaller and is protected by hardening. Fewer defensive missiles are needed, since the attacking missile must eventually be channeled into a "threat tube." This reduces the HPDS discrimination and acquisition problems and allows a simpler and cheaper radar. It also reduces the data-processing requirements. Since the target is hardened, defensive warhead detonation lower in the atmosphere is possible, allowing the close-in ABM to wait longer before launching, while the atmosphere filters the decoys. The HPDS is less provocative than an urban defense system, because the former is protecting the retaliatory forces while the latter protects the population. However, the logic of the argument that protecting the population is provocative is quite tenuous, in the author's mind.

The UDS concept presents a more difficult problem, in that a single missile, once through the defense, will do as much damage as if there had been no defense at all. Any solution to this problem hinges on the development of a system which cannot be countered cheaply by using decoys or penetration aids and a comprehensive civil defense program.

technical capability of the Soviet Union to build and deploy its own BMD and the effect an American BMD deployment would have on Soviet strategic and political thinking. Writing on "Urban Defense and Hard Point Defense Concepts," James Trainor in *Missiles and Rockets* said:

> Basically, leaders in the Administration feel that past U.S. weapons system developments have actually aggravated the arms race and contributed to the instability of the deterrent concept. Past U.S. actions, they claim, have actually forced the Soviet Union into weapons development they probably would not have undertaken otherwise.
>
> Therefore, several potentially unstabilizing weapons will not be developed and deployed because of the conviction that such action will be met by similar restraint in the Soviet Union. An Urban Defense System almost falls into this category but, depending on the nature of the Soviet missile threat in terms of both warhead yield and guidance accuracy, the Hard Point system may or may not fall into the "Not-to-be-developed-and-deployed" class. [47]

This passage, remarkable for 1962, was prophetic of the SENTINEL/SAFEGUARD debate in the late 1960s. Almost four years later the Johnson Administration publicly revealed such a policy in its attempt to halt an unwanted and unwarranted BMD race [48]. Yet to hedge against the failure of such a policy the Administration pursued a vigorous missile defense research program. The dual policy dating back to 1958 was to fund R&D but withhold deployment.

By year's end, the Army was hoping for BMD production approval from the Defense Department. Within the Defense Department considerable optimism prevailed that some form of missile defense was now feasible, even though ZEUS was three to four years from operational status. Studies on the SPRINT missile, a high-acceleration rocket system, were due for completion in February 1963. With this missile the Army hoped to supplement ZEUS with a system capable of close-in intercept, using the atmosphere to strip away the decoys and reveal the warhead. Using two missiles, the Army began to evolve an operational missile defense system consisting of both area and terminal defense. The range of ZEUS would have to be extended before an area defense would be possible.

In 1962 Senator Thurmond continued the campaign in the Congress to get NIKE-ZEUS into production. Thurmond insisted that nothing was more vital in the cold war than to maintain the balance of power.

> Without question, the side which first develops a defense, even a partial defense, against ballistic missile attack will win a tremendous psychological and military advantage in the cold war. This is important, not

so much because we would capitalize on any advantage we may have, but rather because the enemy will, as he always has, push any advantage to the maximum, whether it be to effect nuclear blackmail or nuclear holocaust, in order to attain his goal of world domination.

He continued:

If we continue to delay production of ZEUS parts until the development phase is completed—and the Secretary of Defense recently indicated we might not even go into production then—we may not have any missile defense capability until 1970 or later because of the production lead-time required. On the other hand, it is within the realm of possibility that the Soviets may have their system in operation within the next few years. [49]

References

[1] John W. Finney, "Army Aides Warn on Anti-ICBM Race," *The New York Times,* February 18, 1961, p. 5.

[2] U.S. Senate, Hearings Before the Committee on Armed Services, *Military Procurement Authorization, Fiscal Year 1962,* 87th Cong., 1st Sess., 1961, p. 14, hereafter cited as *Military Procurement Authorization FY 1962.*

[3] U.S. House of Representatives, Hearings Before a Subcommittee of the Committee on Appropriations, *Department of Defense Appropriations for 1962,* Part 3, 87th Cong., 1st Sess., 1961, pp. 16–17, cited hereafter as *House Defense Appropriations FY 1962.*

[4] *House Defense Appropriations FY 1962,* Part 3, p. 17.

[5] *Military Procurement Authorization FY 1962,* p. 37.

[6] *House Defense Appropriations FY 1962,* Part 3, p. 31.

[7] *House Defense Appropriations FY 1962,* Part 3, p. 31.

[8] *House Defense Appropriations FY 1962,* Part 3, p. 40.

[9] "Terminal ICBM Defense," *Aviation Week and Space Technology,* 15[1961]26.

[10] *House Defense Appropriations FY 1962,* p. 112.

[11] *House Defense Appropriations FY 1962,* p. 141.

[12] *House Defense Appropriations FY 1962,* p. 37.

[13] *House Defense Appropriations FY 1962,* p. 166.

[14] *U.S. Congressional Record,* 87th Cong., 1st Sess., February 2, 1961, p. 1659.

[15] *U.S. Congressional Record,* 87th Cong., 1st Sess., February 13, 1961, p. 1822.

[16] *U.S. Congressional Record,* 87th Cong., 1st Sess., February 13, 1961, p. 2133.

[17] Text of the White House reply to Flood's letter in the *U.S. Congressional Record,* 87th Cong., 1st Sess., March 13, 1961, p. 3800.

[18] U.S. Arms Control and Disarmament Agency, *Documents on Disarmament 1961,* Publication 5, GPO, 1962, pp. 475–482.

[19] G. P. Coates, "ICBM's and Military Satellites—What Defense Is Possible?" *The Aeroplane and Astronautics,* 2608[1961]483, October 12, 1961.

[20] Hanson Baldwin, "Soviet Antimissile System Spurs New U.S. Weapons," *The New York Times,* February 5, 1967, p. 76.

[21] U.S. Library of Congress, Legislative Reference Service, *United States Defense Policies in 1961,* House Document No. 502, 87th Cong., 2nd Sess., 1962, p. 160, hereafter cited as *U.S. Defense Policies in 1961.*

[22] Theodore Shabad, "Russian Reports Solving Rocket Defense Problem," *The New York Times,* October 24, 1961, p. 1.

[23] "Transcript of the President's News Conference on Foreign and Domestic Affairs," *The New York Times,* November 9, 1961, p. 14.

[24] Walter Sullivan, "Spot Check Urged on Arms Solution," *The New York Times,* January 1, 1962, p. 1.

[25] "Transcript of Kennedy's News Conference on Foreign and Domestic Affairs," *The New York Times,* February 8, 1962, p. 14.

[26] See *U.S. Department of State Bulletin,* Vol. 46, No. 1186, March 19, 1962, for a text of President Kennedy's "Nuclear Testing and Disarmament" speech, p. 445.

[27] *U.S. Defense Policies in 1961,* p. 161.

[28] U.S. House of Representatives, Hearings Before a Subcommittee of the Committee on Appropriations, *Department of Defense Appropriations for FY 1963,* 87th Cong., 2nd Sess., 1962, Part 2, p. 43, hereafter cited as *House Defense Appropriations for FY 1963.*

[29] *House Defense Appropriations for FY 1963,* p. 43.

[30] *House Defense Appropriations for FY 1963,* p. 46.

[31] U.S. Senate, Hearings Before the Committee on Armed Services, *Military Procurement Authorization FY 1963,* 87th Cong., 2nd Sess., 1962, p. 206, cited hereafter as *Senate Authorization FY 1963.*

[32] *Military Procurement Authorization, FY 1962,* pp. 140–142.

[33] *House Defense Appropriations for FY 1963,* Part 2, p. 348.

[34] *House Defense Appropriations for FY 1963,* Part 2, p. 257.

[35] *House Defense Appropriations for FY 1963*, Part 5, p. 85.

[36] *House Defense Appropriations for FY 1963*, Part 5, p. 153.

[37] *House Defense Appropriations for FY 1963*, Part 5, p. 177.

[38] *House Defense Appropriations for FY 1963*, Part 2, p. 349.

[39] *House Defense Appropriations for FY 1963*, Part 2, p. 349.

[40] *House Defense Appropriations for FY 1963*, Part 2, pp. 347–349.

[41] *House Defense Appropriations for FY 1963*, Part 5, pp. 175–176.

[42] U.S. Arms Control and Disarmament Agency, *Documents on Disarmament 1962*, Vol. 1, Publication 19, GPO, 1963, p. 355.

[43] George C. Wilson, "President, Dr. Bethe, Differ Over Usefulness of Anti-Missile Missile," *Aviation Week and Space Technology*, 12[1962]29.

[44] John W. Finney, "Nike-Zeus Intercepts a Missile Fired from U.S. over Pacific," *The New York Times*, July 20, 1962, p. 1.

[45] U.S. Library of Congress, Legislative Reference Service, *A Compilation of Material Relating to United States Defense Policies in 1962*, House Document No. 155, 88th Cong., 1st Sess., p. 48. Prepared by Charles Donnelly. Hereafter cited as *U.S. Defense Policies in 1962*.

[46] U.S. House, Committee on Armed Services, *Hearings on Military Posture and H.R. 2440* (No. 4), 88th Cong., 1st Sess., 1963, p. 324, hereafter cited as *Hearings on Military Posture FY 1964*.

[47] James Trainor, "DOD Says AICBM Is Feasible," *Missiles and Rockets*, 26[1962]14.

[48] John W. Finney, "Rusk Seeks Curb in Missiles Race," *The New York Times*, December 22, 1966, p. 1. See also John W. Finney, "U.S. Will Suggest Missile Moratorium at Geneva," *The New York Times*, December 20, 1966, p. 20.

[49] *U.S. Congressional Record*, 87th Cong., 2nd Sess., April 25, 1962, p. 7158.

PART II
Nike-X

CHAPTER 5

Zeus Plus Sprint Equals X—1963

In seven short years missile defense had evolved from a dream to a reality, albeit only an unsophisticated threat could be handled by ZEUS. In anticipation of the emergence of a more sophisticated threat in the late 1960s, the Defense Department in 1963 decided to skip alternatives which presented only marginal improvements in missile defense and concentrate:

> . . . on an urgent basis with the development of the more advanced system (NIKE-X), incorporating SPRINT missile and advanced radars and deferring the decision to deploy the system. [1]

In his 1963 testimony before the House Armed Services Committee, Defense Secretary McNamara explained the reasons for not producing ZEUS:

> We still have a great deal to learn about re-entry phenomena and techniques for discriminating between warheads and decoys. We also have a great deal to learn about the effects of a nuclear detonation from one of our intercepting missiles on other elements of the defensive system. On balance, therefore, we believe that it is premature at this time to commit ourselves to the production of any system and certainly not to an interim system with admittedly limited capabilities. Instead, we propose to proceed with the greatest urgency in the development of the NIKE-X system, retaining the option to move ahead with actual production and deployment of such a system, if the capabilities of the system and the circumstances should warrant such a decision at some later time. [2]

With this pronouncement, NIKE-X was born.

NIKE-X involved a vastly improved radar system and a mix of missiles designed to overcome the weaknesses of the ZEUS system. The technical decisions which led to the development of NIKE-X were a result of extensive reentry body tests, which indicated atmospheric filtering was the most effective means for discriminating warheads from decoys. NIKE-X incorporated the ZEUS missile for intercepting targets at altitudes of 70 to

100 miles, while SPRINT was designed to kill at 20 to 30 miles after the atmosphere had filtered the decoys.

The principal system elements which differentiated NIKE-X from its predecessor were the multifaced phased-array radar (MAR); SPRINT, the high-acceleration missile; and a smaller phased-array radar called the missile site radar (MSR), which combined the functions of the target tracking radar (TTR) and the discrimination radar (DDR).

Because low-altitude nuclear detonations made the NIKE-ZEUS radars vulnerable, a means to protect them had to be found. Several years earlier the Army initiated development of a phased-array radar which combined many of the functions of the existent ZEUS radars. Developed at Sylvania, the system required no large moving parts such as mechanically slewed radars, because the radar beams were shifted electrically through 360 degrees. With the exception of the exposed flat faces (which could be made moderately blast resistant), the radars could be housed almost completely in hardened concrete structures. MAR could handle multiple ZEUS and SPRINT launchings. Compared with earlier radars, MAR made possible superior discrimination of reentry object size, shape, and mass. Also, it could acquire and track far larger numbers of incoming warheads and objects than could the earlier ZEUS radar systems.

Late in 1962 Bell Telephone Laboratories awarded contracts to North American Aviation, Lockheed Aircraft, Douglas Aircraft, and the Martin-Marietta Company for SPRINT system studies. Early in 1963 the SPRINT program was awarded to Martin. SPRINT was housed in an underground silo and, when launched, would pop out, ignite, and simultaneously be pitched in the direction of the incoming target. SPRINT was designed to operate against a sophisticated missile attack employing penaids. With its high rate of acceleration, SPRINT could wait until atmospheric filtering had taken place [3]. SPRINT was developed because of the disadvantages of ZEUS, with its large-yield warhead and too slow acceleration rate. The need for atmospheric filtering resulted in too low a commitment altitude for practical use. With the development of SPRINT and the multifaced phased-array radars, the acquisition of a complete—area and terminal—missile defense was being attained.

More and more, strategic weapons requirements, as discussed in Secretary McNamara's Annual Posture Statements, reflected an attempt to reconcile forces with the missions and overall defense policy of the United States [4].

With his decision to proceed with NIKE-X already made, McNamara explained his reasoning for delaying the production and deployment of a BMD. A BMD deployed now, he said, might reduce U.S. casualties in the case of a "small" or "medium" Soviet attack on our urban areas. Further, it would complicate the design of and tactics for the attacker's offensive weapons. But there are even better reasons why we should *not* proceed with actual deployment of a system: (1) we still have a great deal to learn about reentry phenomena and techniques for discriminating between real warheads and decoys; and (2) we also have a great deal to learn about the effects of a nuclear detonation from one of our intercepting missiles on other elements of the defensive system [5]. Given these considerations, McNamara emphasized:

> . . . the effectiveness of an active ballistic missile defense system in saving lives depends in large part upon the existence of an adequate civil defense system. Indeed, in the absence of adequate fallout shelters, an active defense (ABM) might not significantly increase the proportion of the population surviving an all-out nuclear attack. For this reason, the very austere civil defense program recommended by the President . . . should be given priority over any major additions to the active defense. [6]

In describing the relation of BMD to civil defense, McNamara said:

> . . . because there will be such a huge amount of fallout generated by our own anti-ICBM system and the incoming warheads of the strike that it would be foolhardy to spend funds of this magnitude without accompanying it with a civil defense program. [7]
>
> . . .
>
> I personally will never recommend an anti-ICBM program unless a fallout program does accompany it. I believe that even if we do not have an anti-ICBM program, we nonetheless should proceed with the fallout shelter program. [8]

McNamara reassured the committee that the Administration's policy was to continue further development of an ABM even though the decision was not to deploy it.

Dr. Brown elaborated upon the need for fallout shelters in these same hearings (Part 6, pp. 8–9) by emphasizing that an enemy could detonate weapons outside or upwind of the defended target and allow the wind to carry fallout over the defended site. Shelters were also necessary to protect the defended population from the detonation of both the offensive and defensive warheads. If interception could be made to take place at higher altitudes, then there would be less danger from nuclear effects. Conversely, if missile defense guidance were improved so that accuracy increased, smaller defensive warheads could be used. In any event, the real fallout danger would come from the exploding ICBM warhead.

The decision to deploy NIKE-X appeared to rest squarely on the acceptance of a Civil Defense (CD) program by the American public. Yet the public had no way of making its feelings about civil defense known, while Congress believed that the American people wanted no part of CD.

Responding to a question by Representative Flood concerning ZEUS, McNamara claimed that if the Administration had pushed ahead with ZEUS in 1960 or 1961, a system would have been deployed which would not have granted adequate protection against the Soviet threat the Defense Department saw developing in the 1964–1968 period. Explaining why NIKE-X was not revealed publicly in 1962, he said the program was under consideration during 1962 among Bell Laboratories, Western Electric, and himself, but the decision to begin work on NIKE-X was not made until late in the year [9].

As in the past, McNamara was forced to justify his decision not to deploy NIKE-ZEUS to members of the Appropriations Committee. Arguing from his assumptions and his hypothetical alternatives, he was able to rationalize his favored choice; i.e., to continue with development of NIKE-X but not to produce it. While the committee considered the system's growth potential, McNamara summed up his argument, saying the committee should address itself to the degree of protection that either the NIKE-X or NIKE-ZEUS would give. By postulating a variety of Soviet missile threat levels and making certain assumptions about decoys and Soviet targeting doctrine, his examples provided sufficient doubt as to the attractiveness of NIKE-X under the particular circumstances he postulated [10].

As in previous years, much of the questioning revolved around the degree of protection ZEUS would have provided had it been deployed when the Army wanted to deploy it several years earlier. McNamara claimed it would have offered little or no protection beyond 1964.

General Taylor, Chairman of the Joint Chiefs of Staff, agreed with McNamara's contention that if ZEUS were not deployed, there was a greater likelihood a better system would become available—thus making ZEUS obsolete. However, as Taylor saw it, the problem was to go into production immediately so at least some weapon system would be operational. Taylor recognized the advantages of working for a better system, contending that if ZEUS had been deployed two things would have happened:

> One, we would now be learning by doing; and . . . we would have had a technological triumph over the Soviets. Some day there will be a great ballyhoo that the Soviets have an anti-ballistic missile and we do not. The claim may be largely sham and propaganda, but we face that possibility of a cold war defeat. [11]

Dr. Finn Larsen, Army Secretary for R&D, believed NIKE-X would be deployed ultimately for two reasons: (1) it would have the capability of locating warheads at altitudes where discrimination was possible and destruction feasible, and (2) whereas the Army was arguing in opposition to the Office of the Secretary of Defense on NIKE-ZEUS, both were in agreement on NIKE-X [12].

General Earle Wheeler, the new Army Chief of Staff, was a strong proponent of NIKE-ZEUS and carried his recommendation for its deployment not only through the JCS and Department of Defense but to the President [13].

General Wheeler suggested that NIKE-ZEUS be deployed as soon as possible with whatever feasibility the state of the art would permit, and then move into NIKE-X. Even at the cost of $2.8 billion it was worth something to protect a large number of people and a large segment of the economy. On the possibility of a Soviet BMD, Wheeler felt that it would certainly cause us to perceive a change in the balance of power. If it were good, it might result in the inability of our missiles to penetrate Soviet defenses, thereby reducing the credibility of the deterrent and weakening our overall military posture. The gap caused by the Soviets' obtaining a BMD while we did not could be disastrous and have a powerful psychological effect on the world. Since we have a lot of other "military things," Wheeler believed, we should also have a BMD because there was nothing now in our arsenal to defend against ICBMs [14].

On April 11, 1963, Senator Strom Thurmond requested and received permission to hold a closed session of the Senate, the first since World War II. The closed session was held in an effort to try to retain $196 million in the military procurement bill to begin production of NIKE-ZEUS. While the authorization had been favorably reported out of the Armed Services Committee (9 to 8), Chairman Richard Russell (D-Ga.) found himself in disagreement with the majority of his Committee. He offered an amendment to reduce the authorization for Army missiles by eliminating the $196 million for the production of component parts of NIKE-ZEUS. The proponents of the Russell amendment were not against BMD per se, as were later Senate votes and debates, but rather against the deployment of this particular (NIKE-ZEUS) missile defense system which they believed was obsolete and uneconomical compared to NIKE-X, whose deployment they favored. Furthermore, they contended, since the Defense Department was not in favor of deploying ZEUS and requested, instead, $335 million for research on SPRINT and the array radars, the cost of retrofitting these improvements into the ZEUS system installations would cost $2.8 billion. Supporting Senator Thurmond's position was the testimony, given earlier in the year, of Army Chief of Staff General Earle G. Wheeler, who felt the advantage of deploying NIKE-ZEUS to protect our population was well worth the cost now. General Maxwell Taylor likewise supported the Army's position and contended that ZEUS should go into production immediately because an effective missile defense could tip the balance of power in favor of the United States. The reason for calling an executive session was Senator Thurmond's desire to introduce classified material in his argument against the amendment. The vote (58 to 16) resulted in the adoption of the amendment, eliminating funds for production [15].[1]

In June 1963 Senator Thurmond described his position on missile defense in an article which more than likely contained some of the information he presented in defense of his position during the closed session in April. This article at the time represented the best and only reasoned argument for missile defense.

Thurmond argued:

> The capability of causing *mutual destruction* is not an acceptable basis of deterrence. A deterrence depends for its effectiveness not only on existing power, but on the belief by the one sought to be deterred that upon some level of provocation, the deterrent power will be unleashed. The range of provocations against which one can make the threat of unleashing mutual destruction believable is unacceptably limited.
>
> A deterrence consisting of the power of *mutual destruction* is the necessary result of a relative parity of strategic striking power. An acceptable deterrence, consisting of the power of unilateral destruction of the one sought to be deterred, can only be founded on a superiority of strategic force. [16]

Furthermore:

> The road to continued superiority can also be in the development and deployment of an effective ballistic missile defense system. Indeed, either side which achieves such a defense capability *first* will gain superiority for at least a temporary period of time. [17]

He said:

> The acquisition of an effective operational defense against ballistic missiles is the most immediate and vital requirement of U.S. military security today. The degree of success and speed with which we must meet this requirement might well be the crucial factor which determines whether general war can be deterred and prevented in the next decade. [18]

Thurmond indicated that two Administrations resisted recommendations for the production of ZEUS in 1958, 1961, and 1963, because they felt that the system was not perfected. While the system is limited against

---

[1] See Table 2 for a breakdown of this vote.

penaids and decoys and has a four-year lead time, no effort has been made to deploy it, despite its crucial urgency. He added that the Soviets were apparently deploying a system around Leningrad, while the earliest any U.S. system could be deployed was 1967 for ZEUS or 1969 for NIKE-X.

Indeed, in the absence of a much greater sense of urgency in the U.S. program, the Soviets may well accomplish for a period their frantically sought goal of strategic superiority by this means. [19]

Thurmond agreed that for the return on the investment, the cost of this weapon system—as is the case with any other—is high but certainly not excessive. Concerning the system's vulnerability to decoys and penaids, he said:

Such arguments discount the fact that penetration aids, decoys and multiple warheads are still very much in the planning stages, and the U.S. has no such devices operational. If the Soviets have made developmental progress on such devices, they have at least not yet equipped their operational missiles with such devices. From our own research, we know that a program to refit or replace existing ballistic missiles with such modifications would be a major undertaking for either the U.S. or the Soviets, in resources, scientific and engineering manpower and time. [20]

Thurmond discounted the argument that deployment would freeze the system because, during the four years it would take to deploy it, R&D could go on and improvements could be incorporated. If deployment were to wait until perfection had been achieved, the system would never be deployed. The argument that a massive Soviet attack could saturate the ZEUS system was spurious, since it was not believed the Soviets had sufficient numbers of missiles ". . . to permit a massive attack on each of a large numbers of first priority targets." [21]

One of the problems associated with BMD development, however, is "what effect the detonation of a warhead on the intercepting missile would have on the total defense system, and we have not ascertained an answer because we have declined to engage in nuclear tests in the atmosphere." [22] The failure to begin deployment of an ABM by the spring of 1964 would preclude strategic superiority for the United States in the coming years. Those who desired the NIKE-ZEUS deployment as an interim measure felt that "it is a lot safer and, in the long run, cheaper to build weapons and not use them than it is to need weapons and not have them." [23]

As 1963 ended, a number of articles told of the United States' improved offensive capability and reported that Secretary McNamara would not authorize any BMD production and deployment unless Congress authorized a full-scale $2.5 billion shelter program. All indications were,

Table 2

	DEMOCRATS		1963	1966	1968a	1968b	1968c	
State	Name	Committee	Y N NV	Y N NV	Y N NV	Y N NV	Y N NV	Y
Ala.	Allen							
N.M.	Anderson	4	x	N	x	x	N	
Alsk.	Bartlett		Y	PF	Y	Y	x	
Tenn.	Bass			N				
Ind.	Bayh		Y	N	PF	AN	N	
Nev.	Bible		Y	N	x	x	N	
Md.	Brewster	2	Y	N	N	N	N	
N.D.	Burdick		Y	x	x	x	Y	
Va.	Byrd	2	Y	N	N	N	N	
W.Va.	Byrd	2	x	N	N	N	N	
Nev.	Cannon	2	Y	N	N	N	N	
Idaho	Church	3	Y	Y	x	x	x	
Pa.	Clark	3	AY	Y	PF	PF	Y	Y
Calif.	Cranston							
Conn.	Dodd	3	N	N	PA	PA	N	
Ill.	Douglas		N	x				
Mo.	Eagleton							
Miss.	Eastland		AY	N	x	x	N	
Okla.	Edmondson		AY				N	
La.	Ellender	1	AY	N	N	N	Y	
Calif.	Engle	2	Y					
N.C.	Ervin	2	N	N	AN	AN	N	
Ark.	Fulbright	3	Y	Y	Y	Y	x	
Tenn.	Gore	3, 4	Y	N	x	x	Y	
Alsk.	Gravel							
Alsk.	Grueing		Y	Y	Y	Y	x	
Okla.	Harris			N	x	x	N	
Mich.	Hart		Y	N	Y	Y	Y	Y
Ind.	Hartke		N	N	Y	Y	PF	
Ariz.	Hayden	1	Y	x	N	N	N	
Ala.	Hill	1	x	x	x	x	N	
Fla.	Holland		AY	N	N	N	N	
S.C.	Hollings				PA	PA	N	
Iowa	Hughes							
Minn.	Humphrey	3	Y					
Hawaii	Inouye	2	N	N	Y	Y	N	
Wash.	Jackson	2, 4 (1)	N	N	PA	PA	N	
S.Car.	Johnston		Y					
N.Car.	Jordan		N	N	x	x	N	
Tenn.	Kefauver		AY					
Mass.	Kennedy, E.		Y	Y	PF	PF	x	
N.Y.	Kennedy, R.			Y	PF	PF		
O.	Lausche	3		N	x	x	Y	
La.	Long	3	Y	N	x	x	N	
Mo.	Long		AY	N	x	x	x	
Wash.	Magnuson	1	Y	N	PA	AN	N	
Mont.	Mansfield	3, 1	Y	N	Y	Y	Y	
Minn.	McCarthy	3	Y	x	x	x	Y	
Ark.	McClellan	1	N	N	N	N	N	
Wyo.	McGee	3	Y	N	N	N	N	
S.D.	McGovern		Y	Y	Y	Y	Y	
N.H.	McIntyre	2	Y	N	N	N	PA	
Mich.	McNamara		x					
Mont.	Metcalf		Y	Y	PF	PF	Y	
Minn.	Mondale			N	PF	Y	Y	
Okla.	Monroney	1	Y	N	PA	PA	x	
N.Mex.	Montoya			N	N	N	x	
Ore.	Morse	3	Y	PA	PF	PF	Y	
Utah	Moss		Y	N	N	Y	Y	
Me.	Muskie		Y	N	N	N	Y	
Wis.	Nelson		Y	Y	Y	Y	Y	
Ore.	Neuberger		Y	Y				
R.I.	Pastore	1, 4	Y	N	N	N	N	
R.I.	Pell	3	Y	N	N	Y	Y	
Wis.	Proxmire		Y	Y	Y	Y	Y	
W.Va.	Randolph		Y	N	PA	PA	Y	
Conn.	Ribicoff		Y	N	PA	N	PF	
Va.	Robertson	1	Y	N				
Ga.	Russell	2, 4, 1	Y	N	N	N	N	
S.C.	Russell			N				
Fla.	Smathers	3	Y	x	x	x	N	
Ala.	Sparkman	3	N	x	N	N	N	
Va.	Spong				N	N	N	
Miss.	Stennis	1	Y	N	N	N	N	
Mo.	Symington	3, 2, (1)	x	N	Y	Y	Y	
Ga.	Talmadge		Y	N	N	N	N	
S.C.	Thurmond	2	N					
Md.	Tydings			Y	Y	Y	Y	
N.J.	Williams		N	Y	Y	Y	Y	
Tex.	Yarborough		x	x	N	N	PA	
O.	Young	2	AY	Y	Y	Y	Y	
	Subtotal		42 11 14	14 43 10	14 21 29	17 20 27	22 30 12	

	1968f	1969a	1969b	1969c	1969d	1969e	1970a	1970b	1970c
Y N NV	Y N NV	Y N NV	Y N NV	Y N NV	Y N NV	Y N NV	Y N NV	Y N NV	Y N NV
		N	N	N	N	N	N	N	N
PF	N	N	N	N	N	x	N	N	Y
	PF								
	x	N	Y	Y	Y	Y	Y	Y	Y
PA	x	N	N	N	N	N	N	N	N
	PA								
	N	N	Y	Y	N	N	N	Y	Y
	N	N	N	N	N	N	N	N	N
	N	N	N	N	N	N	PA	N	N
	N	PF	Y	Y	N	N	N	N	N
	PF	Y	Y	Y	Y	Y	Y	Y	Y
	Y								
	N	N	Y	Y	Y	Y	Y	Y	Y
		N	N	N	N	N	N	N	N
	N	N	Y	Y	N	Y	Y	Y	Y
		N	N	N	N	N	N	N	N
	PA	N	Y	Y	N	Y	N	Y	N
	N	N	N	N	N	N	N	N	N
x	Y	Y	Y	Y	PA	Y	Y	Y	Y
x	Y	Y	Y	Y	PF	Y	Y	Y	Y
PF	Y	N	Y	Y	Y	Y	Y	Y	Y
	N	N	Y	Y	Y	Y	Y	Y	Y
	Y	N	Y	Y	N	Y	Y	Y	Y
	x	N	Y	Y	Y	Y	Y	Y	Y
	N								
	N								
	N	N	N	N	N	N	N	N	N
	x	N	N	N	N	N	N	N	N
		N	Y	Y	Y	Y	Y	Y	Y
Y	N	Y	Y	Y	Y	Y	Y	Y	Y
	N	N	N	N	N	PA	N	N	N
	x	N	N	N	N	N	N	N	N
	Y	N	Y	Y	N	Y	Y	Y	Y
A	N								
	N	N	N	N	x	N	x	N	N
	x								
F	N	N	Y	Y	N	PF	N	Y	Y
	Y	N	Y	Y	N	PA	N	Y	Y
	x	Y	Y	Y	Y	Y	x	Y	Y
	N	N	N	N	N	N	N	N	N
	x	N	N	N	N	N	N	N	N
	x	Y	Y	Y	Y	Y	Y	Y	Y
	N	N	Y	Y	Y	N	N	N	Y
	Y	N	Y	Y	Y	PF	Y	Y	Y
	x	N	Y	Y	Y	Y	Y	Y	Y
	x								
	N	N	Y	Y	Y	Y	Y	Y	Y
	PF								
	Y	N	Y	Y	Y	Y	Y	Y	Y
	x	Y	Y	Y	N	Y	Y	Y	Y
	x	Y	Y	Y	N	Y	Y	Y	Y
	N	N	N	N	N	N	N	Y	Y
	Y	N	Y	Y	Y	Y	Y	Y	Y
	Y	N	Y	Y	Y	Y	Y	Y	Y
	Y	N	Y	Y	N	Y	N	Y	N
	x	Y	Y	Y	Y	Y	N	Y	Y
	N	N	N	N	N	PA	N	N	N
	PA						N		
	N	N	N	N	N	PA	N	N	N
	N	N	N	N	N	N	N	N	N
	N	N	N	N	N	N	N	N	N
	Y	N	Y	Y	N	AY	N	Y	Y
	N	N	N	N	N	N	N	N	N
	Y	N	Y	Y	Y	PF	x	Y	Y
	Y	N	Y	Y	Y	PF	Y	Y	Y
	x	N	Y	Y	Y	Y	N	Y	Y
	Y	Y	Y	Y	Y	Y	Y	Y	Y
17 25 21	8 49 0	36 21 0	36 21 0	22 32 3	27 20 10	24 29 4	35 22 0	35 22 0

Table 2 (*continued*)

	REPUBLICANS		1963	1966	1968a	1968b	1968c	
State	Name	Committee	Y N NV	Y N NV	Y N NV	Y N NV	Y N NV	Y
Vt.	Aiken	3, 4, 1	AY	N	N	Y	Y	
Colo.	Allott	1	PF	N	AN	AN	N	
Tenn.	Baker				x	x	N	
Md.	Beall	2	PA					
Okla.	Bellmon							
Utah	Bennett	4	x	AN	N	N	N	
Del.	Boggs		Y	N	N	Y	N	
Mass.	Brooke	2			Y	Y	Y	
Kan.	Carlson	3	PF	N	N	N	N	
N.J.	Case	2, 3	N	N	x	x	Y	Y
Ky.	Cook							
Ky.	Cooper	3	Y	N	N	Y	Y	Y
N.H.	Cotton		Y	N	x	x	N	
Neb.	Curtis	4	N	N	AN	AN	N	
Ill.	Dirksen		Y	N	AN	AN	N	
Kan.	Dole							
Colo.	Dominick	2	Y	N	N	N	N	
Ariz.	Fannin			N	AN	AN	N	
Hawaii	Fong		N	N	N	N	N	
Ariz.	Goldwater	2	x					
N.Y.	Goodell							
Mich.	Griffin			N	N	N	N	
Fla.	Gurney							
Wyo.	Hansen				x	x	N	
Ore.	Hatfield				Y	Y	Y	Y
Iowa	Hickenlooper	3, 4	Y	N	N	N	N	
Neb.	Hruska	1	N	N	N	N	x	
N.Y.	Javits	3	Y	N	N	Y	Y	
Idaho	Jordan		Y	N	N	Y	N	
N.Y.	Keating		Y					
Calif.	Kuchel	1	Y	N	AN	AN	N	
Md.	Mathias							
N.M.	Mecham		PA					
Iowa	Miller	2	Y	N	AN	x	N	
Ky.	Morton		AY	AN	x	AN	Y	
S.D.	Mundt	3, 1	PA	N	N	N	N	
Calif.	Murphy	2			AN	AN	N	
Ore.	Packwood							
Kan.	Pearson	2	Y	N	AN	AN	N	
Ill.	Percy				N	Y	Y	
Vt.	Prouty		Y	N	N	Y	Y	
Mass.	Saltonstall	2, 1	Y	N				
O.	Saxbie							
Pa.	Schweiker	2						
Pa.	Scott		AY	N	N	Y	Y	
Wyo.	Simpson		PF	N				
Me.	Smith	2, 1	N	N	Y	N	Y	
Alsk.	Stevens							
S.C.	Thurmond	(1), 2		N	N	N	N	
Tex.	Tower	2	x	N	N	N	N	
Del.	Williams	3	Y	N	N	Y	Y	
N.D.	Young	1	Y	N	N	x	N	
Ill.	Smith							
Subtotal			16 5 12	0 30 3	3 20 13	11 11 14	12 22 1	
Total			58 16 26	14 73 13	17 41 42	28 31 41	34 52 13	1
Source, Congressional Record			4/11/63; S6428-29	8/18/66; S18993-94	4/18/68; S4257-58	4/18/68; S4262	6/24/68; S7653	6 S

Vote Description:		Yea(Y)	Nay(N)	Not Voting (NV)
1963	Delete ZEUS production funds	58	16	26
1966	Clark Amendment— Delete NIKE-X pre-production funds	14	73	13
1968a	Nelson Amendment— Delete SENTINEL procurement funds	17	41	42
1968b	Cooper Amendment— No funds to be spent on BMD deployment	28	31	41
1968c	Cooper-Hart Amendment— Against further BMD expenditures	34	52	13
1968d	Young Amendment— Delete SENTINEL construction funds	12	72	15
1968e	Nelson Amendment— Delete BMD construction appropriations	27	46	24
1968f	Cooper Amendment— Delete funds for production and deployment	25	45	30

e	1968f	1969a	1969b	1969c	1969d	1969e	1970a	1970b	1970c
V	Y N NV	Y N NV	Y N NV	Y N NV	Y N NV	Y N NV	Y N NV	Y N NV	Y N NV
A	x	Y	Y	Y	Y	N	N	Y	Y
	N	N	N	N	N	N	N	N	N
	N	N	N	N	N	N	N	N	N
		N	N	N	N	N	N	N	N
	PA	N	N	N	N	N	N	N	N
	N	N	N	N	N	N	N	N	N
	Y	N	Y	Y	Y	Y	Y	Y	Y
	N								
	Y	N	Y	Y	N	Y	Y	Y	Y
		N	Y	Y	N	PF	N	N	Y
F	Y	N	Y	Y	N	AY	N	Y	Y
	x	N	N	N	N	N	N	N	N
A	N	N	N	N	N	N	N	N	N
A	N	N	N	N	N				
		N	N	N	N	N	N	N	N
	N	N	N	N	N	N	N	N	N
	PA	N	N	N	N	N	N	N	N
	N	N	N	N	N	N	N	N	N
		N	N	N	N	N	N	N	N
	Y	N	Y	Y	Y	Y	Y	Y	Y
	N	N	N	N	N	N	N	N	N
		N	N	N	N	N	N	N	N
	N	N	N	N	N	N	N	N	N
	Y	N	Y	Y	N	Y	Y	Y	Y
	N								
A	N	N	N	N	N	N	N	N	N
?	PF	N	Y	Y	Y	Y	Y	Y	Y
	N	N	N	N	N	N	N	N	N
	N								
		N	Y	Y	N	Y	Y	Y	Y
	N	N	N	N	N	PA	N	N	N
	PF					PA			
	N	N	N	N	N	N	x	x	x
	AN	N	N	N	N	N	N	N	N
		N	N	N	N	N	N	N	N
	N	N	Y	Y	N	N	N	N	N
	Y	N	Y	Y	N	Y	N	Y	N
	Y	N	N	N	N	N	N	N	N
		Y	Y	Y	N	PF	Y	Y	x
		N	Y	Y	Y	Y	Y	Y	Y
	Y	N	N	N	N	N	N	N	N
		AY	Y	Y	N	N	Y	Y	Y
		Y	Y	N	N	Y	Y	Y	N
		N	N	N	N	N	N	N	N
	N	N	N	N	N	N	N	N	N
	AN	N	N	N	N	N	N	N	N
		N	N	N	N	N	N	N	N
	N	N	N	N	N	N	N	N	N
	N	N	N	N	N	N	N	N	N
						N			
7	8 20 9	3 40 0	14 29 0	13 30 0	5 38 0	9 29 15	9 33 1	12 30 1	10 31
5	25 45 30	11 89 0	50 50 0	49 51 0	27 70 3	36 49 15	33 62 5	47 52 1	45 53 2
	10/2/68; S11885	8/6/69; S9253	8/6/69; S9282	8/6/69; S9282	8/7/69; S9341	12/15/69; S16781	8/12/70; S13281	8/12/70; S13304	8/19/70; S13696

			Not Voting	
Description:		Yea(Y)	Nay(N)	(NV)
Smith I Amendment — Delete all SAFEGUARD money		11	89	0
Smith II Amendment—other BMD, R&D OK				
Cooper-Hart Substitute No SAFEGUARD spending		50	51*	0
Hughes Amendment — Bar all SAFEGUARD deployment		33	62	5
Cooper-Hart Amendment — No further expansion of SAFEGUARD beyond Phase 1				1
Brooke Amendment — Limit expansion money only to Phase 1 sites		45	53	2

* President Agnew as President of the Senate cast an additional but necessary vote, as a tie vote in the Senate defeats an amendment.

Committee Key:
1 - Defense Appropriations Subcommittee
2 - Armed Services
3 - Foreign Relations
4 - Joint Atomic Energy
( )- Ex-officio member from Armed Services

Key:
NV - Not Voting
AY - Absent but would have voted "yea"
PF - Paired for
PA - Paired against
AN - Absent but would have voted "nay"

however, that the Defense Secretary would not authorize the missile's production, since it was not far enough along in development. The cost of a BMD was compounded by the fact that if it were successfully deployed, other means of penetration might be found by the enemy. Consequently, into the total cost of a BMD must be figured the cost for new improved air defenses to prevent the Soviets from avoiding the missile defense by employing aircraft.

References

[1] *Hearings on Military Posture FY 1964*, p. 324.

[2] *Hearings on Military Posture FY 1964*, p. 325.

[3] U.S. House, Hearings before Subcommittees of the Committee on Appropriations, *Safeguard Antiballistic Missile System*, 91st Cong., 1st Sess., 1969, pp. 18, 23.

[4] U.S. Department of Defense, *Statement of Secretary of Defense Robert S. McNamara Before the House Armed Services Committee of the Fiscal Year 1964–1968 Defense Program and 1964 Defense Budget*, mimeographed, January 30, 1963, p. 28, hereafter cited as *1963 Annual Posture Statement*.

[5] *1963 Annual Posture Statement*, p. 48.

[6] *1963 Annual Posture Statement*, p. 49.

[7] U.S. House, Hearings before a Subcommittee of the Committee on Appropriations, *Department of Defense Appropriations for FY 1964*, Part 1, 88th Cong., 1st Sess., 1963, pp. 438–439, hereafter cited as *House Defense Appropriations FY 1964*.

[8] *House Defense Appropriations FY 1964*, p. 439.

[9] *House Defense Appropriations FY 1964*, pp. 427–429.

[10] *House Defense Appropriations FY 1964*, pp. 432–434.

[11] *House Defense Appropriations FY 1964*, p. 435.

[12] *House Defense Appropriations FY 1964*, Part 6, p. 270.

[13] U.S. Senate, Hearings Before the Committee on Armed Services, *Military Procurement Authorizations Fiscal Year 1964*, 88th Cong., 1st Sess., 1963, p. 131, hereafter cited as *Senate Procurement Authorizations FY 1964*.

[14] *Senate Procurement Authorizations FY 1964*, pp. 548–549.

[15] *U.S. Congressional Record*, 88th Cong., 1st Sess., April 1, 1963, p. 6407.

[16] Senator Strom Thurmond, "The Gap in Ballistic Missile Defense," *Data*, 6[1963]42, hereafter cited as *Thurmond*.

[17] *Thurmond*, p. 44.
[18] *Thurmond*, p. 42.
[19] *Thurmond*, p. 44.
[20] *Thurmond*, p. 45.
[21] *Thurmond*, p. 45.
[22] *Thurmond*, p. 45.
[23] *Thurmond*, p. 45.

CHAPTER 6

Missile Defense and the Partial Nuclear Test Ban Treaty

The signing of the Partial Nuclear Test Ban Treaty in August 1963 was a landmark in the cold war, and a culmination of 17 years of effort at arms control beginning in 1946 with the Baruch Plan. In addition to its obvious political content, the treaty bore heavily on military and technical questions, especially missile defense development and the risks involved in the U.S. acceptance of such a treaty. Two Senate committees held hearings on the treaty: the Foreign Relations Committee and the Preparedness Investigating Subcommittee of the Senate Armed Services Committee. The witnesses called by the former included not only high-ranking government civilian and military personnel, but scientists, political scientists, private citizens, union officials, and peace and disarmament advocates; whereas the Preparedness Committee called witnesses only from the military, the Atomic Energy Commission (AEC), and Arms Control and Disarmament Agency (ACDA). In addition, Dr. John Foster, then Director of Lawrence Radiation Laboratory of the University of California at Livermore and now Director of DDR&E, and Dr. Edward Teller of the University of California were called as witnesses. Although the testimony of the key individuals who appeared before both committees is the same, the conclusions reached by the committees were remarkably different. The Preparedness Subcommittee concluded:

> From the extensive evidence presented to us, we have come to the conclusion that the proposed treaty banning nuclear testing in the atmosphere, underwater, and in space will affect adversely the future quality of this Nation's arms and that it will result in serious, and perhaps formidable, military and technical disadvantages. These disadvantages, in our judgment, are not outweighed or counterbalanced by the claimed military advantages. At the same time, we are not convinced that comparable military disadvantages will accrue to the nuclear weapon programs of the U.S.S.R. [1]

The Foreign Relations Committee concluded:

Missile Defense and Nuclear Test Ban Treaty

> . . . the treaty represents a net advantage to the United States; that the risks it contains are acceptable . . . . [2]

Both Committees dealt with the missile defense question. The Preparedness Subcommittee concluded:

> The United States will be unable to determine with confidence the performance and reliability of any ABM system developed without benefit of atmospheric operational system tests. [3]

The Foreign Relations Committee concluded:

> . . . that the treaty should not restrict—not to any appreciable degree—the development of such a system, if, indeed, an anti-ballistic-missile system can be developed with sufficient effectiveness to justify the enormous cost of deploying it. [4]

In the following, the reader should keep in mind that there are at least three areas of knowledge necessary for missile defense development which depend on atmospheric nuclear testing: (1) the effect of nuclear explosions on radar (blackout problems), (2) warhead development and design, and (3) warhead lethality.

Many times during the hearings, interception and penetration were observed to be opposite sides of the same coin, and, consequently, that missile defense turned "on the great disparity between offensive and defensive capabilities in the nuclear art." [5] For example, Dr. Herbert York testified that despite defensive ingenuity, offensive weapons would invariably beat any and all defensive systems. He compared this race to one between a tortoise and a hare, which the former would only win if the latter went to sleep.

Secretary McNamara pointed out:

> . . . in designing an anti-ballistic-missile system the major factors are reaction, speed, missile performance, traffic handling capacity, capacity for decoy discrimination, resistance to blackout effects, and warhead technology. The last two of these items, resistance to blackout effects and warhead technology, depend on nuclear testing. [6]

After testifying: (1) the United States had the capability to produce a BMD warhead without further testing, (2) we knew enough about the blackout problem to design around the remaining uncertainties, and (3) Soviet ABM efforts were no better than ZEUS, he said:

> One important point stands out in connection with the anti-ballistic missile: The ABM problem is dominated by factors unrelated to the threat. . . . A fuller understanding of the blackout phenomenon, which

would result from tests prohibited by the treaty, might at most permit some reduction in the number of ABM radars required per ABM site [7].

The Chairman of the Atomic Energy Commission, Dr. Glenn Seaborg, when asked whether a BMD could be perfected without resorting to atmospheric testing,[1] replied that:

> ... quite clearly that kind of test cannot be carried out under the terms of the treaty. But neither is that kind of test necessary to reach a reasoned conclusion that we should or should not deploy such a system. [8]

The chief critics of the treaty, Dr. Edward Teller and Dr. John Foster, were both concerned with the blackout effect on BMD defensive radars, especially the blackout caused by defensive missiles. Dr. Teller pointed out: if an ideal BMD (one designed to neutralize an ICBM in space) were to be developed, it could not be tested under the treaty's provisions.[2]

Dr. George Kistiakowsky, President Eisenhower's Science Advisor, felt offensive weapons technology had a commanding lead over the defense. He suggested the committee seriously consider the views of Dr. Harold Brown, Director of DDR&E, whose assessment of the Soviet and American BMD efforts was "we are about equal . . . ." [9]

In conclusion:

> ... the Committee [the Foreign Relations Committee] is doubtful that either the United States or the Soviet Union will develop an ABM system capable of protecting major population centers and military targets in a general nuclear exchange. Yet the importance of the program is such that the Committee can only urge that the research and development funds regarded as necessary for this program should be made available. [10]

The test ban hearings provided an extremely valuable source of technical information and insight into BMD, especially blackout and high-altitude weapon effects. Secretary McNamara's testimony during these hearings revealed the peculiar political nature of the BMD affair and some

---

[1] Atmospheric testing is considered to be within the altitude at which aircraft can fly—up to about 90,000 to 100,000 feet. High-altitude testing is above this range.

[2] Teller's position on missile defense had changed considerably from his 1959–60 belief that such a system could not be developed because it was too difficult. See U.S. Senate, Hearings Before the Preparedness Investigating Subcommittee on Armed Services, *Military Aspects and Implications of Nuclear Test Ban Proposals and Related Matters,* Part 2, 88th Cong., 2nd Sess., 1964, pp. 579–580, hereafter referred to as *Military Implications.* The change in Teller's position was the result of a gruelling 13 hour symposium (the Teller Symposium) in late 1961 held at the Stanford Research Institute and conducted by the Director of its Strategic Studies Center, Mr. Richard Foster. See Marc Geneste, "La Bataille des Anti-Missiles Aux U.S.A." *Revue de Defense Nationale,* March 1967, pp 420–430.

of the motivation behind his later decisions not to deploy NIKE-X. Six months earlier before the House Appropriations Committee and, later, the Senate Armed Services Committee, McNamara had stated that a great amount of knowledge was needed about the effect of nuclear detonations in the atmosphere; indeed, this knowledge could only be obtained by high-altitude testing and such testing could only aid the development of a missile defense [11]. But, testifying on behalf of the treaty, McNamara said that we had gained sufficient knowledge and data from prior atmospheric nuclear tests to allow us to design a BMD around the blackout problem.[3] Any additional BMD problems associated with nuclear testing could be solved by testing under ground. To make his position stronger, McNamara cited the Army's insistence as far back as 1958 that NIKE-ZEUS would work. Yet when the Army wanted to deploy the system, McNamara claimed that there were too many technical problems to be solved and that it would be a mistake to follow the Army's advice [12].

In answer to a question asked by Senator John Stennis (D-Miss.), McNamara admitted that such a treaty, prohibiting atmospheric testing, would not allow an entire BMD system to be tested to determine if it would work. While insisting BMD could be developed effectively with the present state of knowledge, he admitted the Soviets had gained considerable knowledge about BMD development in their 1961–62 tests and they might be able to deploy a better system than NIKE-ZEUS. McNamara found himself confronted by Senator Thurmond with the fact that in the fall of 1962 he had admitted before the Senate Armed Services Committee that the Soviets had deployed an ABM; in the test ban hearings he denied it [13].[4] Also, during the test ban hearings he asked for $450 million to continue development work on NIKE-X in fiscal 1964—a request in direct contrast to the President's statement that a BMD could not be developed and was beyond U.S. capability [14]. McNamara's insistence that the treaty would not affect BMD development was in substantial disagreement

---

[3] It should be remembered only a few U.S. atmospheric nuclear tests were relevant to the U.S. BMD program—the three Argus shots of 1958, the Teak and Orange shots of 1958, and the 1962 Starfish, Bluegill Triple Prime, and Kingfish shots. No atmospheric nuclear tests were carried out after the 28 atmospheric tests in the 1962 Pacific series, and none was carried out in 1963. McNamara believed sufficient knowledge had been gained from all these tests to develop a BMD. See *Military Implications*, p. 5.

[4] There is no public record of McNamara's admitting the Soviets deployed an ABM; obviously the system being referred to is the Leningrad deployment, which several Department of Defense (DOD) officials and others had discussed in the two test ban hearings and reports cited here. The author called the Senate Armed Services Committee and was told that in the fall of 1962 a top secret briefing on the international situation had been held before a joint meeting of the Senate Armed Services and Foreign Relations Committees. Apparently, this is what Thurmond had reference to.

with the views of a number of scientists, including Dr. Teller and Dr. Foster.

Not unexpectedly, other Administration witnesses echoed Secretary McNamara's position that the central difficulties of BMD development were generally outside the warhead problem and involved either radars, reaction speed, missile speed, traffic handling capacity, or capacity for decoy discrimination. The Chairman of the Atomic Energy Commission, Dr. Glenn Seaborg, stated that the AEC could develop the necessary BMD warheads through underground testing. In fact, he said, a number of warheads was already available for BMD. Elaborating further, Seaborg felt that both the United States and the Soviet Union were at about the same point in developing BMD. Therefore, he supported the treaty because of its other advantages and:

> ... in recognition of the fact that we are not in a disadvantageous position with respect to the ABM—and that we will not get into a more disadvantageous position with respect to the ABM as a result of the treaty. [15]

The Chairman of the Joint Chiefs of Staff, General Maxwell Taylor, who favored deploying BMD as early as 1958 (now acting as spokesman for the JCS) said:

> In the anti-ballistic missile field, development of the U.S. system does not depend on atmospheric testing and hence this treaty will not significantly influence any imbalance that may exist. [16]

Taylor, like Rusk, McNamara, and Seaborg, used exactly the same argument and almost the same language to state that a prohibition on atmospheric testing would not retard BMD development because the problem with BMD was not in the warhead. While this is partly true, the warhead, the blackout problem, and the effects of high-altitude weapon detonations on other nuclear warheads and defensive systems are irrevocably linked to BMD development. U.S. developments in subsequent years have come to substantiate the fact that insufficient data existed from which to draw positive statements on the effect of nuclear weapons on other weapons in the atmosphere.

These hearings demonstrated a great deal of inconsistency between the Administration's position on the treaty and BMD development. While everyone, even those favoring such a ban, stated that the missile defense problem was inseparable from atmospheric nuclear testing, there were ways of overcoming such a ban if BMD had to be developed. Despite these facts, it was concluded that the treaty would not affect BMD, even if the Soviets gained more knowledge from their 1961–62 tests about high-altitude phenomena than we did. In fact, General Taylor said, "both sides could achieve an anti-ballistic missile, but one with less desirable characteristics than would be the case if additional atmospheric tests were conducted." [17] Finally, he said,

> . . . under this treaty, both sides could make about the same technical progress in the ABM field, although the Soviets may possess some information not available to the United States. [18]

The Joint Chiefs approved the treaty with the proviso that certain safeguards be carried out. Their joint conclusion was "on balance, the political and foreign policy advantages to be derived from the treaty outweighed the limitations which the treaty would impose on the Nation's weapon systems programs." [19] The Joint Chiefs unanimously testified that no political pressure was put on them to accept this treaty, although as General Curtis LeMay, Commander of The Strategic Air Command said, "I think we were all caught a little bit by surprise at the seriousness of the Administration trying to get a treaty signed." [20]

It appears reasonable to conclude that despite the Administration's stated need and priority for developing a missile defense which does depend on atmospheric testing, when the test ban appeared possible, it became more politically attractive than solving certain missile defense problems. To be sure, not all the problems were insurmountable even with a partial test ban.

While certain members of Congress and the Army favored deploying the system because they felt it would do the job assigned it, since 1958 the Eisenhower and Kennedy Administrations had consistently deferred the issue of deployment because a number of technical questions and problems remained to be answered about the feasibility of ZEUS or of using any BMD to cope with a sophisticated attack. Yet, when the possibility of reaching an accord with the Soviet Union on nuclear testing appeared, the Administration was the first to declare BMD could be developed, even though the technical questions raised earlier about its feasibility would remain unanswered to the degree that atmospheric and high-altitude testing might have permitted the technical questions to be answered. Forgotten in these proceedings was the fact that the U.S. resumption of atmospheric nuclear testing in 1962 was caused by the fear, testified to by many during these hearings, that the Soviets had gained considerable knowledge (which the testimony likewise confirmed) about BMD development [5] in their own tests, and may have surpassed the United States in such knowledge.

---

[5] In the early 1960s the Soviets actually did deploy a defensive system around Leningrad designed to stop ICBMs. They used an advanced model of a surface-to-air missile called the GRIFFON. The Soviets appeared to lose faith in the system

The test ban treaty was the major arms control accomplishment of 1963, and while it was being negotiated, William Foster, Director of the U.S. Arms Control and Disarmament Agency (ACDA), made several interesting speeches concerning the treaty and BMD. On March 11, 1963, he told the Joint Committee on Atomic Energy that a test ban would slow down the development of missile defense systems on both sides. [22]

At the Southwest Conference on Arms Control, in October 1963, after the test ban treaty had been signed, Foster twice repeated the statement that an adequate missile defense did not appear feasible, especially against sophisticated attack. "Moreover, in the foreseeable future technology offers no great hope that an effective over-all defense can be devised." He suggested that these basic facts pointed up the need for diplomats and strategists "to provide for the security of the free world, in the absence of a classic defense situation." As a result of this condition, he said, "the present technical infeasibility of a real defense has led us to rely on a strategy of deterrence." [23]

The holding of hearings in 1963 on the test ban treaty by both the Senate Armed Services and Foreign Relations Committees portended the beginning of an ideological and jurisdictional dispute between these two committees which reached epic proportions in the 1966–70 period not only over BMD but over Vietnam. The congressional lines of battle between these two committees were drawn not only because of political and ideological differences among the members of the committees but because of the growing difficulty of separating the impact of weapon technology on foreign affairs and the implications of foreign policy on weapon technology.

References

[1] U.S. Senate, Interim Report by Preparedness Investigating Subcommittee of the Committee on Armed Services, *Military Implications of the Proposed Limited Nuclear Test Ban Treaty*, 88th Cong., 1st Sess., 1963, p. 11, hereafter cited as *Military Implications*.

---

apparently for technical reasons as they stopped work on it at about the time they decided to resume nuclear testing. In fact, there is reason to believe the Soviets resumed testing in order to perfect a nuclear warhead for an improved ABM system to replace the one they had deployed [21]. Note: The names of Soviet weapon systems are NATO code names. The letter-numeral designation, i.e., SS-9, is a U.S. assigned designator.

[2] U.S. Senate, Report of the Committee on Foreign Relations, *The Nuclear Test Ban Treaty*, 88th Cong., 1st Sess., 1963, p. 9, hereafter cited as *Nuclear Test Ban*.

[3] *Military Implications*, p. 7.

[4] *Nuclear Test Ban*, p. 12.

[5] *Nuclear Test Ban*, p. 12.

[6] *Nuclear Test Ban*, p. 12.

[7] *Nuclear Test Ban*, p. 12.

[8] *Nuclear Test Ban*, p. 13.

[9] *Nuclear Test Ban*, p. 14.

[10] *Nuclear Test Ban*, p. 14.

[11] *House Defense Appropriations FY 1963*, Part 2, p. 79.

[12] U.S. Congress, Senate, Hearings Before the Committee on Foreign Relations, *Nuclear Test Ban Treaty*, 88th Cong., 1st Sess., 1963, pp. 103–104, 114–115, 137–138, 158–159, 160–163, 165–166, 173–175, 193–195, and 198, hereafter cited as *Test Ban Hearings*.

[13] *Test Ban Hearings*, p. 166.

[14] "Text of President's News Conference on August 1, 1963," *Washington Post*, August 1, 1963, p. A12.

[15] *Test Ban Hearings*, p. 244.

[16] *Test Ban Hearings*, p. 273.

[17] *Test Ban Hearings*, p. 377.

[18] *Test Ban Hearings*, p. 377.

[19] *Military Implications*, p. 10.

[20] *Test Ban Hearings*, p. 382.

[21] *U.S. Defense Policies in 1962*.

[22] U.S. Congress, Hearings Before the Joint Committee on Atomic Energy, *Developments in Technical Capabilities for Detecting and Identifying Nuclear Weapons Tests*, 88th Cong., 1st Sess., 1963, pp. 435–440.

[23] The text of the speech is found in U.S. Arms Control and Disarmament Agency, *Documents on Disarmament 1963*, Publication 24, GPO, 1964, p. 567.

CHAPTER 7

Nike-X and Damage Limitation—1964

With NIKE-X, the American missile defense effort entered its fourth phase (see Table 1). The third phase saw the introduction of SPRINT and phased-array radars added to overcome ZEUS's weaknesses in discrimination, susceptibility to saturation, radar vulnerability, and limited traffic handling capacity. While NIKE-X still was a terminal defense system, its development illustrates the dynamics of military technology.

ZEUS's ability to intercept an ICBM, which made it a success, and the Soviet BMD program spurred a major effort by both sides to develop penetration aids and decoys. The successful development of these devices meant that the once "simple" defense problem—to shoot down an ICBM—was now complicating by the requirement to find the warhead among the mass of other objects. However, the offense paid a penalty to overcome the first-generation missile defense. This penalty is called virtual attrition—the reduction in explosive payload to make room for penaids and chaff. NIKE-X was necessitated by advancing offensive developments, developments in part foisted upon the offense by the first missile defenses.

President Johnson, in his budget message to Congress in January 1964, said that the Soviet strategic threat to the United States was shifting from bombers to ICBMs.

> Accordingly, the 1965 program provides for continued development work on a priority basis for the NIKE-X anti-missile system along with continued exploration of advanced anti-ballistic missile defense concepts. [1]

In his 1964 testimony, McNamara described various strategic alternatives open to the United States, from finite deterrence to counterforce. With any force level the United States built and under the most favorable circumstances, McNamara reasoned, a nuclear exchange between the Soviet Union and the United States would do enormous damage to both sides. He concluded that the strategic forces required by the United States should be large enough to *ensure* the *destruction* of the national societies and war-making capabilities of the Soviet Union and China; i.e., to deter them while *limiting,* to the extent possible, *damage* to the United States [2]. By postulating a strategy of assured destruction and a damage limitation mission for U.S. strategic retaliatory forces, Secretary McNamara attempted to provide a rational framework for viewing the types, numbers, cost, effectiveness, and contributions that strategic offensive and defensive weapons made to U.S. national security.

Before the House Armed Services Committee on January 29, 1964, McNamara discussed the NIKE-X system:

> . . . the continued testing of the NIKE-ZEUS and preliminary studies of the NIKE-X system's characteristics and effectiveness provide grounds for believing that the technical problems of at least a partial defense against a ballistic missile attack may be solved within the next several years. [3]

The Defense Secretary tempered his optimism, saying:

> . . . major problems have yet to be solved before we will have sufficient data upon which to consider a decision to produce and deploy the system. . . . By next year considerably more information will be available to make a judgment about the system's feasibility. A large number of technical, strategic, and economic problems must be solved, such as components withstanding high acceleration and temperatures, devising mass production techniques for complex components, etc. While none of these problems are insuperable, they could result in delays and increased costs. [4]

If these problems and the discrimination problem were surmounted, the system could be deployed starting in late 1964. The estimated cost of a BMD deployment could be as high as $16 billion; consequently, the potential effectiveness of the system had to be determined to justify the cost of deployment. Until these problems were resolved by testing, a decision to deploy the system would be premature, resulting in delays and increased costs. Contending that the effectiveness of the system would have to be demontsrated because of its high cost, McNamara argued that other defensive measures were needed with a BMD deployment to limit damage. He noted: NIKE-X would be relatively effective against a small-to-moderate missile attack, but against a large, sophisticated Soviet attack the system required expansion at considerable cost compared to the cost to the Soviets to ensure penetration of that defense. Secretary McNamara repeated his argument that a fallout shelter program must accompany any BMD deployment and must be given top priority over BMD.

The relation between shelters and ABMs was described by McNamara:

> The effectiveness of the NIKE-X system against attacks employing decoys would vary with the altitude at which the incoming warheads must be

engaged. The lower the altitude, the better the chance of discrimination, but the greater the chance that the weapon might be detonated before it is intercepted. But, the lower the altitude at which the weapon is detonated, the higher the blast and thermal effects on the ground for any given yield. Thus, to the extent that we can protect the population against the blast and heat of a nuclear explosion, we can wait longer before engaging an enemy missile and can thus be surer that we engage the warhead, not a decoy. [5]

General William Dick, Chief of Army Research and Development, testified on January 20, 1964, that no real production decision could be made until at least 1966, since test results of MAR, the most critical aspect of the system, would not be available until late 1964, which would be too late for consideration in the fiscal 1966 budget. Therefore, barring any unforeseen developments, a deployment decision was at least one to two years away [6].

For the first time, there appeared to be no disagreement between the Army and Secretary McNamara on this decision. Interestingly, neither General Wheeler, Army Chief of Staff, nor Secretary of the Army Stephen Ailes commented on the BMD effort during the hearings, at least not in publicly released testimony.

Dr. Brown, Director of DDR&E, who had much to do with the reorientation of NIKE-ZEUS to NIKE-X, said during hearings:

> . . . the decision on NIKE-X will not be made, or should not be made merely on the basis of technical capability. That is, even though the system does what we say it will do, that does not mean necessarily that we should deploy the system. [7]

This appears to be the first public and official governmental statement indicating that considerations other than technical-military ones might affect the decision to deploy a BMD. These considerations included: (1) what types of targets were to be defended, (2) enactment of a civil defense program, (3) what effect deployment would have on an adversary (would it be provocative?), and (4) was the nuclear threat sufficient to warrant the cost of deployment? As U.S. missile defense policy evolved in the middle and late 1960s, items (3) and (4) played a predominant role in any BMD deployment decision. This is clear from the following statement of Secretary McNamara:

> As the arms race continues and the weapons multiply and become more swift and deadly, the possibility of a global catastrophe, either by miscalculation or design, becomes ever more real. More armaments, whether offensive or defensive, cannot solve this dilemma. We are approaching

an era when it will become increasingly improbable that either side could destroy a sufficiently large portion of the other's strategic nuclear force, either by surprise or otherwise, to preclude a devastating retaliatory blow. This may result in mutual deterrence, but it is still a grim prospect. It underscores the need for a renewed effort to find some way, if not to eliminate these deadly weapons completely, then at least to slow down or halt their further accumulation, and to create institutional arrangements which would reduce the need for either side to resort to their immediate use in moments of acute international tension. [8]

In February Hanson Baldwin asserted the Soviets were deploying a BMD not only around Leningrad but around Moscow. Although American experts thought the Soviet system no further advanced technically than the U.S. system, the Soviet deployment gained them precious lead time, since the U.S. system could not be deployed before 1969 and only if a decision were made by January 1965 [9].

On May 18, 1964, the first of a two-part series on the NIKE-X program appeared in *Missiles and Rockets*. The article discussed the existence of a massive, comprehensive Threat Analysis Study on missile defense, begun for the Defense Department in July 1963 and headed by Major General Austin W. Betts, former head of ARPA. The object of this study, subsequently known as the Betts Report, was to provide the broadest possible base of information on which to make a decision to produce and deploy the NIKE-X system. The study covered every aspect of the BMD problem, including the strategic implications of deployment, the North Atlantic Treaty Organization (NATO), the Soviet ICBM threat, and Soviet BMD progress. It contained 23 volumes when completed and is still classified. War game scenarios were postulated to see how nuclear wars might begin and to demonstrate contributions ballistic-missile defense could make in combination with other strategic forces and various levels of civil defense to a war's outcome.

The study also considered whether NIKE-X should be deployed and if it were destabilizing. (Those who held this view contended BMD decreases, not increases, national security by adding another weapon to the inventory of both sides: a weapon which has the potential for altering the balance of power by altering the state of mutual deterrence.) During the 1963 test ban treaty hearings, Dr. Harold Brown, Director of DDR&E, expressed the view that arms development offers no permanent security and that the test ban treaty might be the first step in slowing down the arms race, thereby improving the security of the United States.[1] In fact,

---

[1] This theme is discussed in Chapter 8.

Dr. Brown said:

> I don't consider arms limitation and arms development opposites. I think they are opposites of the same coin. They are both roads that I think we have to pursue to improve our security. [10]

Dr. Brown stated that in spite of all the technical developments and improvements in weaponry initiated by the Defense Department, these had not resulted in any greater security for the United States. The Betts Report considered the issue of deploying NIKE-X because it was expected to weigh heavily on the arms race and the balance of power.

Another issue addressed in the Betts Report was the value of BMD for arms control and as a hedge against the Nth-country threat. In an arms limitation agreement, NIKE-X could provide protection against cheating and provide a defensive nuclear umbrella while the number of ICBMs was being reduced.

The Report suggested deploying BMD to protect Western Europe against Soviet IRBM-MRBMs. A BMD system, if deployed in the United States, could contribute to the credibility of the extended deterrent which the United States provides for Europe [11].

In 1964 the Army began improving NIKE-X to counter the blackout problem. This led to another phase of BMD evolution—the modular approach. The internetting of MAR and MSR, but placing the MSR far enough from MAR so that the MAR-MSR combination would be able to "see" around the ionized blackout caused by a nuclear blast, would reduce the blackout effect on BMD. This modification led eventually to development of the TACMAR unit. A new long-range surveillance radar, PAR (perimeter acquisition radar), was developed to take over the surveillance function of MAR.

SPRINT design work was not expected to be completed until early 1965, making any NIKE-X deployment decision unlikely before 1966. ZEUS was aerodynamically modified for its role as the high-altitude, long-range, exo-atmospheric interceptor. A new first-stage propellant was incorporated, and the repackaging and refinement of third-stage components were initiated [12].

At a news conference on July 15, 1964, Secretary McNamara suggested the possibility of deploying NIKE-X could be decided in late 1964 if certain development milestones were met. The major question affecting deployment was whether the system's effectiveness justified its cost. McNamara estimated that protecting "some 20-odd cities containing about 30 percent of the population of the country," would cost about $15 billion to $17 billion, with an annual operating cost of $1 billion to $2 billion thereafter.

Nike-X and Damage Limitation—1964

In October the Chinese detonated their first atomic bomb. Information and discussion pertaining to NIKE-X for the last half of 1964 were rather scarce, except for two reports, one in *Ordnance,* the other in the December 24, 1964, *Wall Street Journal.* According to *Ordnance,* the cost of a BMD, not its technical feasibility, was the key to its development. Unlike the debate over ZEUS, the decision on NIKE-X hinged on the number of lives saved in conjunction with a shelter program, how much the United States was willing to spend to achieve this program, and whether there might be better ways to achieve damage limitation [13].

William Beecher reported in the *Wall Street Journal* that the 4,000-page Betts Report was delivered to Secretary McNamara with a $30-billion price tag. Like the article in *Ordnance,* Beecher's article suggested that any BMD decision would be a function of cost. However, if a decision to deploy NIKE-X were made, money would be no object. Beecher cautioned that there were many ways to defeat BMD but the cost of doing so continued to be much less than the cost of the BMD. He said Secretary McNamara considered deploying NIKE-X early in 1964 but apparently decided to refine the system to make it a better weapon [14]. Beecher's report about a better system was confirmed by Secretary McNamara in a statement before the Democratic Platform Committee in August 1964:

> The new NIKE-X, which will give us the option to deploy—if the national security requires it—is the most advanced anti-ballistic missile yet conceived by any nation. [15]

This statement suggests doubt that U.S. security would warrant deployment of a missile defense. Such a suggestion was not new, however, as several scientists, and ex-government and academic officials earlier had expressed opposition to deployment of BMD on the grounds it was destabilizing and provocative, would lead to a new arms race, not enhance U.S. security, and was technically ineffective.[2]

When the Eighteen Nation Disarmament Committee (ENDC) reconvened on January 21, 1964, President Johnson sent a message proposing a five-point arms control program. Point Two of this arms control program referred to BMD.

> While we continue our efforts to achieve general and complete disarmament under effective control, we must first endeavor to halt further increases in strategic armaments now. The United States, the Soviet Union, and the respective allies should agree to explore a verified freeze

---

[2] If the latter were true, why was the United States spending hundreds of millions of dollars for devices to penetrate Soviet defenses? Was Soviet missile defense development ahead of ours?

of the number and characteristics of strategic nuclear offensive and defensive vehicles. For our part, we are convinced that the security of all nations can be safeguarded within the scope of such an agreement and that this initial measure preventing the further expansion of the deadly and costly arms race will open the path to reductions in all types of forces from present levels. [16]

Had such a freeze been adopted, the United States would have then remained strategically superior in offensive weapons while neither side would have deployed a defensive system. The justification for the freeze was provided by William Foster on January 31, 1964, before the ENDC:

We have singled them (strategic nuclear vehicles) out for three reasons. We believe, first, attention should be directed to the long-range weapons of greatest destructiveness. We believe a freeze on these weapons can be achieved with effective inspection requirements [the bane of all previous (General and Complete Disarmament) (GCD) proposals] which would be less than those required for a general and complete disarmament programme limiting all major armament across the board. Finally, we believe we should focus on these weapons because they are among the most expensive to develop and produce. [17]

The reason the BMD should be included, said Foster, was that a freeze on strategic delivery systems without one on BMDs would be destabilizing and therefore unacceptable. Among other advantages the freeze would: (1) curb a key area of the arms race; (2) inhibit development of costly, new, and more destructive weapon systems; (3) reduce any fears which might exist that either side could achieve a first-strike capability; and (4) help reduce tensions and accelerate the forward movement toward general disarmament. Except for Deputy Director of ACDA Adrian Fisher's statement: ". . . further technical discussions will be required in order to formulate a workable and acceptable definition of 'anti-missile missile system,'" [18] little more was said publicly by the Government during 1964 about BMD limitation or the NIKE-X program.

References

[1] "Text of President's Message and an Analysis of Federal Budget of $97.8 Billion," *The New York Times*, January 22, 1964, p. 21.

[2] U.S. Department of Defense, *Statement of Secretary of Defense Robert S. McNamara Before the House Armed Services Committee on the Fiscal Year 1965–1969 Defense Program and 1965 Defense Budget*, mimeographed, January 27, 1964, p. 32, hereafter referred to as *1964 Annual Posture Statement*.

[3] U.S. House, Committee on Armed Services, *Hearings on Military Posture and H.R. 9637,* No. 36, 88th Cong., 2nd Sess., 1964, p. 7016, hereafter cited as *House Military Posture FY 1963.*

[4] *House Military Posture FY 1963,* p. 7016.

[5] *1964 Annual Posture Statement,* p. 53.

[6] *House Military Posture FY 1963,* p. 7698.

[7] U.S. Senate, Hearings Before the Subcommittee on Department of Defense of the Committee on Appropriations and the Committee on Armed Services, *Department of Defense Appropriations, 1965,* Part 1, 88th Cong., 2nd Sess., 1964, p. 397.

[8] *1963 Annual Posture Statement,* p. 27.

[9] Hanson Baldwin, "U.S. Missile Defense," *The New York Times,* February 15, 1964, p. 8.

[10] *Test Ban Hearings,* p. 550.

[11] James Trainor, "Nike-X Fate Keyed to DOD Study," *Missiles and Rockets,* 20[1964]14.

[12] James Trainor, "Missile Site Radar Paces Nike-X," *Missiles and Rockets,* 21[1964]14.

[13] "Ballistic Missile Defense," *Ordnance,* September-October 1964, p. 128.

[14] William Beecher, "Fending Off Missiles," *Wall Street Journal,* December 24, 1964, p. 1.

[15] *The New York Times,* August 18, 1964, p. 18.

[16] U.S. Arms Control and Disarmament Agency, *Documents on Disarmament 1964,* Publication 27, GPO, 1965, p. 8. Point Five of this proposal later led to the Draft Treaty to Prevent the Spread of Nuclear Weapons.

[17] *Documents on Disarmament 1964,* pp. 19–20.

[18] *Documents on Disarmament 1964,* p. 159.

CHAPTER 8

Opposition to Missile Defense Begins—1964

The first signs of opposition to missile defense appeared in late 1963 and 1964. Until then, opposition to missile defense, civil defense, or defense by other strategic weapons appeared only in specialized journals such as the *Bulletin of the Atomic Scientists* or the arms control literature of the late 1950s and early 1960s. Dr. Wiesner, shortly before assuming the position as President Kennedy's scientific advisor, in a paper presented at the Sixth Pugwash Conference in Moscow, urged that missile defenses not be deployed or developed. The 1960 Summer Study on Arms Control, sponsored by the American Academy of Arts and Sciences at Brookline, Massachusetts, contained similar urgings. It is interesting to note that these efforts urging nondeployment were evident in 1960, almost 2 years before actual tests were carried out with ZEUS to determine if missile defense was possible.

The arguments to limit BMD deployment were stated or pressed at arms control conferences, East-West scientific meetings, in arms control literature, in the corridors of power, and in the halls of universities and laboratories by officials, government consultants, advisors, and ex-government officials. What had appeared only in specialized and limited circles and writings before 1964 now appeared in several large-circulation, select, science, and foreign policy journals.

Opposition to BMD stems from a belief that the consequences of its deployment, or even existence, would lead to an escalation of the arms race; that it represents a frightful waste of money, which could be spent more appropriately on domestic needs; and that its presence would provide no more security than is now available with offensive weapons. In addition, it would heighten international tension, jeopardize the détente and Soviet-American relations, and accelerate weapon technology. To BMD opponents, this weapon represents a destabilizing and provocative threat. Why?

The attempt to prevent development and production of an ABM had been organized and led, among others, by a number of prominent individuals who were to serve, were already serving, or had served in the Government. Several significant articles appeared in 1963 and 1964 presenting the rationale and arguments opposing deployment of BMD. The authors of these articles had been high-ranking members of the Kennedy Administration or advisors and consultants to that Administration. The underlying theme of the BMD opponents was best stated in a report by a group of independent specialists in April 1963:

> Offensive capabilities have become so varied and deadly that there is no basis for assuming the feasibility of constructing reliable defensive systems against all possible warhead delivery methods. *Defensive methods of every conceivable sort can be saturated and overwhelmed by the variety and quantity of offensive weapons.*
>
> On the offensive side, destructive capability, having already gone far beyond the overkill mark, calls for no further improvement on military grounds. [1]

The authors suggested that a massive civil defense program could be construed by a potential enemy as an intent to initiate a first strike. An ideal method for protecting the nation, they felt, was to maintain a finite deterrent ICBM force which would be so emplaced as to be reasonably secure against attack. A limited number of these powerful nuclear weapon delivery systems would be sufficient to threaten an aggressor with the destruction of his country as predictable punishment for an act of aggression against the United States.

In 1964 Roswell T. Gilpatric, former Deputy Secretary of Defense (1960–1964), argued:

> We cannot afford a policy which, in effect, deliberately avoids seeking a reduction of tensions in order to keep the public alert to dangers. Nor can we afford a policy which deliberately seeks to lull the public, and ignore dangers where they exist, in order to make it easier to build support for a policy of peaceful accommodations. [2]

Gilpatric suggested the kind of strategic policy which might be appropriate for the United States in the event East-West tensions continued to ease. If the détente continued, Gilpatric said, the military forces of the United States could be reduced by 1970 to a finite deterrent level where, among other things,

> . . . there would be no production or deployment of anti-ballistic-missile systems in the absence of Soviet moves to proceed beyond experimental installations of such systems. [3]

Gilpatric questioned the effect BMD would have if it were deployed, given limitations on the effectiveness of any such system capable of development in the foreseeable future. He suggested that the best way to maintain the security of the United States was to maintain the capability to meet aggression while seeking a détente.

Gilpatric suggested missile defense might wisely be limited not only to produce some confidence-building measures between the United States and the Soviet Union but to provide the impetus for slowing down the arms race. According to Gilpatric, from the start of the arms race, certain fundamental differences began to appear, such as a Soviet propensity for defense and the U.S. investment of resources in offensive delivery vehicles. Development and incorporation of ICBMs into the inventories of both sides led to BMD development on both sides, too. The Soviets eventually deployed BMD, while the United States kept its system in the engineering/development stage, relying instead on increased offensive capability to ensure penetration of the Soviet BMD and to maintain a credible deterrent.

Gilpatric described certain arms control efforts which would suffer if a BMD were deployed. These efforts would include: (1) a nuclear non-proliferation treaty, (2) a strategic delivery weapon freeze, (3) a comprehensive test ban treaty, (4) establishment of nuclear free zones, and (5) a cutoff in the production of nuclear materials. Additionally, a BMD could disrupt an already weakened NATO alliance and upset the minimal progress being made at the ENDC in Geneva. Gilpatric, like others desirous of halting an American BMD deployment, felt the Soviet deployment of BMD could be the result of internal pressures, especially in the armed forces; a historic need for defense; and fear of the Chinese threat. While the price tag of another arms race is not prohibitive to the United States, the real problem for the United States is whether to:

> . . . re-engage in an armament contest with the Soviet Union, or should it strive for more progress toward arms control and the substitution of political, economic and sociological measures for military force as means for insuring world peace? [4]

As early as 1964, the Federation of American Scientists (FAS), a nationwide organization of approximately 2,500 scientists and engineers concerned with the impact of science on national and international affairs, opposed any BMD deployment:

> It is the view of the FAS that there is today no known way to construct a satisfactory defense against ICBM's. Indeed, in the foreseeable future there is not going to be any satisfactory defense. This does not mean that single nuclear missiles cannot be knocked down or rendered harmless by anti-missile missiles, or that several nuclear missiles cannot be knocked out. Rather, it means that any foreseeable defense system can

be annulled by means that are technically feasible and economically practicable. [5]

Since the offense can use penaids, saturation, and decoys, it was "the firm belief of the FAS that these factors render any missile defense unfeasible at present and for the foreseeable future." [6] Additional reasons mustered by the FAS include: (1) the high cost, (2) the system's unreliability against an ICBM buildup, (3) its leading to an increase in international tensions, and (4) the need for shelters and a civil defense program:

> Our civilian population would have to be trained, to some extent regimented, and taught unquestioning obedience to authority. This would mean a hardening of our society, a striking change in our American attitudes, and a weakening of our democratic institutions. [7]

The statement concluded that no matter what the Soviets do about BMD, the United States should not deploy its own system.

Two years later in 1966 the FAS, supporting McNamara's contention that a BMD would not add to anyone's security, released another statement against deployment. Reiterating the argument that an increase in the tempo of the arms race would occur if BMD were deployed, the Federation said:

> Neither the technical implications of a decision to deploy nor the political ones, internal or external, are likely in any important way to further our domestic progress or our aspirations for control of the arms race abroad. Instead such a decision will, if it does anything, be disruptive and divisive in its impact upon us and upon those relations with the Soviets from which eventual control of arms can spring. Finally, other nations consider our progress toward arms limitations relevant to their decision to acquire nuclear weapons; thus a new round of arms race will make the achievement of a non-proliferation treaty more difficult. [8]

In June 1964 Dr. Freeman J. Dyson of the Institute for Advanced Study, a former consultant to the Arms Control and Disarmament Agency, Atomic Energy Commission, and Department of Defense, and national chairman of the Federation of American Scientists, suggested that a limited defense against missiles was possible.[1] The major consideration of any defensive system was not its feasibility, Dr. Dyson said, but the effect the deployment of an American BMD would have on the Soviets.

---

[1] This has become a classic statement of those opposed to BMD and is cited by those in favor as indicative of the thinking of mutual deterrence supporters. Dyson, though, has since changed his mind and favors a limited BMD deployment. See Freeman Dyson, "A Case for Missile Defense," *Bulletin of the Atomic Scientists,* April 1969, p. 31.

The military issues concerned the incompatibility of deterrence and defense and the difference between the long and short war doctrines of nuclear war.[2] Developing the logic of these two points, Dyson concluded "the consensus among American civilian strategists is against the deployment of BMD." He suggested the deployment of BMD threatens the stability of the deterrent:

> A country which deploys BMD is expressing a serious intention to make itself invulnerable, and is thus automatically threatening to upset stability. This reasoning has led the majority of American civilian experts to oppose violently the deployment of BMD by either side. [9]

The political issues of deployment, Dyson considered, were internal to the countries concerned. In the United States a limited deployment was politically impossible, since certain cities were likely to be left unprotected. Dyson argued that interservice rivalry played a part in the deployment decision because of the Army's preoccupation with defense and the Air Force's emphasis on offense. He pointed out that a great deal of interservice rivalry existed in the Soviet Union between the air and space defense forces and long-range rocket forces, which would affect BMD, but the Soviets have a propensity to defense and BMD would be compatible with such behavior. In addition, with their decision-making process, as contrasted to ours, they could deploy BMD gradually, "as any rational military man would wish to do without committing himself at once to a countrywide program." For Dyson, a pattern emerged from his analysis:

> For many and diverse reasons, the Soviet military and political leaders find the deployment of an ABM system convenient and reassuring to their feelings of security. For equally diverse reasons, deployment of ABM in the U.S. would be neither convenient nor reassuring to us. It is therefore logical to expect that, as time goes on, a Soviet ABM system will be deployed, whereas an American ABM system will not. Such a course of events would answer to the objective needs of both countries. American security would be assured by an invulnerable retaliatory missile force equipped with the most modern pentration aids, and Soviet security would be assured by the possession of the most modern defensive weapons combined with modest offensive forces. [10]

Unfortunately, Dyson said, this objectively tolerable situation is upset by "the intense political pressure that exists in both countries to duplicate

---

[2] For an understanding of the long and short war doctrines, consult Thomas W. Wolfe, *Soviet Strategy at the Crossroads,* Harvard University Press, 1964, pp. 17–18, 46, and 305.

whatever the other side does." Dyson concluded, "there is no reason why we should consider the Soviet ABM deployment to be threatening to us."

> The crucial problem that remains is to convince the American Congress and public that Soviet ABM systems are not necessarily a deadly threat. The American people must become accustomed to the idea that they may be better off without an ABM system, even if the Soviet people believe they are better off with one. [11]

Opposition to BMD is also prevalent among both civilian strategists and scientists. Dr. Jeremy Stone, now Director of the Federation of American Scientists organization and formerly of the Hudson Institute, Pomona College, and the Council on Foreign Relations, is an advocate of BMD limitation and arms control.

In 1964 he wrote that any decision by either the Soviet Union or the United States to reallocate missile resources and increase expenditures for BMD was made more difficult by the limited value of such a system. While missile defense systems appear ineffective now:

> . . . they alone show any prospect, even in concept of neutralizing offenses, and the possibility that they will be effective in 15 or 20 years cannot be discounted. [12]

Hence, they represent a new round in the arms race.

> Because costs are so high, and the strategic motives for procurement fairly marginal, a U.S. or a Soviet decision to embark on a program of large scale procurement of defenses would indicate in psychological terms a decision to push ahead in the arms race. [13]

Stone, seeing reasons for both sides to acquire BMD, asked what both sides were likely to do about its deployment, especially as the United States may want BMD to protect its retaliatory forces. Using the arguments already presented, Stone concluded each power was more likely to gain additional security by persuading the other to forgo strategic defensive weapons and not buy additional offensive ones. He suggested while this is obvious, neither side is going to show restraint, and herein lies the weakness in Soviet-American arms competition, for neither side would rest content with just BMD.

> As the defense achieved more than token efficiency, it would quickly become evident that a race to achieve both deterrence and defense is unlike a race to achieve deterrence only, one in which both sides cannot be successful simultaneously. At the end of an arms race that neglects defense lies some kind of strategic nuclear stalemate; but at the

end of a race involving large expenditures for defensive weapons systems lies great waste or great instability. [14]

Based on his assessment, Stone felt that the United States should make known its intentions to procure a BMD if the Soviets do, but if the Soviets do procure BMD, it would be a misallocation of resources on their part, and the United States should then *not* carry out its stated intention.

In a later article Stone reiterated his contention BMD does not constrain competition but encourages it. Adopting the Schelling thesis of the communicative value of weapons, Stone maintained that the spiraling arms race would decrease in intensity if neither side bought BMD. Given the choice of buying more offense or defense—the choice now confronting both sides—he felt the political, strategic, and technological pressures which favored the offense would continue to prevail. To oppose the forces of the offense meant to engage in a continuing technological struggle which could only upset stability and make for a new arms race. To support the forces of the offense provided the greatest hope for relative tranquility [15].

The October 1964 *Scientific American* featured an article by Dr. Jerome Wiesner, former scientific advisor to President Kennedy, and Dr. Herbert F. York, head of ARPA during the Eisenhower Administration and later Director of DDR&E during the Kennedy Administration. The authors' theme was that, while both sides had increased their military power, they had not increased their security, because military technology could no longer enhance the nation's security. One of the major potential destabilizing elements in the present confrontation, Wiesner and York believed, was the possibility one side or the other might develop and deploy BMD, thereby nullifying the deterrent force of the other. However, the authors believed defense against thermonuclear attack was impossible and even hopeless. Using the ZEUS and NIKE-X systems as illustrations of how offensive technology made defensive weapons obsolete, they concluded: there was nothing on the horizon to indicate a solution to the missile defense problem. Indeed, "the practical fact is that work on defensive systems turns out to be the best way to promote invention of the penetration aids that nullify them." [16]

While it was not an official statement of U.S. policy, the Report of the Committee on Arms Control and Disarmament of the National Citizens' Commission on International Cooperation in 1966 did contain the efforts of many ex-government officials, including Wiesner and Gilpatric. Basing their hopes and recommendations on the fact that arms limitations agreements had been reached in 1963–64, they believed the climate was then ripe to continue the process of reducing the costs and dangers of military and political competition. "Two imperatives are uppermost," the report stated:

> ... first, to halt the spread of nuclear weapons beyond the present five atomic powers; second, to curb and then reduce the arms build-up taking place among and within these same five countries, a spiral driven upward by new technological possibilities and by the uncertainties resulting from nuclear proliferation. [17]

One of their several recommendations urged:

> ... the United States and the Soviet Union to agree—explicitly or tacitly—to a moratorium of at least three years on new deployment (but not on the unverifiable research and development) of systems for ballistic missile defense. [18]

Conclusions of the Arms Committee report were that the initial American BMD deployment might be against the growing Chinese threat, but eventually a Soviet or American BMD deployment

> ... would almost certainly induce both Superpowers to step up their strategic weapon program in an effort to ensure their respective 'deterrent' capabilities. [19]

It was their opinion that the time was inappropriate to make a decision to deploy BMD. Beyond the technical, military, and economic problems still facing BMD, the Committee believed that sufficient thought had not been given to the political consequences of BMD deployment. No attempt had been given to ascertain the manner in which the United States and the U.S.S.R. could avoid the unintended effects of BMD on the other's deterrent force. The Committee's panel report raised a number of important questions concerning BMD and international relations:

> Shall the systems be emplaced in Europe? Will they be sold to allies by ourselves or by the Soviets? Can we and the Soviet Union devise ways by which we acquiesce in reduced, but still enormous deterrent capabilities? Will our action simply play into the hands of the Communist Chinese effort to disrupt U.S.-Soviet relations in general, and arms limitation efforts in particular? Does the Chinese threat really require immediate action on the part of the U.S. and the Soviets? And how far are we and the Soviets planning to go in building active defenses? The costs involved in the systems under discussion are measured in tens of billions of dollars; their strategic implications are enormous and long-lasting, and their political impact may be the most startling of all—especially in Europe. The matter deserves the closest and most intense discussion and thought; a three-year moratorium would produce it. [20]

A number of other organizations had in previous years (1964–67) come out strongly against deploying BMD. On January 30, 1967, the Council for Christian Social Action of the United Church of Christ adopted a resolution at its convention in Cleveland urging the United States "to seek Soviet agreement upon an indefinite moratorium on the deployment of major anti-ballistic missile systems." The impetus for this declaration, the Council said, stemmed from the Administration's need to decide whether to deploy BMD in view of the Soviet deployment. The Council felt while it might be true the Soviets were deploying BMD, this did not indicate they had any intention of launching an attack against the United States:

> We welcome recent statements by President Johnson and other Administration spokesmen, which indicate that the Administration is extremely reluctant to commence and deploy a multi-billion dollar American anti-ballistic missile system. We believe that such a decision would be a tragic waste of American resources which could be better used to overcome massive human suffering at home and abroad. It would, moreover, increase United States responsibility for a serious escalation of the arms race. While an anti-ballistic missile system and the civil defense effort which would almost certainly accompany it might be defensive in our own intentions, they would probably raise the level of threat and insecurity to an intolerable pitch. We acknowledge that there are risks in any conceivable United States response to this new crisis in military technology. However, we believe that the risks of escalation are immeasurably more difficult to justify in this instance than the risks of restraint. [21]

In 1966 an unsigned article in *Commonweal,* entitled "Containing ABM," ridiculed the idea of deploying BMD, saying such a step would only compound the madness of an irrational world where hundreds of millions of fatalities were part of the normal political discourse. Citing the Arms Control Panel Report of the White House Conference on International Cooperation, the author said, even though efforts at reaching an agreement with the Soviets on a BMD moratorium have proved fruitless, "much of the Committee's argument remains as relevant for unilateral American restraint." [22]

The arguments against missile defense have included at one time or another: (1) its cost is high; (2) the money spent on BMD could be used to buy more offensive deterrent weapons; (3) buying BMD is a waste of money as the money might be better used for domestic and civilian needs; (4) the offense can overcome any defense for less money than the defense costs; (5) civil defense must accompany missile defense; (6) missile defense cannot discriminate decoys from warheads; (7) chaff can jam the

BMD radars; (8) BMD radars are vulnerable to attack; (9) BMD can be saturated; (10) damage limitation can be purchased in much less expensive ways; (11) the system is unreliable; (12) the computer software and hardware provide insurmountable problems; (13) the system is not perfect; (14) it will escalate the arms race by introducing a new weapon; (15) it will provoke the Soviets into finding a counter to it or launching a preemptive attack; (16) BMD is not feasible; and (17) it is destabilizing, since it upsets the deterrent balance and does not allow for a stabilization of strategic weapons. By 1967 every one of these arguments had been put forth. In the great debate of 1969 and the "mini debate" in 1970, not a single new argument was made against missile defense, except that it would upset the Strategic Arms Limitation Talks (SALT), SAFEGUARD was not designed for hard point defense, and the Soviet SS-9 ICBM was configured for a first strike.

It is important for the reader to know the rationale for *not* deploying a missile defense if the developments in missile defense policy in the subsequent years are to be understood.

The BMD concept and its technology evolved during a period (1955 to early 1960) of technological innovation and invention—the period of the revolution in strategic weaponry. The practicality and utility of BMD became apparent during a time (mid-1962 to 1966) when the technology which had created it was being reappraised in view of its effect on the international system. Decisionmakers were faced with a dilemma: the accelerating exploitation of technology for military purposes might be a threat to the very existence of the political system the technology was designed to preserve. During this period (separating the 1955 to early-1960 and the mid-1962 to 1966 phases in BMD development) voluminous literature on military strategy (both analytic and prescriptive) began to appear, evaluating the deterrent's balance, its elements, its stability, and its effects on world politics. This was followed by arms control and disarmament studies, and, finally, by the recognition that a strategy of deterrence had to be discussed in terms of the particular effect any one weapon might have on the nuclear equation. After 1960, when an invulnerable strategic deterrent force composed of ICBMs became possible, mutual deterrence appeared as a practical means for halting or slowing down the spiraling arms race.

By 1962 it became apparent:

> . . . in addition to weapons systems, other elements not of a military dimension were necessary for deterrence in the broader modern sense [that any kind of armaments for any purpose, limited war or conventional or nuclear war, contribute to deterrence]. Diplomacy, signals given to the other side, proposals for arms control, statements of policy, doing or

not doing, disclosure of secrets to the other side, and penetration into the secrets of the potential enemy had to be understood as being quite as important as weapons. Weapons could, in fact, be considered as a deterrent only in the context of a much wider set of measures which, taken together, amount to a strategy [23].

BMD is and was revolutionary. During the first period, it was revolutionary per se, like all of the strategic weapons that technology has made possible. In the second period, when the decisionmaker had acquired the means to carry out any strategy he considered appropriate, BMD was revolutionary because it could upset the strategic status quo—in the context of mutual deterrence. By this time technology and its military by-products were identified with instability, since they could be viewed as capable of accelerating the arms race and thereby upsetting the strategic balance. Since the goal of mutual deterrence was to halt the arms race, stabilize the nuclear equation, and improve Soviet-American relations, the two developments, advancing military technology and mutual deterrence, were incompatible. This is why the technological-plateau thesis was introduced, to provide a "scientific" rationale for not pursuing further strategic weapon development. The existence of BMD was a threat to the technological-plateau thesis and to mutual deterrence and its hoped-for political goals.

The strategy of mutual deterrence is premised on a number of peculiar assumptions deriving from historical experiences of the last quarter-century. The experience of Pearl Harbor and then the use of the atomic bomb against Japan led the creators of the atomic bomb to believe the next war would open with a surprise nuclear strike, which would result in the utter destruction of civilization. This placed nuclear weapons in a class by themselves. Fear of their use led to demands that they be placed under international control. This fear was exacerbated by the failure of the Soviets to accept the Baruch Plan for such control. The scientists who created the bomb, shocked at their achievements and the prospect of the further use to which these weapons might be put, determined to make people realize the peril of atomic arms. A feeling of guilt [3] for having developed these weapons, plus technical understanding of the consequences if these weapons were used, in no small way contributed to the politicization and polarization of the scientists and scientific community as participants in

---

[3] The "guilt feeling for having participated in the development of nuclear weapons" theme was part of the major post-World War II Soviet peace and disarmament campaigns. This theme was a recurring one at the early Pugwash Conferences. See U.S. Senate, Subcommittee to Investigate the Administration of the Internal Security Laws of the Committee on the Judiciary, *The Pugwash Conference,* 87th Cong., 1st Sess., 1961, p. 26.

defense policy formation and at arms control and disarmament efforts agreements.[4]

Hanson Baldwin, former military editor for *The New York Times*, has written of the scientists' guilt feelings.

> This kind of thinking stems from the collective guilt complex felt by many atomic scientists who worked in the Manhattan Project in the Second World War and by their proteges. It reflects, too, the scientists' occupational distaste for secrecy and for what many of them feel to be the prostitution of their science to destructive purposes. But in a larger sense, as some of the wiser of them admit, it also displays the physical scientists' naivete about political science. [24]

Eugene Rabinowitch, editor of the *Bulletin of the Atomic Scientists,* which was founded along with the Federation of American Scientists in 1945 to lobby on the perils of nuclear arms, has written that scientists who developed nuclear weapons have a responsibility to prevent their use. In the February 1967 *Bulletin,* he stated that the equilibrium of mutual deterrence would be destroyed by either side's deploying BMD, an argument propounded by some American scientists a decade ago. Therefore, "American scientists must do all in their power to prevent the U.S. government from unthinking commitment to 'winning' this new arms race, which would only cause further deterioration of world security, and wasteful use of American resources." [25]

This differentiation between nuclear arms and all other arms has given to the concept of deterrence its unique 20th century connotation, although deterrence as a military strategy is as old as man. Fear that these weapons might be used led to the evolution and development of a strategy designed to prevent war by deterring it. Deterrence was to be achieved by threatening and if need be using strategic retaliatory forces capable, under any circumstances, of attacking and destroying an attacker's society. From this emerged the idea that any deterrent strategy which sought a quantitative and qualitative balance between antagonists would be defeated if either side sought unilaterally to redress the balance by introducing new or more advanced weapons.

In such a concept, weapons, whether they were offensive or defensive, were not considered provocative. It was the intention of the user that determined whether a weapon was for aggression or deterrence. Therefore,

---

[4] See Robert Gilpin's *American Scientists and Nuclear Weapons Policy* for a discussion of the scientists' role in defense policy formulation and in arms control and disarmament efforts.

weapons for deterrence could be strategic offensive weapons such as an ICBM, or defensive weapons such as interceptors or BMD. Aggressive weapons could be bombers, BMD, or missiles. It all depended on the kind of strategy—deterrent, war-waging, or war-winning—which the possessor had, and how the weapons would be used within that strategy.

The most desirable form of deterrence to those opposed to BMD deployment was mutual deterrence, which was not measured by equality or symmetry of forces, deliverable megatonnage, or numbers of weapons, but by the stability of the balance. The balance is only stable when neither side by striking first can destroy the other side's ability to retaliate and destroy the attacker.[5] The only acceptable measure is the number of survivable deliverable warheads. Implicit in this concept was that retaliatory forces should be made as secure and invulnerable as possible. Therefore, any measure for increasing or bringing about stability should be directed to the protection of weapons, not people. Stabilization in mutual deterrence is accomplished by enhancing the integrity of a particular, already deployed weapon system, not by introducing new ones. Such a situation, thought Wiesner, would be made possible by creating offensive weapon systems sufficiently invulnerable to prevent their destruction by any practicably achievable force in a surprise attack. If this situation were to prevail for both sides, then neither side would have the incentive to build a counterforce capability. Wiesner continued:

> . . . it is important to note that a missile deterrent system would be unbalanced by the development of a highly effective anti-missile defense system, and if it appears possible to develop one, the agreement should explicitly prohibit the development and deployment of such systems. [26]

From Wiesner's viewpoint, as long as security could be ensured by the ability of the two adversaries to destroy each other's society under all circumstances (i.e., mutual or stable deterrence), BMD could only upset this equilibrium by causing one side to gain an advantage.

The weapons most crucial to a mutual deterrent situation, the ones

---

[5] A corollary of this strategy is: one side alone should not have the capability to render ineffective a retaliatory force or to limit damage to itself in face of retaliation or surprise attack. The occurrence and acceptance of a mutual deterrent situation was dependent on *both* sides' desiring it and communicating their intention to the other. Mutual deterrence by its very definition cannot occur with one side espousing it and the other not. Nor can it tolerate asymmetrical differences in offense or defense on both sides. The danger of mutual deterrence is the assumption: first, one's adversary desires it, when he does not; and, second, he is complying with and understanding one's suggestions and signals to achieve a mutual deterrent situation, when in fact he is not.

which must be protected and made survivable, are those most destructive of people; the ones designed to retaliate, to punish, not to fight with or disarm the enemy. "A weapon that can hurt only *people,* and cannot possibly damage the other side's striking force, is profoundly defensive; it provides its possessor no incentive to strike first." [27] Conversely, weapons capable of destroying strategic weapons are destabilizing and provocative.

The theme—to acquire and then maintain a stabilized deterrent composed of an invulnerable second-strike ICBM or SLBM retaliatory force— pervades every discussion for slowing down the arms race. The belief is: any measures, including defensive ones, which enable one nation to acquire protection for itself or gain an advantage over its adversary will enhance the feasibility and probability of war by upsetting the stability of the environment created by the vulnerability of cities. Obviously BMD and mutual deterrence are incompatible. Unfortunately, the opponents of BMD never point out that the Soviets deployed a BMD first or that they should refrain from deploying BMD as they urge their own country to do.

A variety of political problems is associated with formal arms control arrangements; e.g., inspection, safeguards, and controls. Arms control agreements unless formally enacted cannot halt the tempo of the arms race or slow down weapon technology development. In informal agreements, where mutual goals and benefits exist for both sides, unilateral actions, freezes, and self-imposed constraints and restraints may be the forerunners for building the mutual confidence between parties so necessary for more formal measures.

Underlying informal measures of arms control is the belief, despite past Soviet-American behavior, that now, during a period of great instability caused by the arms race and rapidly accelerating weapons technology and its attendant costs, there are compelling reasons why both sides should reach a common understanding, an interdependence, with each other. The argument runs: To create mutual trust between the Soviet Union and the United States, so the Soviets will have a common interest and desire to adopt informal arms control policies, the United States should communicate, by some concrete unilateral action, its willingness to enter into an informal restraining agreement. Simultaneously with this psychopolitical strategy to develop mutual confidence, in the absence of successful disarmament agreements, both sides should rely on a military strategy which recognizes the commonality of interests between them, the reality of the world situation, and the need to halt the arms race. One solution may be to ensure each side's security by permitting mutual vulnerability of cities and populations and the retention of invulnerable offensive forces designed to survive a first strike and then retaliate against the aggressor's society. This is stable or mutual deterrence. No attempt to upset this situation, such as deploying

BMD or building shelters, would be permitted. The mutual fear of having one's society destroyed is the deterrent; to protect the society is destabilizing, since it makes war possible. A great similarity between this theory and the Johnson Administration's national security policy of 1965–1967 is evident.

References

[1] Seymour Melman, ed., *A Strategy for American Security: An Alternative to the 1964 Military Budget,* Lee Offset, 1964, p. 3.

[2] Roswell Gilpatric, "Our Defense Needs," *Foreign Affairs,* 3[1964]368–369.

[3] Gilpatric, p. 371.

[4] Roswell Gilpatric, "Are We on the Brink of Another Arms Race?" *The New York Times Magazine,* January 15, 1967, p. 85.

[5] "FAS Statement on Ballistic Missile Defense," *FAS Newsletter,* June 1964, p. 3, hereafter cited as *FAS-BMD 1964.*

[6] *FAS-BMD 1964,* p. 3.

[7] *FAS-BMD 1964,* p. 3.

[8] "Scientists Group Supports McNamara's Opposition to Anti-Missile Fund Increase," *Federation of American Scientists Press Release,* May 8, 1966, p. 2.

[9] J. Freeman Dyson, "Defense Against Ballistic Missiles," *Bulletin of the Atomic Scientists,* 6[1964]13, hereafter cited as "Defense Against Ballistic Missiles."

[10] "Defense Against Ballistic Missiles," p. 18.

[11] "Defense Against Ballistic Missiles," p. 18.

[12] Jeremy Stone. "Arms Race or Disarmament?" *Bulletin of the Atomic Scientists,* 7[1964]21, hereafter cited as "Arms Race or Disarmament?"

[13] "Arms Race or Disarmament?" p. 21.

[14] "Arms Race or Disarmament?" p. 22.

[15] Jeremy Stone, "Containing the Arms Race," *Bulletin of the Atomic Scientists,* 7[1965]18.

[16] Jerome Wiesner and Herbert F. York, *Scientific American,* 4[1964]34.

[17] *Report of the Committee on Arms Control and Disarmament of the National Citizens' Commission Prepared for the White House Conference on International Cooperation,* New York, United Nations Association of the United States of America, 1966, p. 16, hereafter cited as *Arms Control Report of the ICC.*

[18] *Arms Control Report of the ICC,* p. 16.

[19] *Arms Control Report of the ICC,* p. 16.

[20] *Arms Control Report of the ICC,* p. 17.

[21] "On Anti-Ballistic Missiles and the Arms Race," A text of the *Statements of the Council for Christian Social Action of the United Church of Christ* at the 1967 Cleveland Convention, New York, Council for Christian Social Action, United Church of Christ, 1967.

[22] "Containing ABM," *Commonweal,* 10[1966]272.

[23] Urs Schwarz, *American Strategy: A New Perspective,* Doubleday Anchor, 1967, pp. 101–102.

[24] Hanson Baldwin, "The Great Missile Debate," *The Reporter,* 13[1967]25.

[25] Eugene Rabinowitch, "The Editor Comments: Missile Gap and Wheat Gap," *Bulletin of the Atomic Scientists,* 2[1967]3.

[26] Jerome B. Wiesner, "Comprehensive Arms Limitation Systems," Donald G. Brennan, ed., *Arms Control, Disarmament and National Security,* George Braziller, 1961, p. 216.

[27] Thomas C. Schelling, *The Strategy of Conflict,* Oxford University Press, 1963, p. 233.

CHAPTER 9

Missile Defense—The Modular Approach—1965

On January 19, 1965, President Johnson delivered his Budget Message to Congress, in which he said:

> Our investment has effected an enormous improvement in the design of antiballistic missile systems. We will pursue our program for the development of the NIKE-X antimissile system, to permit deployment of this anti-ballistic missile should the national security require. Research will continue on even more advanced antimissile components and concepts. [1]

However, before spending large sums of money on the NIKE-X system, the President wanted to be certain the system would provide adequate protection against attack. Such protection, he pointed out, would lose all effectiveness if it were not accompanied with a fallout shelter program. He added:

> . . . we will continue our existing programs and start a program to increase the total inventory of shelters through survey of private homes and other small structures. We shall continue the research and development which retains the options to deploy an antiballistic missile system. . . . [2]

A year earlier, McNamara introduced the concept of assured destruction/damage limitation. He now suggested if the United States and the Soviet Union had the same general strategic objectives—i.e., deterrence of the other—then the U.S. assured destruction problem was the Soviet's damage limiting problem. Since the BMD question was but one aspect of the U.S. strategic retaliatory force structure, understanding the BMD issue in 1965–1966 depended on comprehending the ever more complex strategic issues. In his 1965 Posture Statement McNamara discussed U.S. strategic nuclear war forces and issues.

Certain basic qualifications apply to damage-limiting forces, McNamara said, because it is virtually impossible to provide anything approaching perfect protection for the U.S. population. For any given level of enemy offensive capability, successive additions to each of the various

U.S. strategic systems would have a diminishing marginal value. No matter how large general nuclear war forces might be, strategic offensive forces and their targeting doctrine would affect the damage and population losses of the United States; i.e., were U.S. forces targeted countervalue or counterforce? The Soviets have within their technical and economic means the capability to prevent the United States from keeping its own fatalities below a tolerable level, even if it were to deploy an active defense.

Since the Soviets could inflict severe damage on the United States with bombers, submarine-launched missiles, and ICBMs, a very good defense against only one form of attack would have limited value:

> A meaningful capability to limit the damage of a determined enemy attack, therefore, requires an integrated, balanced combination of strategic defensive forces, area defense forces, terminal defense forces and passive defenses. [3]

In effect, these principles meant every weapon system competed with every other weapon system to see which combination of systems would optimally ensure an adequate assured destruction/damage limitation force. In practical terms the defensive NIKE-X must compete against the ICBM on a cost-effectiveness basis to determine whether the high cost of NIKE-X warrants its deployment or whether its mission can be accomplished more cheaply by the counterforce targeted ICBM. Moreover, if the NIKE-X should be deployed, to its actual cost must be added the cost of strengthening bomber defenses and antisubmarine-warfare (ASW) forces, in order to prevent the enemy from circumventing the defense and gaining a "free ride."

Secretary McNamara's testimony before the Senate Armed Services and Appropriations Committees shed additional light on his own reasoning and the President's decision. For the first time, all strategic forces—offensive and defensive—were considered together. Going into unprecedented detail about the complexities and economics of nuclear war, the Defense Secretary described the problems involved in finding a combination of weapons which would save the most lives per dollar invested. His 33-page analysis concluded that "there is no defense program within this general range of expenditures which would reduce fatalities to a level much below 80 million. . . ." [4] While the argument is not conclusive, Secretary McNamara said:

> . . . it does underscore the fact that beyond a certain level of defense, the cost advantage lies increasingly with the offense, and this fact must be taken into account in any decision to commit ourselves to large outlays for additional defensive measures. [5]

In light of his analysis, the Secretary announced that six major issues were involved in the fiscal 1966-1970 general nuclear war programs. Two of these were questions as to whether NIKE-X should be produced and deployed and whether fallout shelters should be constructed for the entire population.

Secretary McNamara said that in the past year United States missile defense systems had improved greatly with respect to cost and effectiveness and to alternate forms of deployment. While system development had progressed satisfactorily, however, many technical problems still remained to be solved. Therefore, he suggested that it was premature to make any commitment to production and deployment:

> Over and above the technical problems there are even greater uncertainties concerning the preferred concept of deployment, the relationship of the NIKE-X system to other elements of a balanced Damage Limiting effort, the timing of the attainment of an effective nationwide fallout shelter system and the nature and effect of an opponent's possible reaction to our NIKE-X deployment. [6]

The Army again recommended production of NIKE-X, using already appropriated funds, but McNamara said it would be very unwise to follow the Army's advice because:

> . . . the development work has not progressed to the point where the system has been fully tested, and if we begin to lay out the production process and long lead time tooling before development is completed, almost surely we will have to go back and revise the production process and redesign the tooling as the design changes are introduced into the system. I think it would be unwise to initiate production with fiscal 1966 funds even if we had already decided to deploy it. We are not really in a position to decide that at the present time. I think that decision could be better made in fiscal 1967, and therefore, for both reasons I think it would be unwise to include procurement funds for that system in the fiscal 1966 budget. For example, we would require quite a different system for the expected less sophisticated Chinese threat than we would for the Soviet threat. For the Soviet threat we need a much higher capability at a given point and therefore would deploy this system at fewer points. [7]

Accordingly, NIKE-X was provided with $400 million for development, and the issue of deployment was deferred for another year.

Since the BMD concept was closely tied to the civil defense program, Secretary McNamara proposed to spend $23 million to continue the efforts to identify, stock, and determine the exact nature of the residual shelter requirements. The chief problem of the civil defense program was the reluctance of Congress to approve a fallout shelter program. Much of the fiscal 1966 Appropriations testimony was concerned with civil defense.

Under questioning by Representative Mahon, Secretary McNamara said he thought that if the United States deployed the present system, it would still suffer 80 million casualties in a nuclear attack. If a much more effective system than the present NIKE-X was deployed, McNamara said, he would expect the Soviets to construe this as an aggressive move and increase their expenditures (for ICBMs and probably for an ABM). While discussing the cost of NIKE-X and what it would provide, he illustrated its relation to civil defense.

Since one cannot be sure of destroying all the attacking warheads, McNamara noted, fallout shelters are necessary to supplement the NIKE-X. He used the following examples: a Soviet attack in 1970 would result in 100 million to 150 million fatalities if nothing had been done to protect or defend the population. If $5 billion had been spent on defense, 20 million people could be saved, although 80 million to 100 million would still perish. If an additional $20 billion were spent for a full NIKE-X deployment, an additional 10 million people would be saved. The question he asked was, does it pay to invest $20 billion to save 10 million people when upwards of 75 million are still going to perish? As he pointed out, if spending $20 billion meant the difference between zero fatalities and 10 million, then the cost would be justified. While a BMD deployment against a Soviet threat was ruled out, despite the growing Soviet threat, McNamara hinted at the possibility of considering deploying NIKE-X against a primitive Chinese threat [8].

Departing from their position of the previous year, the Joint Chiefs unanimously recommended that $200 million be put into the budget for pre-production of NIKE-X components [9].[1] Once again, the JCS and the Administration were at odds over the immediate necessity for deploying NIKE-X.[2] According to General William Dick, the major reasons for

---

[1] On p. 355 of the Senate Appropriations Hearings the amount to be allocated for NIKE-X pre-production is deleted for security.

[2] An interesting aspect is found on p. 890 of the *House Defense Appropriations FY 1966*, in which it is reported Air Force Chief of Staff General McConnell believed, until NIKE-X became more acceptable, it should not be deployed. He also believed this was the opinion of the JCS. Yet on p. 397 it is reported General Wheeler, as Chairman of the Joint Chiefs, recommended the deployment of the NIKE-X to DOD, but a contrary decision was made. This may indicate that within the Joint Chiefs there was not a unanimous position on the question of BMD deployment. In fact, the decision within the JCS for deployment was not unanimous, nor was there a consensus. Two years later Wheeler revealed that the lack of consensus at the time was over the speed of deployment rather than disagreement as to whether

disagreement were NIKE-X's vulnerability to saturation and the lack of a fallout shelter program.

The Betts Report of 1964 contained a number of interesting factors bearing directly on the decision to deploy NIKE-X. First, the report refuted the idea that offensive technology had an insurmountable lead over defensive technology; rather, it suggested that the two were closer to a standoff. Second, ballistic-missile defense was considered a useful contribution to a damage-limiting strategy. Not unexpectedly, the report said, the utility and value of BMD varied with the war game scenario used. For example, in the event of a surprise attack, the system would have great value; in a gradually worsening international crisis, however, it might not.[3] The report concluded that the period of mutual deterrence would continue whether a BMD system were deployed or not. The threat of destabilization was not considered as serious as at first thought. The report made no recommendation for deployment, but provided an arithmetic underpinning to any future decision regarding the system [10].

Dr. Harold Brown described in his testimony the new approach NIKE-X was taking toward tailoring a deployment to a specific threat:

> Because of the future uncertainties of the level and sophistication of the possible attacks which we may face, we have been working very hard in the NIKE-X program on a design concept representing the maximum flexibility in our choice of capability and the corresponding cost. We propose in fiscal year 1966 to concentrate on the "building block" concept of NIKE-X to permit maximum flexibility in deployment options against various threats, including those less than a massive all-out attack by a sophisticated opponent. [11]

Brown explained the basic nature of the cost-effectiveness argument presented by McNamara:

> At low U.S. casualty levels the exchange ratio—number of dollars expended by the defense per dollar expended by the offense—is unfavorable to the defense—for example, the ratio is approximately 4 to 1 at a [deleted] U.S. casualty level. That is, to maintain the capability to limit U.S. casualties to less than [deleted] with NIKE-X, the United States would have to spend about four times as much on defense to limit damage as the Soviets would have to spend on ICBM's to create damage.

NIKE-X should be deployed. See U.S. Senate, Hearings Before the Subcommittee on Disarmament of the Committee on Foreign Relations, *United States Armament and Disarmament Problems,* 90th Cong., 1st Sess., 1967, p. 92.

[3] The author believes the opposite of this might be true.

At higher casualty levels, the exchange ratio shifts toward the defense [deleted]. [12]

Asked by Senator Levett Saltonstall (R-Mass.) whether he was giving more emphasis this year than in years past to defense forces, McNamara replied:

... without question, offensive capability or what I will call the capability for assuring the destruction of the Soviet Union is far and away the most important requirements we have to meet. [13]

In fact, McNamara was not sure what action the United States should ultimately take regarding defensive systems, once the offense was provided for. He appeared to have relegated defense to a subordinate role compared to offense. Consequently, as long as he remained at the Defense Department, U.S. nuclear strategy could be assumed to rely primarily on offensive retaliatory power to deter the Soviet Union and perhaps a mix of offensive and defensive forces to deter the Chinese.

In the search for a credible deterrent, would the solution be more apt to be found in a combination of offensive and defensive systems? Or would it be found in an assured destruction capability which rests on some number of *offensive* vehicles certain to survive a nuclear attack and then retaliate? So long as evidence existed that the Soviets were developing BMD, the United States would have to assume they will have some capability to intercept the U.S. assured destruction forces threatening them. If, as McNamara says, assured destruction and damage limitation are the opposite sides of the coin for the United States and the Soviet Union, respectively, then compared to the Soviet Union the United States would have less damage-limiting potential. To the author, this reveals a weakness in logic and politics; as the credibility of the U.S. deterrent would be less, so conceivably the United States could not take as much punishment as the Soviets in a nuclear attack. Such an asymmetrical condition in the deterrent equation is not favorable to a mutual deterrence condition.

By March 1965 several things were apparent about the possible deployment of BMD. Despite its high cost, this country could decide then to begin deployment of NIKE-X, or some modular form of BMD based on NIKE-X, to protect against an unsophisticated attack or to protect hardened missile sites. Both forms of deployment, hard point defense and limited city deployment, were gaining considerable attention in ARPA and the Defense Department.[4] Either system's cost would be in the neighborhood

---

[4] In January 1965, Douglas Missile and Space Systems Division delivered a report to ARPA entitled *Characteristics of Anti-Ballistic Missile Systems Optimized for Defense Against Small Attacks*. The contents of this report indicated that ARPA

of $5 billion to $8 billion, and a comprehensive fallout shelter program would not be required. A BMD deployment against a lesser threat than the Soviet Union posed was consistent with the Betts Report, which concluded that the Nth-country problem, although serious, could be made less critical by deploying a limited city missile defense.

The Defense Department felt, without shelters and in the face of a determined attack, the utility of a BMD system was not such as to warrant the cost of its deployment. The Army contended shelters and BMD were really not dependent on each other, although it would be advantageous to have both, especially if Secretary McNamara's damage limitation assumptions were not shared.[5]

Intelligence reports pointed to the existence of second- and third-generation Soviet ICBMs by 1970–1971. If BMD defense were to be deployed against this threat, a decision to deploy NIKE-X had to be made during the fiscal 1967 budget review (i.e., by early 1966). [14]

In 1965 the United States appeared to be increasingly concerned with the effect a BMD might have on the Soviet Union. Would the Soviets view it as tipping the balance of strategic power in favor of the United States? Would they accept it as a normal increment to U.S. security? Would they make plans to increase their own penetration capabilities? Would they deploy a new BMD of their own? Would the Soviets worry about the effect of their deployment on the United States as the United States worried about the effect of deployment on the Soviets? Should the United States voluntarily withhold its system from deployment because of these doubts and hope the Soviets might do the same?

Meanwhile, NIKE-X continued its technical progress. The system had two phased-array radars (MAR and MSR) for guiding the SPRINT and ZEUS missiles. By early 1965, NIKE-X could have provided a high quality terminal defense. But because of ZEUS's range (the only carry-over from the NIKE-ZEUS system), the area defended in a single-site terminal deployment was about 20 miles. Hence, the cost per defended city was so great that only a few cities could be defended. During the 1963–1965 period, missile defense came to be viewed as an integral part of the U.S. strategic weapons inventory. The damage-limitation studies made during

---

was interested in limited missile defense concepts using the modular or building block approach. See "Douglas Delivers A-ICBM Study," *Missiles and Rockets*, January 25, 1965, p. 7.

[5] Ironically, on the subject of shelters, the reaction of Congress is the opposite of that of the Defense Department (i.e., Congress did not want shelters but wanted BMD, while the Defense Department felt it absolutely necessary to have shelters before BMD could be deployed).

this period clearly showed that the presence of missile defense required a diversion of enemy warhead payloads to provide for penaids. A diversion in warhead payload resulted in smaller warheads. This meant, if the enemy adopted a city targeting doctrine, etiher fewer casualties would result or the enemy would have to put more ICBM *boosters* on each target (this was before MRV and MIRV). These same damage-limitation studies showed the higher the percentage of population survival the defender tried to guarantee, the more the cost ratio between offense and defense favored the offense by a wide margin. At lower percentage levels of survival the cost ratio between offense and defense approached unity. In short, a city defense required the defense to protect all its population in order to deny the enemy the ability to destroy any percentage of it, and each defense site had to be capable of handling the total number of missiles the enemy could allocate to the target. ZEUS's range and payload capability were extended to 400 miles, and a new missile evolved from ZEUS called DM15X2. This interceptor came to be known as SPARTAN.

Howard Margolis of the *Washington Post* reported in April 1965 that, as a result of its intensive efforts to learn how to stop a sophisticated ICBM attack, the United States might inadvertently have found a solution. By combining ZEUS with NIKE-X radars, a better system could be developed (than if ZEUS were deployed with its own radars) at a cost of $1 billion to $2 billion. Hence, for a relatively modest cost, a wide area defense might be possible. In fact, with a modular BMD, NIKE-X, combined with a massive fallout shelter program, could be effective against a sophisticated attack; while ZEUS alone, combined with MAR, might constitute a light area defense [15]. A month later both *The New York Times* and the *Washington Post* reported that any U.S. decision to deploy BMD would be based on the rapidity with which the Chinese threat emerged [16]. The cost of the "Chinese" ABM was reported to be between $6 billion and $10 billion. The following week, *Missiles and Rockets* carried a short article confirming the *Times* and *Post* reports, adding that the Defense Department felt even a minimum deployment would have growth potential beyond a light defense, since SPRINT and more advanced radars could be added [17].

Even the most pessimistic proponents of BMD, those who had lived through the successive rejections of the systems by the Eisenhower, Kennedy, and Johnson Administrations, now foresaw the likelihood a BMD system would be deployed, most likely against a presumed Chinese threat. Still to be solved were some technical problems and the answer to "the cost for what it will buy" question of the Defense Department. However, a greater sense of urgency was added to the decision as evidence appeared the Soviets were deploying a BMD system across northwestern Russia and in other areas southwest and east of the Urals [18].[6]

By this time, most of the concepts essential to the operation of NIKE-X were proved, and the remaining technical problems were of an engineering nature. A number of questions and problems about deployment, however, did need answering. These included: (1) deciding on the deployment configuration (i.e., the proper mixture of ZEUS and SPRINT missiles with their accompanying radars), (2) estimating the number of shelters needed in conjunction with a particular BMD deployment for any given level of damage limitation, and (3) assessing the impact of an American BMD on Soviet strategic policy and ICBM force structure. Essential to the deployment question, too, as it would affect the size of the deployment and consequently the cost, were: (1) the likely number of nations possessing a deliverable nuclear arsenal and (2) the extent of damage limitation as a function of other strategic system mixes.

For example, if NIKE-X were deployed to guard against a possible Chinese threat, the most likely configuration would be (1) an area defense employing ZEUS and (2) a limited number of SPRINT missiles defending selected cities. Because of possible enemy targeting strategies, it would be economically inefficient to deploy SPRINT alone as a point defense system around some or all major cities. The Chinese would then have the option of launching terror attacks against the undefended targets, an option that makes an area defense more attractive.

The complexity of the deployment problem is illustrated further. For example, the cost of deployment is affected by the possibility that the ABM site itself, or any target protected by an ABM, may be subject to non-ballistic attack in the form of aircraft or air-breathing missiles. A NIKE-X deployment costing about $8.5 billion might therefore have to include an additional expenditure of $15 billion for an air defense system.

Still another issue affecting the deployment configuration stemmed from BMD kill mechanisms. ICBM RV destruction can be accomplished by heat, blast, EMP, X ray, neutron, and other forms of radiation. Each of

---

[6] This was the so-called Tallinn Line which for several years was to be the subject of much debate in the American intelligence community as to whether it was an advanced air defense system or a missile defense system. Most now agree it is an air defense system, but it might have the potential for upgrading to a missile defense system. The upgrading argument can be found in John W. Finney, "Dispute on Soviet Missiles Hampers U.S. Arms Stand," *The New York Times*, January 1, 1970, p. 1, and in Dr. John Foster's testimony to the House Subcommittee on National Security Policy and Scientific Developments of the Committee on Foreign Affairs, *Diplomatic and Strategic Impact of Multiple Warhead Missiles*, 91st Cong., 1st Sess., 1969, pp. 276–278.

these effects varies with altitude of detonation, time of day, and warhead design.[7] Nuclear effects not only affect the design and deployment of a BMD system, but affect the kinds and numbers of fallout shelters required. Together, the type of BMD deployment, its operational capabilities, and the passive defense accompanying it affect both the enemy's targeting strategy and the damage-limiting capabilities of the United States.

Another problem is public awareness. The results of a public opinion survey on missile defense (called here the General Electric (G.E.) Report) carried out during 1965 by the National Opinion Research Center of the University of Chicago for General Electric TEMPO and for ARPA are rather startling [19]. The purpose of this study was to assess public attitudes about BMD in the event a decision to deploy or withhold deployment were made. The survey pointed up an apparent contradiction between U.S. arms control policy (wherein the United States has indicated a willingness to forgo, under certain conditions, BMD deployment) and the popular conception of missile-age defense, which views BMD deployment as being beneficial to the nation's security. This lack of accurate information about the status of BMD is typical of the communications gap between the Government and the public, and the public's lack of interest in defense matters.

One of the major findings was that two-thirds of those interviewed believed this country was already protected by BMD.

The G.E. Report also dealt with shelters and their relation to BMD. The G.E. TEMPO Report indicated a basic public acceptability and desire for shelters, too. Clearly, the opinion of Congress concerning the shelter program was unrealistic, was based on mistaken information, and did not derive from public opinion. Had Congress been willing to enact civil defense legislation based on accurate knowledge of public feeling and to comport with the Defense Department's view that shelters were a basic prerequisite for a ballistic missile defense program, then a BMD might have been deployed years earlier.

As early as the fall of 1965, evidence was accumulating that the development and deployment of NIKE-X would be competing with the cost of the Vietnam war. The Administration's efforts to meet the financial burden of the war without increasing taxes, while holding defense spending down in the coming election year, meant the Defense Department might reject the Army's proposal to initiate production of long leadtime items for NIKE-X. This decision would not be so critical to U.S. security if the only threat in the coming decade were the Chinese. However, evidence

---

[7] The reason for resumption of nuclear testing in 1961 (and the cause for opposition to the test ban treaty of 1963) was the need to know more about these nuclear phenomena and their effects on BMD warhead design and ICBM kill.

was accumulating that the Soviets were deploying a BMD and their ICBM force was being increased. BMD proponents felt that, aside from these threats, technical progress was being made at such a rate operational deployment of NIKE-X could not but help to spur further BMD developments and breakthroughs.

In November 1965, Dr. Charles M. Herzfeld, Deputy Director of ARPA, in a paper delivered to the New York Academy of Sciences, revealed that the Defense Department was actively studying the feasibility of developing a relatively low-cost, less sophisticated missile defense system for cities. Its purpose would be to provide urban area protection from an accidental or Nth-power ICBM firing, but not from a deliberate and sophisticated nuclear attack.

He described ARPA's role in missile defense, especially in terminal defense measures, and held that atmospheric sorting was the only feasible discrimination technique. Dr. Herzfeld said both nuclear and nonnuclear kill mechanisms should be looked into because of the blackout problem with the use of the former and the need for exact guidance intercept with the use of the latter. He agreed with the Betts Report: no target could be completely protected from a determined attacker; but he argued that a BMD system, coupled with fallout shelters, would save lives and "up" the price of attack. Dr. Herzfeld explained there are many reasons other than cost-effectiveness for deploying even a less than perfect defense. One reason was to gain operational experience which might lead to new developments in missile defense. Second, BMD would raise the price of entry for an aggressor determined to saturate a target, causing him to buy more missiles. Third, enough ABMs might be deployed in such a manner:

> . . . that the larger defended targets would be as unattractive to the attacker as the undefended smaller ones, so that he would not be able to do more damage to the country as a whole by ignoring the defended cities and concentrating on the undefended ones. [20]

Fourth, the existence of BMD could force changes in an enemy's targeting doctrine. He would have to choose whether to attack cities only, a mixture of cities and strategic offensive force bases, or the latter only. It would be necessary for him to calculate whether he had enough offensive capability to carry out such an attack in face of the defender's invulnerable second-strike force and BMD.

Fifth, even a poor defense, Herzfeld said, would make a significant difference, depending on the kind of target being protected. If the target were an ICBM silo, a less than perfect defense would still increase the number of survivable missiles. With such a BMD it would be irrelevant which silos were hit, since some fraction would be successfully defended:

This would enable one to increase the survivability of one's own missile forces without increasing the number of missiles which one has, and would therefore be a relatively non-threatening way to strengthen one's retaliatory force; in other words, it would be a stabilizing factor. [21]

Sixth, Herzfeld argued "only in a few situations does defense produce an obviously stabilizing or destabilizing influence." [22]

By December 1965 no decision had been announced to deploy NIKE-X. However, William Beecher, writing in the journal of the AIAA (American Institute of Astronautics and Aeronautics), *Astronautics and Aeronautics,* reported Secretary McNamara had not changed his position on deployment; some of his aides had. At the December news conference the Defense Secretary said the Russian anti-missile missile:

> . . . is not as advanced as ours and . . . neither one (either the U.S. or Soviet ABM) is an effective defense against the strategic nuclear forces which we have available to us today and which we will have available in the future. [23]

In the end, President Johnson would be the final arbiter of the decision to deploy BMD. However, despite the development of a new ZEUS missile (DM15X2) with a longer range, which provided a reasonable basis for developing an area defense, capable of destroying and intercepting intercontinental and submarine-launched missile, no decision was expected in 1966 to deploy NIKE-X.[8]

On December 1, 1965, *The New York Times* reported that a further postponement of the NIKE-X decision was likely, although research and development activities would continue at a high level during 1966 [24].

A major conflict appeared to be shaping up in 1966 between the Defense Department and the Army (which had JCS and congressional support) over the advisability of continuing to withhold production and deployment authorization in the face of the growing Soviet and Chinese strategic threats. The Army felt any further delay would place the United States in a dangerous position vis-à-vis the Soviet Union in the post-1970 military environment. The Administration's intransigence against a BMD was based on cost, the Vietnam war, the continuing East-West détente, and Soviet interpretation of such a deployment. Pressure not to deploy the system was gaining momentum outside the Government; and failure to get a shelter program through Congress upset the Administration's rationale for damage limitation.

---

[8] Since the new missile could intercept ICBMs farther out in space, it could use a larger nuclear warhead than would be the case if interception were closer to earth, thereby maximizing the radiation emission effect and increasing the kill probability.

The BMD issue remained relatively muted, at least in Congress, during 1964–1965 as the NIKE-X program moved ahead. Contributing to this situation was the belief by BMD proponents that after the first and second Chinese nuclear weapon tests some form of BMD would surely be deployed against a future Chinese missile threat. When such action was not forthcoming, despite the JCS recommendations and additional congressional authorizations for NIKE-X production, proponents of the BMD began anew their fight to have the system deployed.

Because the controversy over whether to deploy NIKE-X increased both within and outside the Government, it is important for the reader to understand the arguments used for deploying missile defense. Until General Wheeler's 1967 statement arguing for deployment of BMD, the single best statement favoring BMD was made by the late Major General Nicolai Talensky, a Soviet military historian and strategic analyst: [9]

> . . . the long development of the means of warfare has revealed one characteristic law: there is a kind of struggle between the means of attack and the means of defense. Sooner or later every new means of attack leads to the emergence of a means of defense. The latter did not always have a specific form in its initial stage, and was frequently the same means of attack, but improved and used in greater numbers. But in the subsequent stages of the competition between the means of attack and of defense, specific means of defense gradually become the rule. [25]

Furthermore:

> . . . it frequently turned out that a new type of weapon was more effective at its initial stages than later. This happened because, as the new means of attack was developed and accepted, new means of combating it were also developed. Every rationally designed arms system tends to be a harmonious combination of the means of attack and the means of defense against it, of offensive and defensive armaments. [27]

Talensky considered the possibilities that science and technology would eventually counterbalance the absolute weapons of attack with absolute weapons of defense. He pointed out that BMD is strictly defensive:

> The advantage of antimissile systems in the political and international law context is that their use is caused by an act of aggression, and they

---

[9] Talensky reached the conclusion a BMD was only provocative if it was deployed by an "aggressive" nation. In fact, only an "aggressive" nation desired a BMD freeze. The only solution to the arms race, he said, is general and complete disarmament. Despite the cold war semantics and the Aesopian language, it is easy to see how his logic lent itself to the peculiarities of Soviet-American relations [26].

will simply not work unless an aggressor's rocket makes its appearance in flight over a given area. [28]

He continued:

An effective antimissile defense merely seems to build up the security of the peaceable, nonaggressive state; the fact that it is in possession of a combination of antimissile means and effective nuclear-rocket forces serves to promote the task of deterring a potential aggressor, insuring its own security, and maintaining the stability of world peace. [29]

Thus:

... in such conditions, the creation of an effective antimissile system enables the state to make its defenses dependent chiefly on its own possibilities, and not only on mutual deterrence, that is, on the goodwill of the other side. [30]

In addition, strategic offensive and defensive forces when taken together "substantially increase the stability of mutual deterrence, for any partial shifts in the qualitative and quantitative balance of these two component elements of mutual deterrence tend to be correspondingly compensated and equalized." [10] [31]

In the context of the assured destruction/damage-limitation strategy, Talensky said a deterrent strategy which relies solely on offensive forces to destroy the fabric of the enemy's society will cause instability because the incentive to strike first is always present. Accordingly, stability was increased by maintaining a deterrent strategy which included both offensive and defensive forces. This was the antithesis of the argument propounded by opponents of BMD who saw stability as a function of mutually deterring offensive forces. The underlying assumption of those favoring deployment of BMD ran counter to the mutual-deterrence thesis in recognizing the possibility that national security may be better obtained through a combination of strategic offensive and defensive forces. BMD proponents believed a mix of strategic forces would provide more security against a deliberate strike or a technological breakthrough in either the offense or defense than would a single force; i.e., offense only or defense only.

In April 1965 Major General Austin W. Betts, Deputy Chief of Research and Development (now Lieutenant General and Army Chief of R&D), spoke at Purdue University to the Student Branch of the American Institute of Aeronautics and Astronautics about NIKE-X. One reason for

---

[10] The remainder of his discourse was designed to refute the major arguments of Western arms control specialists who were against BMD deployment. This was done by equating Western arguments against BMD to the designs of an "aggressive" state.

deploying a BMD, he said, was the uncertain nature and direction of the strategic offensive and defensive Soviet threat. He averred that every year since 1960 the Army had been able to improve the NIKE system to meet each of the objections raised by its detractors "and is in a better position today to talk about an effective ballistic missile defense than we were in 1960." For example, he referred to the limited traffic-handling capacity of NIKE-ZEUS as a fundamental weakness, and gave the fact that ZEUS's radars could not be hardened and the presence of decoys as additional reasons for not committing NIKE-ZEUS to production. NIKE-X, Betts pointed out, was designed from the very beginning to overcome these weaknesses. In addition, he said, "the old assessment that the offense would overwhelm the defense with a trivial additional effort is just no longer true." While a 100-percent-effective defense was not likely, there was substantial cost in preparing the offense to penetrate the defense. The Soviets, who do have limited resources, would find such costs relatively high. This reasoning is an additional argument for BMD, as it forces the enemy to allocate resources from other areas. However, he continued:

> . . . we can demonstrate that the system will have a wide range of effectiveness against the wide range of targets that might be brought against it. Just how effective it could be now becomes a matter of estimating the cost of possible deployment, and assessing the protection that might be afforded by each of those deployments against all reasonably possible threats. These results must then be compared with other ways of spending the defense dollars—for example, civil defense, antisubmarine warfare, or strategic attack forces. [32]

Betts attempted to refute Dyson's contention that the high cost of a BMD precludes its deployment, arguing instead that expenditures for missile defense could provide significant levels of protection. On the question of upsetting stability, he said Dyson's argument fails to be convincing for several reasons, one of which is there is no way to guarantee a 100-percent-effective defense:

> Therefore, even with a considerable commitment to defense on both sides, nuclear attack forces are so powerful that mutual deterrence will continue to exist. The contribution defense can make is not to seek illusive invulnerability, but rather to save lives and property in the event that deterrence fails.[11] [33]

The critical question for Betts was not, "should we have insurance?" but, "how much?" [34]

---

[11] Putting it another way, he said, "buying seat belts doesn't mean that you intend to smash into the car of someone you don't like."

The emergence of the Chinese nuclear threat, coupled with the technological breakthrough in missile defense during 1965, led George Boehm, in an article in *Fortune,* to introduce a new argument for deploying a BMD:

> NIKE-X promises extremely good protection at relatively modest cost against a nuclear adversary of the Chinese magnitude. In fact, the system should be so successful in thwarting relatively feeble ICBM attacks that its very existence might discourage other nations hostile to the U.S. from even trying to develop long-range nuclear weapons for the rest of this century. [35]

In addition, NIKE-X would provide a defense from the accidental firing of an ICBM. Boehm noted additional reasons for deploying BMD now. If it proved necessary to deploy one against the Soviet Union, it would be easier to do it from the existing Chinese version than "to start from scratch"; and if a nuclear war were to involve the controlled exchange of ICBM's, then BMD would be a distinct advantage to its possessor.

References

[1] "Text of President Johnson's Budget Speech," *The New York Times,* January 15, p. 16.

[2] *Fiscal 1966 Budget* reprinted in *The New York Times,* January 26, 1965, p. 27.

[3] U.S. Department of Defense, *Statement of Secretary of Defense Robert S. McNamara Before the House Armed Services Committee on the Fiscal Year 1966–70 Defense Program and 1966 Defense Budget,* mimeographed, February 18, 1965, p. 39, hereafter cited as *1965 Annual Posture Statement.*

[4] U.S. Congress, Senate, Hearings Before the Subcommittee on Department of Defense of the Committee on Armed Services, *Department of Defense Appropriations FY 1966,* Part I, 89th Cong., 1st Sess., 1965, p. 55, hereafter cited *as Senate Defense Appropriations 1966.*

[5] *Senate Defense Appropriations 1966,* pp. 55–56.

[6] *Senate Defense Appropriations 1966,* p. 67.

[7] U.S. Congress, House, Hearings Before a Subcommittee of the Committee on Appropriations, *Department of Defense Appropriations for 1966,* Part 3, 89th Cong., 1st Sess., 1965, p. 355, hereafter cited as *House Defense Appropriations FY 1966.*

[8] *Senate Defense Appropriations 1966,* p. 357.

[9] *Senate Defense Appropriations 1966,* p. 611.

[10] James Trainor, "Study Aids Case of Nike-X," *Missiles and Rockets,* 1[1965]12.

[11] *House Defense Appropriations 1966,* Part 5, p. 7.

[12] U.S. Congress, House, Committee on Armed Services, *Hearings on Military Posture and H.R. 4016,* No. 7, 89th Cong., 1st Sess., 1965, p. 551, hereafter cited as *House Authorizations for 1965.*

[13] *Senate Defense Appropriations 1966,* p. 229.

[14] "Decision Time Grows Shorter for Nike-X," *Aviation Week and Space Technology,* 11[1965]149.

[15] Howard Margolis, "U.S. Plans Cheaper, Better Missile System," *Washington Post,* April 14, 1965, p. 1.

[16] "McNamara Assays Anti-Missile Plan," *The New York Times,* May 15, 1965, p. 2 and Howard Margolis, "U.S. Missile Defense Plans Pegged to Chinese Threat," *Washington Post,* May 26, 1965, p. 1.

[17] "Chinese Nuclear Threat Pushes Studies of Nike-X Option," *Missiles and Rockets,* 22[1965]17.

[18] William Beecher, "Missile Killing Gains," *Wall Street Journal,* July 26, 1965, p. 1.

[19] *Public Opinion and Ballistic Missile Defense: Report of an Exploratory Study* (RM 64TMP-50, General Electric TEMPO, Santa Barbara, 1964), p. 88.

[20] Charles Herzfeld, "BMD and National Security," *Survival,* 3[1966]74.

[21] Herzfeld, p. 75.

[22] Herzfeld, p. 75.

[23] William Beecher, "NIKE-X in the Balance," *Astronautics and Aeronautics,* 12[1965]5.

[24] Jack Raymond, "New U.S. Delay Likely in Building Missile Defense," *The New York Times,* December 1, 1965, p. 1.

[25] N. Talensky, "Antimissile Systems and Disarmament," *Bulletin of the Atomic Scientists,* 2[1965]26.

[26] Talensky, p. 26.

[27] Talensky, p. 26.

[28] Talensky, p. 26.

[29] Talensky, p. 28.

[30] Talensky, p. 28.

[31] Talensky, p. 28.

[32] Major General Austin Betts, *Role of Ballistic Missile Defense,* Purdue University Chapter of the AIAA, Lafayette, Indiana, April 27, 1965, text of speech, mimeographed, p. 11.

[33] Betts, p. 2.

[34] Betts, p. 12.

[35] George Boehm, "Countdown for Nike-X," *Fortune,* 5[1965]136.

CHAPTER 10

The Year of Surprises—1966

In his Posture Statement to the House Armed Services Committee in 1966, Secretary McNamara discussed the role of damage-limiting forces. From this analysis, he reached several conclusions relevant to missile defense:

1. Against likely Soviet postures for the 1970s, appropriate mixes of Damage Limiting measures could effect substantial reductions in the maximum damage the Soviets could inflict, but only at substantial additional cost to the U.S. over and above that required for Assured Destruction. Even so, against a massive and sophisticated Soviet surprise attack on civil targets, there would be little hope of reducing fatalities below 50 or more millions.

2. An efficient Damage Limiting effort against the kinds of postures which the Soviets could achieve in the 1970s would require a mix of measures, including a full Civil Defense Fallout Shelter Program, ballistic missile defenses, anti-submarine (SLBM) defense, and improved bomber defenses. Against a very rapid buildup of Soviet missile forces based in hard silos, additional U.S. missile payload might have to be added.

5. An ABM system employing long range exoatmospheric interceptors in addition to lower altitude interceptors could complicate even a sophisticated attacker's ballistic missile penetration problem. It could also improve overall system performance compared to an equal cost system employing lower altitude interceptors only. However, this conclusion is based on a preliminary analysis and there are still many unresolved questions about the design and performance of a system employing both exoatmospheric and low altitude interceptors.

6. The entire problem of the extent and kind of efforts we should make to limit damage is dominated by the great uncertainties about Soviet responses to those efforts. How far we should go in hedging against these uncertainties is one of the most difficult judgments which have to be made. Analytical techniques can focus the issue but no mechanical rule can substitute for such judgments. Accordingly, we should not now commit ourselves to a particular level of Damage Limitation against the

Soviet threat—first, because our deterrent makes general nuclear war unlikely, and second, because attempting to assure with confidence against all reasonably likely levels and types of attack is very costly, and even then the results are uncertain. Our choices should be responsive to prejections based upon the observed development of the Soviet threat and our evolving knowledge of the technical capabilities of our own forces. [1]

Besides the Soviet threat, the Nth-country threat must be considered, a threat McNamara claimed was real, especially from China. Against the Chinese threat a moderately priced defense appeared promising. Of the Chinese, he said:

> . . . the development and deployment of even a small force of ICBM's might seem attractive to them as a token, but still highly visible, threat to the U.S., designed to undermine our military prestige and credibility of any guarantee which we might offer to friendly countries. The prospect of an effective U.S. defense against such a force might not only be able to negate that threat, but might possibly weaken the incentives to produce and deploy such weapons altogether. [2]

There appeared to be a high degree of confidence that not just a few cities, but the entire nation, might be protected by deploying some form of NIKE-X against the type of ICBM attack the Chinese might launch in the 1970s. Such a deployment could be the basis for augmenting its effectiveness against larger or more sophisticated threats by adding more long-range ZEUS interceptor missiles, by improving the radars, or by increasing the number of cities with terminal defenses. Consequently:

> . . . on the basis of our present knowledge of Chinese Communist nuclear progress, no deployment decision need be made now. However, the development of the essential components should be pressed forward vigorously. [3]

On the basis of this rationale, the Defense Secretary did not recommend deployment. Instead, he requested $447 million for research, development, testing, and evaluation programs. This was in addition to the $119 million asked for by ARPA to continue: (1) missile defense studies, particularly Defender, which included the HIBEX, an extremely high-acceleration missile, and HAPDAR, a complementary hard point defense phased-array radar; (2) reentry measurements; (3) penetration aids; and (4) satellite defense. Elaborating, he said:

> Considering all of the uncertainties involved, including the nature and consequences of the Soviet reaction, the technical problems yet to be

solved, and the great cost of such deployment, I do not believe that a decision should be made now to undertake an all-out Damage Limiting effort against the Soviet threat. [4]

To support this decision, McNamara reminded the committee that in three of the last five years he had asked for a full fallout shelter program but was turned down each time.

The tenor of the questions asked during these hearings indicated that Congress believed—as in past years—McNamara had unilaterally made the decision about NIKE-X. In 1965 General Wheeler testified that the Secretary of Defense:

. . . not only seeks but listens to and heeds the views of the Joint Chiefs of Staff on every occasion. He is always most careful to indicate in his various memoranda to the President or in his appearances here, for example, before the Congress, wherein he has disagreed with the Chiefs on a particular item. There is certainly no inclination on Secretary McNamara's part to avoid getting the counsel of the Joint Chiefs of Staff fully and completely. [5]

Wheeler pointed out that McNamara has his own views, and is a man of:

. . . strong opinions and views . . . while receptive to the views of others, and he certainly listens to the views of others, he is the man who makes the final decision. This is the role of the Secretary of Defense according to law, as compared with that of the Joint Chiefs of Staff. [6]

The Secretary provided additional information on the decisionmaking process. First, the subject had been discussed thoroughly with the Army. Second, the prime and major subcontractors aided him with his decision. McNamara also asked that certain additional studies be carried out. In addition, offices within the Defense Department participated in these studies; for example, the Director of Defense Research and Engineering and the Army Staff. The efforts of all these groups were brought together at the quarterly meetings attended by the Chiefs of Staff, the Secretary of the Army, and the primary contractors [7].

Despite all the recommendations and programs, McNamara insisted he would never sanction a BMD deployment against the Soviet threat because: (1) the Soviets can offset the defenses at a lower cost than the U.S. deployment, (2) it would cost $25 billion to $30 billion to deploy, and (3) the United States would still suffer upwards of 50 million fatalities. The BMD effort would continue to be funded at the $500 million to $600 million level because of the knowledge it provided for developing penetration aids and advancing the state of the art in defensive systems:

> It is possible that we will discover some technology or achieve the performance characteristics in some system that will so protect us as to warrant deployment, or the situation may change in some presently unforeseen way so as to make its deployment desirable. [8]

Secretary McNamara revealed that NIKE-X underwent another change in 1965. See Table 1. The earliest NIKE-X (incorporating ZEUS, SPRINT, MAR, and MSR) had been designed to meet a multiple-object threat and had relied on atmospheric separation to discriminate decoys from real warheads:

> Initially, the deployment concept for NIKE-X contemplated the point defense of only a relatively small number of the larger cities against a heavy Soviet attack. [Then] . . . it became possible to consider extending protection to smaller cities by modifying certain NIKE-X subsystems and using less extensive and sophisticated deployments. [9]

The new system, the Defense Secretary said, would include a number of different types of radars: MAR, MSR, and perhaps VHF radars for long-range search.

Dr. John Foster, who had recently replaced Dr. Harold Brown as Director of Defense Research and Engineering, discussed the major change which now made an area defense possible. This capability had been achieved by the addition of a new long-range interceptor (DM15X2) which increased the system's effectiveness against an unsophisticated attack. This missile, Dr. Foster said, supplemented the terminal defense components of NIKE-X. He said the United States had pushed:

> . . . the modular (building bloc) design concept for NIKE-X still further in the direction of being able to provide a family of radars whose mix and quantity can be made to match various threat and required defense levels. In this connection, the MAR radar is being designed so that the version originally installed at operational sites will be considerably cheaper, with the capability to be upgraded as the threat becomes more sophisticated. [10]

All of these components, Dr. Foster said, had a potential for hard point defense. The modified MAR was described by General Dick, Chief of Army R&D, as having resulted from varying the electronic components in MAR to develop a tactical MAR (TACMAR) which could be tailored to a specific deployment requirement.

Again, as in 1965, the Joint Chiefs recommended the beginning of production on long leadtime items for NIKE-X. The Army asked for $188 million for pre-production funds, which was turned down by the Defense Department. The Army did not believe that BMD (the modular concept), air defense, and fallout shelters were as irrevocably linked as McNamara and the JCS believed they were, arguing that a start on defense had to be made at some point [11].

There was some disagreement among the Chiefs over the question of shelters. Wheeler felt the nation would have a better chance of survival if there were 40, 60, or 70 million fewer fatalities, as would be the case if the United States had both a shelter program and BMD. Notwithstanding the costs, he believed BMD should be funded "in an effort to save as much of our population as possible and to pose to the Soviets an additional complicating factor in their offensive actions." [12] Wheeler's statement is even more striking because he indicated an awareness of the central argument of BMD deployment:

> The first charge on the resources of this country, from a military point of view, is our strategic striking force. However, I try to look at this on both sides, and I believe that an additional damage limiting force, as well as an assured destruction force, is needed. [13]

General Harold Donnelly, Director of the Defense Atomic Support Agency, argued that the NIKE-X could not be satisfactorily tested without violating the test ban treaty. Nevertheless, General Donnelly felt a BMD should be deployed in order to protect the country from the Soviets and to test the system to determine if it was effective [14].

Dr. Harold Brown, Secretary of the Air Force in 1965, said that while it is worth quite a lot to reduce casualties from 120 million to 60 million, it is not necessarily true that BMD will help deterrence [15].

During April it was revealed that a large-scale effort was under way to improve U.S. offensive capabilities in order to ensure that under the worst circumstances the United States possessed the capability to penetrate Soviet defenses. The decision to ensure penetration rather than provide the United States with a defensive system reflected part of the reasoning behind the Administration's decision not to deploy NIKE-X. According to the decisionmakers, it was cheaper, more efficient, and more effective to ensure penetration than it was to build an uncertain defense for protection of targets which could probably be destroyed in an all-out attack. This reasoning did not apply in the case of the Chinese (since their threat was not considered sophisticated) nor to the hard point defense missile sites which would contribute to the survivability of the assured destruction retaliatory forces.

Indicative of the differences of opinion between Congress and the

Administration over NIKE-X, the Senate Armed Forces Committee during April took the initiative and recommended the appropriation of $167.9 million in order to buy long leadtime items to shorten the date to initial operational capability (IOC) and to spur the Administration into deployment of the NIKE-X [16]. However, the committee could not compel the Administration to spend the money. Congress' action in recommending these additional funds for production showed its growing concern over the Soviet strategic threat—in particular the BMD program—and the Administration's refusal to deploy NIKE-X despite the advice and urging of the JCS.[1]

Because McNamara had decided to override the JCS recommendation on NIKE-X deployment, the Senate hoped to force a reopening of the deployment issue and other, more fundamental, defense policy issues, especially those related to the possibility of a Soviet technical coup in strategic offensive and defensive missile systems. Early in May the House Armed Services Committee announced unanimous support for the Senate committee's NIKE-X appropriation recommendation [17]. This prompted Secretary McNamara to reiterate his position that (1) the cost of an ABM compared to other forms of damage-limitation protection was high; (2) there was uncertainty as to Soviet reaction to an American BMD deployment; (3) the Chinese threat was not yet well enough advanced to warrant deployment of NIKE-X; and (4) without the inclusion of a meaningful fallout shelter program, the lowered potential of this system to save lives did not warrant its production. In May 1966 the Chinese exploded their first hydrogen device.

Opposition to BMD deployment was not confined to the Executive Branch, its advisors, and certain civilian strategists and scientists. In 1966, a vociferous minority had developed in the Congress against BMD. This group was enlarged considerably in both houses by 1968. Aside from the Annual Defense Appropriations and Authorizations Hearings in which the BMD program was discussed, in three instances before 1968 the deployment issue was the subject of debate and vote. Each of the debates had transpired as a result of an amendment to delete funds for BMD production and deployment. Of the three instances before 1968, only two were subject to a roll-call vote; both in the Senate, one in 1963.

---

[1] In early 1966 it appeared that a heightening feud was taking place between the Secretary of Defense and the Joint Chiefs of Staff. The areas of controversy included not only missile defense but the gravity of the Soviet technological threat and the ability of the United States to maintain its military superiority. Moreover, members of Congress were lining up with the JCS on these matters and conduct of the Vietnam war. See Robert Hotz, "A Vital Probe," *Aviation Week and Space Technology*, February 28, 1966, p. 11, and George C. Wilson, "Joint Chiefs Fear Soviet Technical Coup," *Aviation Week and Space Technology*, February 28, 1966, p. 16.

The House Armed Services Committee authorized the additional $153.3 million for NIKE-X procurement because:

> We have long felt that the Department of Defense did not have a proper sense of urgency in the field of the anti-ballistic missile defense system. This added authority could save about 1 year in the time required between a deployment decision and achievement of the first operational capability. [18]

Representative Melvin Price (D-Ill.) presented the case for providing money toward NIKE-X production. First, the threat from Russia and China was changing and growing in sophistication and complexity; so long as the nation depended on deterrence alone for its security, tens of millions of casualties would result from a nuclear attack. Second, deployment of a Soviet BMD would certainly upset the favorable balance of military power for the United States. Third, the cost and complexity of NIKE-X would demand the earliest possible start [19].

In July 1966, during the House Appropriations Committee meeting, Representative Jeffrey Cohelan (D-Calif.) offered an amendment to an Appropriations Bill then before the Committee to strike $163.3 million for pre-production of the NIKE-X. Cohelan said:

> We are taking the first step . . . in the procurement of this costly weapons system, without adequate public debate, without adequate consideration of the system's effectiveness or reflection on its consequences. [20]

He felt there was no evidence to warrant an expenditure of this nature, when there was still evidence that the system could be saturated in a massive attack using sophisticated decoys and penetration aids. Also, the NIKE-X system had a fallout shelter prerequisite, the decision for which neither "the Congress nor the country has been asked to make." In addition, this system would not be the best one available; therefore, since neither the President nor DOD wanted this money, and probably would not spend it even if it were appropriated, why appropriate it? To appropriate this money would be to force a deployment decision prematurely, according to what Cohelan had gathered in discussions with scientists at the University of California, in Washington, and in other places. If money were to be spent on defense, it should be spent on increasing the capabilities of U.S. offensive weapons by adding to their penetration effectiveness, not spent to procure a BMD. Cohelan, like others opposed to deploying BMD, pointed out the international effects of an American BMD deployment on the arms race, arms control negotiations, and Soviet-American relations. Additional arguments were put forth by Representative Weston Vivian (D-Mich.).

He argued that any defense would be weak and ineffective; it would upset the balance of power; and now was not the time to make the decision, especially since the President, who must make the decision, had not yet said we need BMD [21].

Representative Mahon thought it wise to vote for the authorization, since it would contribute to progress and be a further down payment on the eventual deployment of BMD. Representative Sikes said:

> We cannot wait until there is a missile attack before we start building a defense against missiles. It takes years. I do not want to expose the American people unnecessarily to the possibility of attack. [22]

Commenting on the objection that our deploying BMD might provoke the Soviets to a greater effort and precipitate an arms race, Sikes said it would be silly even to approve the bill being considered if we are going to operate on the premise that we cannot undertake the defense of this country because it may make the Russians unhappy, angry, cause them to build more weapons, or cause them to attack us:

> No, we do not provoke the enemy to attack by defending ourselves. We deter attack. The only real security the free world has is in our military strength and defense capability, in the invulnerability of this Nation to attack; not in hopeful pronouncements by diplomats, and even less in the wishful thinking of those who believe that all problems can be settled through negotiation. [23]

The whole reason for the appropriation was to buy a little time, since the Soviets were already ahead of the United States. The cost was small compared to the lives that could be saved and the war it might prevent; if the Soviets could afford it, declared Sikes, I think the United States can, too.

The late Representative Glenard Lipscomb (R-Calif.) explained that the whole purpose of including the NIKE-X production funds was to make it possible for the President to save one year between a decision to deploy and an operational capability, and that the failure of Congress to act would delay an Executive Branch decision.

> The decision as to whether or not to produce and deploy an antiballistic missile system in this country is one of major significance. Such a decision involves consideration of an almost indescribably complex combination of factors including psychological, political, financial, technological and strategic ones. It is a decision in which military departments, our State Department, the President, and the Congress must participate. The final decision, under our form of government, rests with the President in his capacity as Commander in Chief.

Congress has the responsibility to act in a responsible fashion and in a cooperative manner so as to make available to the President the legal authority and funds necessary to complement the decision to deploy such a system. [24]

Cohelan's amendment was not voted on in committee or reported out, and the House approved the bill (392 to 1) as reported out of committee [25].

A similar debate took place in the Senate in August 1966 when the Senate was considering an additional appropriation of $153 million for procuring long leadtime items for the NIKE-X. Senator Joseph Clark (D-Pa.) offered an amendment to delete this item. "There are three compelling reasons for refusing to appropriate funds for the deployment of an anti-ballistic missile at this time," said Clark.

> First, we do not now have the know-how to build an anti-missile defense that would give us any reasonable assurance of security. [26]

He thought the Administration should be commended for its decision not "to plunge ahead with the premature deployment of a relatively primitive anti-ballistic missile which would not materially enhance our security from an attack by our most powerful adversary."

> Second, at a time when domestic programs, such as education, mass transit, health, housing, and the war on poverty are being cut back or held back for lack of funds, we certainly should not appropriate funds for a vastly expensive weapons system of such dubious value, which the administration had not requested and does not want. [27]

Citing the Arms Control Panel Report's recommendation for a three-year BMD moratorium, Clark concluded:

> A decision to proceed with a huge new weapons system might very well provoke a similar move by the Russians, escalating the arms race and increasing world tensions.[2] [28]

Senator Stephen Young (D-O.) supported the Clark amendment and stated that no nuclear power is threatening the peace of the world now; the Soviet Union has changed in the last 15 years and is evincing cooperation toward us and hoping for coexistence. "It is inconceivable that while Adrian Fisher at the ENDC in Geneva is urging the United States and the

---

[2] Clark read into the record: James Reston, "McNamara and the Anti-Ballistic Missile," *The New York Times,* July 20, 1966, p. 20, which pointed out that the United States may be slipping into a commitment to deploy against the will and intentions of the Administration.

Soviet Union to renounce the building of ABM systems, Congress wants to appropriate $153 million for pre-production of such a system," said Young. In addition, since BMD requires shelters to make it effective, more money will be added to the "civil defense boondoggle which has to date cost taxpayers more than $1.5 billion." [29]

Those in opposition to this amendment did not attack Clark on his reasoning, but as Senator Saltonstall pointed out:

> We cannot control expenditures of the Executive Branch, but we can—where there is a difference of opinion between men in uniform who have the ultimate responsibility for our defenses and the civilians who have the ultimate responsibility for cost—but the money in and they need not spend it. That is the whole purpose of putting in money for the NIKE-X where, I repeat, the development has been extraordinarily advanced over the past 2 years. [30]

Senator Richard Russell, who until 1966 was vigorously opposed to BMD production, stated why he had changed his opinion:

> . . . because I do not think we had reached the stage of development that justified embarking upon the expenditure of such large amounts of money. We have expended about $2 billion on research and development. But now we have advanced to the stage where we believe we can defend at least some of our cities. [31]

Russell also pointed out:

> The time has come when Congress should share the responsibility for developing an anti-missile system with the President. We cannot do it without this provision ($153 billion appropriation). If the Executive department does not spend the money, it will not be the first time. . . . The Administration has taken that responsibility (not spending funds for other projects), but Congress, in measuring up to its responsibility, provided the funds. [32]

Senator Symington said:

> With all due respect to military authorities, or to scientific minds who for years have preached a doctrine of "If we will only be peaceful, they will be peaceful," I believe this request is needed and therefore worthwhile, and this despite my becoming increasingly worried about the money now being asked from Congress, and appropriated by the Congress. [33]

Senator Russell Long (D-La.) felt this issue was "a matter of being first with the best in defense," because "there is no advantage in being second best in defense." [34] Senator Thurmond made a major speech on behalf of the appropriation, pointing out that for the last 9 years he had been working toward the creation of BMD. He urged the defeat of this amendment especially in view of the fact that for the last two years the JCS had urged the Secretary of Defense to begin pre-production engineering on NIKE-X [35].

Senator Stennis emphasized the fact that if the Soviets should get BMD first, the "game would be up," and therefore we must move ahead. More importantly, he said:

> It is high time that the legislative branch of this Government shares the responsibility of what could be the most momentous decision we have to make this year on our future military program. [36]

Sympathizing with Clark's efforts toward disarmament, Senator John Sherman Cooper (R-Ky.) felt that while millions would die if nuclear weapons were ever used, there was another factor to be considered.

> . . . until some enforceable agreements can be made, the possession is a deterrent to war, a deterrent to this destruction. And if this weapon, awful as it is, but necessary as it is, could be developed and in the possession of the United States, certainly so if the Russians should develop it, that fact is a deterrent which we hope may help avoid war until these agreements could occur. [37]

The amendment was defeated 14–43. (See Table 2).

Late in May, the Army announced the start of a very-high-frequency (VHF) radar project, designed to increase the search range and the acquisition capabilities of NIKE-X. This was the beginning of the perimeter acquisition radar (PAR) which was later developed into an ultra-high-frequency (UHF) radar in order to reduce the effects of ionization phenomena on its performance. This new radar, the fourth (MAR, MSR, and TACMAR) incorporated in the NIKE-X system, was expected to play a key role in any NIKE-X configuration deployed against the Chinese or Nth-power nations.

In the summer of 1966 the United States apparently was preparing to deploy a limited NIKE-X system against the Chinese. The system then being discussed would cost between $8 billion and $12 billion and would employ a dozen ZEUS batteries, associated MSRs, and a small number of VHF acquisition radars. The proposed system would provide a thin area defense using the DM15X2 missile and was tailored to the Chinese threat, differing in deployment concept from anything discussed in connection with NIKE-X. It would have limited growth potential so as not to influence or provoke a Soviet reaction.

Congressional testimony revealed a preponderance of negative opinions within ARPA and the higher echelons of the Defense Department regarding BMD deployment against the Soviets. It was felt that a light area defense could be useful if a nuclear war were long and initial Soviet attacks were directed away from cities. Differences of opinion continued to reflect concern over the warhead kill problem. Improved guidance-intercept technology might lead to smaller warheads' being used to destroy incoming missiles with the same assurance as with the large-yield warhead. This improvement would reduce further the need for shelters, since the damage wrought by a large warhead exploded at 100,000 to 150,000 feet was enough to wreck a modern city, whereas the level of damage was considerably less from a smaller warhead.

Additional research to advance ballistic-missile-defense concepts and technology farther was part of the instructions the Army received from the Defense Department. This order was designed to ensure continued advances in BMD technology, pending an Executive decision to deploy. Any deployment decision was contingent on the findings of three key investigations then in progress. The Army, DDR&E, and a special group of the Defense Department's Defense Science Board (headed by Dr. Richard Latter of The RAND Corporation and Dr. Eugene Fubini, the former Deputy Director of DDR&E) carried out these studies [38].

Despite apparent optimism, similar to that which existed during the summer of 1965, evidence began to appear that a decision to deploy a BMD against the Chinese might be deferred for another year. Three articles in *The New York Times* described the growing Soviet strategic threat [39]. The authors pointed out the American effort to offset Soviet strategic offensive and defensive advantages by developing and deploying more advanced and sophisticated offensive weapons wtih numerous penetration aids rather than deploying a defense of its own. This commitment to increase security through improvements in offensive weapon systems, rather than attempting to create a balanced deterrent using a mix of offensive and defensive forces, pointed up the direction and thinking of the Administration's defense policy. The rationale for not deploying continued to be based on economic and political, rather than technical and military, considerations. [40]

Even with the successful firing of a Chinese nuclear armed missile in late 1966, the Administration held that there was still considerable time to deploy before the Chinese ICBM threat became real, and said it had no intention of spending the additional funds appropriated in 1966 by Congress for BMD.

On November 11, 1966, Secretary McNamara revealed that a Soviet

BMD was being deployed,[3] but that no decision had been made to produce and deploy the NIKE-X system or any component of it in response to this new event [41]. Rather, the Secretary said he would recommend the production and deployment of an advanced POLARIS-type missile (POSEIDON) both of which are launched underwater by submarine which could effectively penetrate any Soviet defense. This was thought to be cheaper than deploying NIKE-X [42].

The announcement that Soviet offensive and defensive missile deployments and improvements would still not result in a NIKE-X deployment sparked a renewed congressional effort to get a missile defense system deployed. The opponents of the BMD were expected to continue their opposition to its deployment because of their fear that this would accelerate the arms race. Many of these opponents, recognizing the potential effect of the increased Soviet offensive and defensive capabilities, argued that the United States should develop and deploy a massive new ICBM force, much as it did in response to the "missile gap" fear of the early 1960s. This, they suggested, would maintain U.S. nuclear superiority and security while precluding the need for a BMD.

In fact, a new round in the arms race had begun long before 1966. Yet opponents of BMD saw in the Soviet deployment of second-generation, hardened, solid-fueled ICBMs, the prospect of a new era of stability, an era which would be upset by the U.S. deployment of BMD, but not by a Soviet missile defense.

Two questions affecting NIKE-X now faced the United States: (1) how good was the Soviet defense and (2) what guarantee was there that the Chinese would adhere to the weapons development timetable Washington had predicted? It was expected that these questions would precipitate a new round of debate concerning deployment of a U.S. missile defense. In any event, the Chinese and Soviet technical and military developments did not appear at the time to alter the White House decision not to deploy NIKE-X. In fact, by late 1966 there were more cogent political and financial reasons (the escalating cost of Vietnam, for one) not to deploy than there were military ones to deploy.

In late November *The New York Times* reported that preliminary discussions had been held with some NATO members concerning the

---

[3] McNamara had long thought the Soviet deployment of BMD was an error and carry-over from its rationale to deploy an air defense system which reflected a philosophy about strategic defense different from the one existing in the United States. See Michael Getler, "McNamara Says Soviets Err on ABM," *Missiles and Rockets*, May 2, 1966, p. 12.

feasibility of a U.S. BMD deployment in Europe.[4] Concurrently, a similar technical study was under way in this country concerning the deployment in Japan of a U.S. BMD (although there had not been any discussions with Japanese officials) [43].

The most startling development in the period following the announcement of the Soviet BMD deployment was a report that the United States was considering asking the Soviet Union for a moratorium on BMD deployment; a recommendation suggested a year earlier by the Arms Control and Disarmament Committee, chaired by Wiesner and Gilpatric of the National Citizens Commission of the White House Conference on International Cooperation. Believing the Soviet BMD effort was not an all-out one and that a costly upward spiral of the arms race would be touched off if either side deployed a BMD system, the Administration hoped to delay or even prevent such a race by seeking the moratorium. While a decision on the possibility of making this request was not expected until January or February, the Administration was said to favor delaying its own BMD decision for at least another year. The decision to wait for a Soviet answer to the proposal was expected to forestall increasing Congressional pressure to deploy NIKE-X [44].

On December 22, 1966, Secretary of State Rusk confirmed for the first time that discussions were taking place within the Administration to find a means to halt the arms race. Secretary Rusk said he hoped both sides would find a means to limit the arms race and thus avoid the "wholly new major levels of expenditure" that would be required by deployment of anti-missile defense systems by the two major powers [45]. This plea reflected the Administration's reluctance to deploy BMD which, in the end, would cost both the United States and the Soviet Union a great deal of money and would not provide any more security than that which already existed.

The year ended with no positive decision taken to deploy the NIKE-X system. However, during 1966 a sense of urgency, communicated by the stepped-up tempo of the arms race, renewed underground nuclear testing,[5] and new developments in the NIKE-X system, indicated that a sharp disagreement (if not a full-scale investigation of the U.S. BMD program and the Administration's position on it) might be upcoming.

The question of missile defense deployment came to figure increasingly

---

[4] A move advocated earlier in the year in the February 1966 issue of *Interavia*, p. 185.
[5] John W. Finney asserted that the accelerating race to develop a missile defense system set off the new round of underground nuclear testing in 1966–1967. See "U.S. and Soviet Begin a New Atomic Test Race," *The New York Times*, December 21, 1966, p. 26.

in international arms control discussions as part of U.S. arms control policy. On August 2, 1966, ACDA Deputy Director Adrian Fisher discussed before the ENDC a freeze on strategic nuclear delivery vehicles. This freeze was the sixth part of a six-part nuclear disarmament program presented by President Johnson on January 27, 1965, to the ENDC.[6] This freeze proposal had been before the ENDC for some time, and in September 1966 U.S. United Nations Ambassador Arthur Goldberg suggested that not only a freeze, but a reduction, in the number of strategic nuclear offensive and defensive vehicles should be explored [46].

Lester Pearson of Canada advocated an agreement between the superpowers not to deploy anti-ballistic missiles, and the British Disarmament Minister Lord Chalfont on June 16, 1966, had said that the deployment of BMD would lead the arms race into a new and irreversible phase and, "furthermore, that a serious threat will be posed to whatever stability is provided by the present balance of power." [47]

On August 16, 1966, Fisher presented the rationale for including BMD in any strategic nuclear weapons freeze. He argued that the basis for stability existed because both sides, with their offensive forces, could inflict unacceptable damage on the other. One side, in the face of the other's BMD deployment, might be concerned with its ability to inflict unacceptable damage to the defender. Such a situation, said Fisher, "would create undesirable tensions and uncertainties and would threaten to destroy the existing stability." [48]

Any nation confronted with the possibility of another's deploying BMD when only an agreement to limit offensive forces existed would have two alternatives: (1) abrogate the agreement and build new offensive forces or (2) build a BMD of its own. "Neither of these choices would be desirable." Fisher concluded:

> If one power displays an anti-missile system in addition to existing offensive systems, other nations might fear that their relative strategic capability was being eroded and therefore undertake one or more counteractions, such as the parallel deployment of an anti-ballistic missile system, increased offensive deployment, or the introduction of new or improved types of weapons capable of penetrating or by-passing ballistic-missile defenses. The resulting arms race would be self-defeating. [49]

---

[6] The other five parts were: (1) nonproliferation, (2) international safeguards over relevant peaceful nuclear activities, (3) strengthening of the U.N. and other international security arrangements so that those nations which forswore nuclear weapons could do so without fear, (4) extension of the limited nuclear test ban treaty to cover underground testing as well, and (5) halting or slowing down of the production of fissionable material for weapons.

These points were reiterated in the letter of transmittal of ACDA's Sixth Annual Report to President Johnson on January 23, 1967. The President, in his transmittal letter to Congress on ACDA's annual report, warned that despite the hope that a nonproliferation treaty would be concluded, missile defenses held the key to any further escalation in the arms race. Any such deployment, he felt, would be a futile step in the nuclear race [50].

References

[1] U.S. Department of Defense, *Statement of Secretary of Defense Robert S. McNamara Before the House Armed Services Committee on the Fiscal Year 1967-71 Defense Programs and 1967 Defense Budget,* mimeographed, March 8, 1966, pp. 55–56, hereafter cited as *1966 Posture Statement.*

[2] *1966 Posture Statement,* p. 5.

[3] *1966 Posture Statement,* p. 58.

[4] *1966 Posture Statement,* p. 70.

[5] U.S. Congress, House, Hearings Before a Subcommittee of the Committee on Appropriations, *Department of Defense Appropriations for FY 1967,* Part 1, 89th Cong., 2nd Sess., 1966, p. 399, hereafter cited as *House Defense Appropriations for FY 1967.*

[6] *House Defense Appropriations for FY 1966,* p. 399.

[7] *House Defense Appropriations for FY 1967,* pp. 116–117.

[8] *House Defense Appropriations for FY 1967,* p. 115.

[9] *House Defense Appropriations for FY 1967,* p. 61.

[10] U.S. Congress, Senate, Hearings Before the Committee on Armed Services and the Subcommittee on Department of Defense of the Committee on Appropriations, *Military Procurement Authorizations for Fiscal Year 1967,* 89th Cong., 2nd Sess., 1966, p. 425, hereafter cited as *Senate Defense Appropriations for FY 1967.*

[11] *Senate Defense Appropriations for FY 1967,* p. 537.

[12] *Senate Defense Appropriations for FY 1967,* p. 254.

[13] *Senate Defense Appropriations for FY 1967,* p. 255.

[14] *Senate Defense Appropriations for FY 1967,* p. 568.

[15] *House Defense Appropriations for FY 1967,* p. 530.

[16] Benjamin Welles, "Senate Panel Adds Anti-Missile Funds," *The New York Times,* April 22, 1966, p. 1.

[17] Michael Getler, "Nike-X Deployment Feud Heightening," *Missiles and Rockets,* 19[1966]12.

[18] *U.S. Congressional Record,* 89th Cong., 2nd Sess., July 20, 1966, pp. 15550–51.

[19] *U.S. Congressional Record,* 89th Cong., 2nd Sess., June 14, 1966, pp. 12469–70.

[20] *U.S. Congressional Record,* July 20, 1966, pp. 15524–25.

[21] *U.S. Congressional Record,* July 20, 1966, pp. 15539–41.

[22] *U.S. Congressional Record,* July 20, 1966, p. 15539.

[23] *U.S. Congressional Record,* July 20, 1966, p. 15539.

[24] *U.S. Congressional Record,* July 20, 1966, p. 15542.

[25] *U.S. Congressional Record,* June 14, 1966, p. 12444.

[26] *U.S. Congressional Record,* 89th Cong., 2nd Sess., August 18, 1966, p. 18981.

[27] *U.S. Congressional Record,* August 18, 1966, p. 18981.

[28] *U.S. Congressional Record,* August 18, 1966, p. 18981.

[29] *U.S. Congressional Record,* August 18, 1966, p. 18971.

[30] *U.S. Congressional Record,* August 18, 1966, p. 18983.

[31] *U.S. Congressional Record,* August 18, 1966, p. 18985.

[32] *U.S. Congressional Record,* August 18, 1966, p. 18985.

[33] *U.S. Congressional Record,* August 18, 1966, p. 18984.

[34] *U.S. Congressional Record,* August 18, 1966, p. 18985.

[35] *U.S. Congressional Record,* August 18, 1966, p. 18987.

[36] *U.S. Congressional Record,* August 18, 1966, p. 18993.

[37] *U.S. Congressional Record,* August 18, 1966, p. 18993.

[38] Michael Getler, "U.S. Opting for New, Low-Cost ABM," *Technology Week* (formerly *Missiles and Rockets*), 25[1966]14.

[39] William Beecher, "Air Force Plans a Giant Missile to Penetrate Enemy's Radar Defenses," *The New York Times,* June 30, 1966, p. 1.; William Beecher, "Now an Anti-Anti Missile Missile?" *The New York Times,* June 26, 1966, p. E3; and, Hanson Baldwin, "U.S. Lead in ICBM's Is Said to Be Reduced by Build-up in Soviet Union," *The New York Times,* July 14, 1966, p. 3.

[40] James Reston. "Washington: McNamara and the Anti-Ballistic Missile," *The New York Times,* July 20, 1966, p. 40.

[41] Robert B. Semple, Jr., "McNamara Hints Soviet Deploys Antimissile Net," *The New York Times,* November 11, 1966, p. 1.

[42] William Beecher, "The Antimissile Issue," *The New York Times*, November 1, 1966, p. 9.

[43] William Beecher, "U.S. Studying Missile Defense of Western Europe and Japan," *The New York Times*, November 27, 1966, p. 18.

[44] "U.S. Studies Appeal to Soviet for a Halt on Missile Defense," *The New York Times*, December 16, 1966, p. 20.

[45] "Transcript of Secretary of State Dean Rusk's News Conference of December 21, 1966," *Department of State Bulletin, No. 1437,* January 9, 1967, p. 43.

[46] U.S. Arms Control and Disarmament Agency, *Documents on Disarmanent 1966,* Publication 43, GPO, 1967, p. 491, hereafter cited as *Documents on Disarmament 1966.*

[47] *Documents on Disarmament 1966,* p. 553.

[48] *Documents on Disarmament 1966,* p. 566.

[49] *Documents on Disarmament 1966,* p. 566.

[50] John W. Finney, "President Warns of 'Futile' Step-Up in Nuclear Race," *The New York Times,* February 18, 1967, p. 6.

PART III
Sentinel

CHAPTER 11

Sentinel—The Chinese Defense System Decision

In his State of the Union Message in January 1967, President Johnson announced a decision to seek an accord with the Soviets to halt BMD deployment. He said:

> We have the solemn duty to slow down the arms race between us, if that is at all possible, in both conventional and nuclear weapons and defenses. And I thought we were making some progress in that direction the first few months I was in office. And I realize that any additional race would impose on our peoples, and on all mankind, for that matter, additional waste of resources with no gain in security to either side. [1]

The President in his message implied that the United States would defer any missile defense deployment decision, hoping the Soviets would slow down or halt their deployment and engage in BMD limitation talks.[1] Ambassador Llewellyn Thompson carried a special message to the Soviet leaders regarding a BMD moratorium [2]. In addition, the United States continued to undertake measures to ensure the continued penetrability of Soviet missile defenses by the U.S. ICBM force.

By 1967, NIKE-X entered another phase. It now consisted of a new, long-range interceptor, called SPARTAN (DM15X2), capable of exo-atmospheric intercept, which replaced ZEUS and a long-range surveillance radar, PAR. Together these developments constituted a substantial base for an area defense system.

A Senate Disarmament Subcommittee favored the idea of a BMD moratorium and was concerned that the President was not showing enough

---

[1] It should be remembered that up until the beginning of 1967 the members of the Administration responsible for BMD policy, in particular Secretary McNamara, believed that *any* form of deployment was against the long-run interests of the United States. The failure of some of the strongest opponents of BMD to realize that certain forms of deployment might be more desirable than none at all complicated the President's decision. It appears rather odd, too, that the United States would take the initiative to talk about limiting missile defenses when it had none deployed and the Soviets did. Any talks would certainly be undertaken by the United States from a position of weakness, since it lacked a BMD.

urgency in the matter. The subcommittee agreed to support the deferment of BMD deployment in return for a Soviet commitment to do likewise. Apparently the President had expected considerable pressure from Congress to deploy NIKE-X after events in 1966 made it likely the deployment issue would reach a climax in 1967. Instead, he was greeted by favorable reaction. Senator Albert Gore (D-Tenn.) indicated that joint hearings would be held between his Disarmament Subcommittee and his Subcommittee on International Agreements of the Joint Atomic Energy Committee. He also suggested to the Administration that it should determine if the Soviets were willing to enter into an agreement before Congress adjourned so Congress could authorize a missile defense deployment if the Soviets declined [3].

Several days later the Administration announced that the Soviets might be interested in a BMD freeze and talks between Rusk and Soviet Ambassador to the United States Anatoliy Dobrynin had taken place several weeks before the President's announcement to seek an accord [4].

In his Budget Message, the President said:

> In [FY] 1968 we will: continue intensive development of NIKE-X but take no action now to deploy an antiballistic missile (ABM) defense; initiate discussions with the Soviet Union on the limitation of ABM deployments; in the event these discussions prove unsuccessful, we will reconsider our deployment decision. To provide for actions that may be required at that time, approximately $375 million has been included in the 1968 budget for the production of NIKE-X for such purposes as *defense of our offensive weapons systems* [author's italics]. [5]

The deployment rationale appeared to have shifted from the Chinese toward the Soviets.

Secretary of Defense McNamara, in his Annual Posture Statement, went into greater detail about missile defense. In light of the Soviet strategic buildup, in particular in its deployment of BMD, the Secretary indicated that the United States would produce and deploy POSEIDON SLBMs and improved penaids, increase the proportion of MINUTEMAN III ICBMs and provide them with an improved third stage, and initiate the development of new RVs specifically designed to penetrate BMD-defended targets [6].[2] McNamara reasoned that if the Soviet deployment were less than his worst case assumption and the United States proceeded to improve

---

[2] This was MIRV, which was not officially reported until December 1967 by Dr. Foster. However, William Beecher broke the story about MIRVs on POSEIDON and MINUTEMAN III in his article in *The New York Times,* "Missile to Carry Warhead Cluster," January 20, 1967, p. 1. Hanson Baldwin used the acronym MIRV in his article in *The New York Times,* "Soviet Antimissile System Spurs New U.S. Weapons," February 5, 1967, p. 1.

Sentinel—The Chinese Defense System Decision

its posture with the worst case in mind, the Soviets would be worse off than if they had not started their deployment. The Secretary expressed concern with the possibility that the Soviets might deploy a hard-target kill capability. He indicated that NIKE-X might be a partial solution if U.S. land-based ICBMs were threatened.

McNamara discussed the use of NIKE-X to protect cities. He postulated two deployments, A and B. The former, costing $9.9 billion, was a light defense of the top 25 U.S. cities, consisting of area and terminal defenses. Only a number of the largest cities would be provided with terminal defenses. Posture B, costing $19.4 billion, was similar to Posture A with respect to overlapping area defenses but had terminal defenses for 50 cities (twice the number in Posture A).[3] Only later, in House Authorization Hearings, were the numbers and identification of the cities revealed [7].

McNamara illustrated the problem associated with deploying NIKE-X to protect cities. With no U.S. BMD, the Soviets could kill 120 million people. With Postures A and B and no Soviet response to them, a Soviet first strike would kill 40 million and 30 million Americans, respectively. If the United States struck first, the United States would lose to Soviet retaliation 100 million, 30 million, and 20 million people, respectively. But if the Soviets, like the United States, were determined to maintain an assured destruction capability—and McNamara believed this to be so—then the Soviets would be forced to respond to U.S. deployment. The Soviets, if they struck first, would be able to inflict 120 million fatalities on the United States whether it had no BMD or had either Posture A or B! He concluded:

> It is the virtual certainty that the Soviets will act to maintain their deterrent which casts such grave doubts on the advisability of our deploying the NIKE-X system for the protection of our cities against the kind of heavy, sophisticated missile attack they could launch in the 1970's. [8]

Earlier, he said:

> It is this interaction between our strategic forces programs and those of the Soviet Union which leads us to believe that there is a mutuality of

---

[3] McNamara pointed out there would be a number of problems with any deployment: (1) the need for proper system integration and computer programming; (2) prototype developments might not be produceable in quantity without extensive re-engineering, which would delay deployment and spiral costs; (3) unprotected taxpayers would demand that they should be protected and not just the big cities; (4) an initial small BMD systems deployment would eventually expand to a $40-billion or $50-billion 10-year cost system; (5) a new bomber defense would be required to prevent the Soviets from end-running NIKE-X; and (6) the shelter program would have to be accelerated. Adding the cost of items 5 and 6 to Postures A and B would increase the cost of A to $12.2 billion and of B to $21.7 billion.

interests in limiting the deployment of anti-ballistic-missile defense systems. If our assumption that the Soviets are also striving to achieve as [an] Assured Destruction capability is correct, and I am convinced that it is, then in all probability all we would accomplish by deploying ABM systems against one another would be to increase greatly our respective defense expenditures, without any gain in real security for either side. [9]

Regarding China, McNamara felt the United States had time to deploy BMD before China developed any significant offensive force and therefore could safely postpone a deployment. In light of his analysis, McNamara proposed a $440-million RDT&E effort and $375 million for pre-production of NIKE-X if the negotiations initiated by the President proved successful.

The Joint Chiefs disagreed with Secretary McNamara's decision, and General Wheeler, speaking for the Chiefs, said

> ... we believe we should go ahead now and start to deploy a light defense as a first step in moving toward possibly the Posture A, which the Secretary outlined in his statement. [10]

The bulk of General Wheeler's statement is presented below as it still represents the single most lucid argument for deployment and stands in contrast to McNamara's assumptions and reasoning. The year before, Wheeler had pointed out that the JCS had recommended a NIKE-X area defense deployment similar to 1967s Posture A for a number of the most densely populated areas. The recommendation was made for two reasons:

> Firstly, we had continued to watch the growing Soviet ability to destroy our population and our industry, and second, the research and development program on NIKE-X had reached a point where we felt that the NIKE-X was ready for deployment. [11]

By 1967 the intelligence community was certain the Soviets were deploying BMD. Moreover, it was believed the Soviets probably would extend and improve their system in the future. Offensively, the Soviets had accelerated the deployment of hardened ICBMs. The reason for this is uncertain, said Wheeler.

> The Joint Chiefs of Staff don't know whether the Soviet overall objective is strategic nuclear parity or superiority. In either case, we believe that their probable aims are one or more of the following:

> First, to reduce the United States assured destruction capability—that is, our ability to destroy their industry and their people.

> Second, to complicate the targeting problem which we have in directing our strategic forces against the Soviet Union.

Third, to reduce our confidence in our ability to penetrate Soviet defenses, thereby reducing the possibility that the United States would undertake a pre-emptory first strike against the Soviet Union, even under extreme provocation.

Fourth, to achieve an exploitable capability, permitting them freedom to pursue their national aims at conflict levels less than general nuclear war. [12]

The fundamental reason for not deploying NIKE-X last year according to Secretary McNamara, observed Wheeler, was that our security with BMD would not be any greater and would not lessen the risk of a Soviet attack or reduce damage to the United States in any meaningful sense if an attack occurred. Wheeler continued:

We feel that this judgment assumes that Soviet reaction to NIKE-X deployment will be equal, opposite, feasible, and possible. We don't think that it gives sufficient weight to important interactions associated with deploying NIKE-X, and importantly, consideration of the interaction of not deploying the NIKE-X appears not to be weighed sufficiently. [13]

In fact, the high price the Soviets must pay to overcome NIKE-X includes: "the economic and technological expenditures necessary to counter the NIKE-X" and "the diversion of resources from other high-priority programs." The remaining portion of General Wheeler's statement is included below, as it presents the best integrative argument for deploying NIKE-X.

Again, we feel that they would also be faced with the grave uncertainties associated with targeting against an ABM defended nation. We believe that the Soviet offensive and defensive buildup does increase the risk of nuclear war because, in the first place, deterrence is a combination of forces in being and state of mind.

Should the Soviets come to believe that their ballistic missile defense, coupled with a nuclear attack on the United States, would limit damage to the Soviet Union to a level acceptable to them, whatever that level is, our forces would no longer deter, and the first principle of our security policy is gone.

I should say here that while I certainly agree—and so do the Joint Chiefs—that the basis of deterrence is the ability to destroy an attacker as a viable nation, as a part of this, there is also the ability of the nation to survive as a nation—in other words, the converse of the first point.

Second, lack of a deployed U.S. ABM increases the possibilities of a nuclear war by accident and by the Nth country triggering.

Third, failure to deploy a U.S. ABM creates a strategic imbalance both within our forces and between the United States and the Soviet forces. It could lead to Soviet and allied belief that we are interested only in the offensive, that is, a first strike, or that our technology is deficient, or that we will not pay to maintain strategic superiority.

We also believe that damage to the United States from a nuclear strike can be reduced by an ABM system in a meaningful way. Now, of course, Mr. Chairman, nobody can say at what point of nuclear destruction a nation is no longer a viable society. We do know, or at least we have estimates, that the Soviets lost something like 25 million people in World War II. Now these losses are not exactly comparable, of course, to what would happen in a nuclear war, because they lost 25 million people perhaps over a period of 4 or 5 years. We are talking here of the loss of 25 or more million people in a matter of hours, and the psychological shock and other effects would be considerably different.

Nevertheless, one nation will probably survive best in a nuclear exchange, and the 30, 40, or 50 million American lives that could be saved by NIKE-X are, therefore, meaningful, we believe, in every sense.

Now the basis of our recommendation—this is a sort of recap, Mr. Chairman—the basis of the recommendation of the Joint Chiefs that we initiate new deployment of NIKE-X with an initial operating capability in [deleted] is based fundamentally on the requirement to maintain the total strategic nuclear capability or balance clearly in favor of the United States.

Specifically, we believe that deployed NIKE-X would do one or more of the following: First, provide a damage limitation capability by attrition of a Soviet attack.

Second, introduce uncertainties which would inhibit Soviet leaders from concluding that the United States could not survive a Soviet first strike or that the United States would not pre-empt under any circumstances.

Third, stabilize the nuclear balance.

Fourth, demonstrate to the Soviets and our allies that the United States is not first-strike minded; in other words, that we don't put all of our eggs in the offensive basket.

Fifth, continue to deny to the Soviets an exploitable capability. And by this I mean to continue the Cuba power environment in the world.

I think that in regard to this last point, and to explain it a bit, I should point out that by this we mean that at the time of Cuba, the strategic nuclear balance was such that the Soviets did not have an exploitable capability, because of our vastly superior nuclear strength. And to bring this forward into the present context, it's also the view of the Joint Chiefs that regardless of anyone's feelings about the situation in Vietnam, we think it quite clear that we would have had even more hesitation in deploying our forces there, had the strategic nuclear balance not been in our favor. [14]

During the fiscal 1968 House Defense Appropriations Hearings, General Wheeler told the Appropriations Committee that, while the JCS disagreed with the Defense Secretary, they agreed with the President's decision to postpone BMD deployment temporarily "while exploring with the Soviet Union the possibilities of arms control implementations of one kind or another." [15]

Representative Jamie Whitten (D-Miss.) remarked during these 1967 hearings, "this is the only time I know the Chairman of the Joint Chiefs of Staff has taken a prepared position in front of this Committee different from the Secretary of Defense." [16] Secretary McNamara replied by noting that the importance of the subject was such it was felt necessary to present both sides of the argument. Opposition to Secretary McNamara's decision not to begin deployment of a missile defense system reached into the civilian leadership of the Pentagon as well. Even though money was budgeted for deployment, no decision had been made and Secretary McNamara was on record (see Chapter 10) as unalterably opposed to deployment.

Representative George Mahon, Chairman of the House Appropriations Subcommittee for the Department of Defense, asked each of the Service Secretaries their opinion about deploying an ABM. Secretary of the Army Stanley Resor said that:

> I agree fully with the Secretary of Defense's proposal that before commencing deployment of an ABM defense, we should attempt, through negotiations with the Soviets, to curb the strategic arms race. If these negotiations do not lead to a significant change in our current estimate of the Soviet threat or a satisfactory agreement, my present view is that I would then favor deploying the light ABM defense for which this budget provides the funds.
>
> This would primarily be an area defense providing some degree of protection for our entire population. Its objective would be threefold: (1) to deny damage from the early Chinese Communist ICBM threats;

(2) to provide increased protection for MINUTEMAN squadrons against Soviet attacks; (3) to safeguard the United States against accidental launches of missiles by other countries. [17]

Air Force Secretary Harold Brown replied to the same question by saying that he agreed with the Defense Department's position

> ... that the Soviets would be able to counter a massive deployment ... with very much less money than it would cost us to deploy it, and that they would have a very strong incentive to do so since they require assured destruction capability against the United States just as we require and insist on having an assured destruction capability against the Soviet Union. [18]

> If these talks do not succeed, then it seems to me it might be well worthwhile to put up a $5 billion system to defend the population against a small attack by the Chinese and to do such things as defend our missiles so that they could be survivable. [19]

Secretary of the Navy Paul Nitze said:

> ... we might be well advised to initiate a light deployment of an anti-ballistic-missile defense subject to the results of proposed negotiations with the Soviet Union. It is a very complicated question. One of the factors involved is the degree of confidence that one can have in the first generation of the anti-ballistic-missile system. [20]

Continuing, Secretary Nitze said it is a moot point as to how the Soviets would offset a U.S. deployment:

> In the long run we ought to know what a first generation system can do. You can learn this by building a light one, and in my view the advantages of a light defense as against any threats that might come from Communist China would warrant so doing. [21]

Whereas McNamara did not want to deploy a BMD, the Service Secretaries thought it prudent to do so under the conditions each stated. Supporting the Chairman of the Joint Chiefs and the civilian Service Secretaries were the Chiefs of Staff of the Army, Navy, Air Force, and Marines, and the Director of ARPA, Dr. Charles Herzfeld. Each service chief, when asked for his personal opinion on the BMD, stood by the JCS recommendation. The sense of frustration in the military's testimony was expressed by General Harold Johnson of the Army:

> The next higher authority above the Joint Chiefs of Staff has not accepted that recommendation, and I, obviously, must support the view of the

next higher authority because I am subordinate to him, and under the law, I take his orders. [22]

Therefore, General Johnson said he supported Secretary McNamara and the Administration. When he could no longer do that, he said, it would be time for him to take off his uniform. He added, however, that he was personally uncomfortable about the decision, because the United States was not deploying (nor were we taking any measures to deploy) a BMD system, while the Soviets were continually improving their deployment capabilities. This was the crucial difference, he suggested: they are moving, we are standing still.

Several interesting developments regarding missile defense occurred in February 1967. *U.S. News and World Report* reported that the Soviets made a breakthrough in exo-atmospheric missile defense by using the X rays released from a thermonuclear blast as the kill mechanism.[4] The article also said that in 1958 both Soviet and American scientists knew from tests that X rays were released from H-bomb explosions, but apparently only the Soviets realized their potential. The article asserted that, having once discovered the X-ray effects, the Soviets agitated for a testing moratorium. The Soviets broke the moratorium in 1961 and during the subsequent test series in 1961–1963 actually destroyed two RVs with one ABM using the X-ray effect. It was only by accident that the United States learned of the phenomenon. A Russian scientist, according to this article, spoke about the X-ray effect at a meeting with U.S. scientists, assuming that everyone knew about the phenomenon.[5] The article quotes one U.S. authority as saying, "they found that the Russians not only had something, and were years ahead in theory, but had already tested it out in space and probably were starting to build their anti-missile system around it." [23]

On February 9, 1967, while in London, Premier Kosygin at a news conference made several interesting statements in his answer to several

---

[4] When X rays from an exo-atmospheric explosion encounter an RV, the energy which they carry is transmuted within the RV into a form of thermal energy. This energy boils, melts, or vaporizes the material inside the RV and the warhead becomes an inert mass. RVs can be hardened to some degree to protect them from this effect. Thermonuclear weapons in the megaton range can be designed to increase the proportion of X rays released.

[5] Not the Russian aspect, but the phenomenon was also reported a month earlier by Rex Pay, "New Effort Aimed at X-Ray Protection," *Technology Week,* January 2, 1967, p. 10. At least by 1967, the United States was aware of the problem for ICBM penetration. The United States was also working along these lines for BMD warhead development. See John Finney, "X-Ray Missile To Be Key in Defense Against China," *The New York Times,* November 16, 1967, p. 1, and by the same author, "U.S. Plans X-Ray Defense Against Missile Warheads," *The New York Times,* May 10, 1967, p. 10.

questions about missile defense. The question asked was, "Do you consider it possible to agree on a moratorium on the development of anti-missile defense systems and, if so, on what conditions?" He answered:

> This is an important question in the military sphere. I should not like to answer it directly, but want in turn to ask the person who submitted this question—I understand that he represents the British Institute of Strategic Research [Studies]—the following: Which weapons should be regarded as a tension factor—offensive or defensive weapons? I think that a defensive system, which prevents attack, is not a cause of the arms race but represents a factor preventing the death of people. Some persons reason thus: Which is cheaper, to have offensive weapons that destroy cities and entire states or to have defensive weapons that can prevent this destruction? At present the theory is current in some places that one should develop whichever system is cheaper. Such "theoreticians" argue also about how much it costs to kill a person— $500,000 or $100,000? An antimissile system may cost more than an offensive one, but it is intended not for killing people but for saving human lives. I understand that I am not answering the question that was put to me, but you can draw appropriate conclusions yourselves.
>
> There are other, far more dependable, ways of solving the security problem, ways that really could suit mankind. You know that we advocate discontinuing nuclear arming altogether and destroying reserves of nuclear weapons. We are ready for this, and not because we have few such weapons, but precisely because we have many, and mankind does not need nuclear weapons. And if the representatives of the press, those who influence the minds of people, treated this question along such lines, it seems to me that there would be far greater results than from talk about which weaponry is cheaper, offensive or defensive. The best thing is to seek renunciation of nuclear armament and the destruction of nuclear weapons.[6] [24]

A week after the Premier's interview, an article in *Pravda* was interpreted by Western analysts as indicating a Soviet shift in favor of a missile defense deployment moratorium. *The New York Times* of February 16, 1967 (p. 10), reported the shift, but the *Washington Post* of February 18, 1967 (p. A10), reported that Russian officials denied any shift and "that basically Russia had no interest at present in negotiating a moratorium with the United States." Murray Marder, in the *Washington Post* of

---

[6] Dana Adams Schmidt of *The New York Times* reported as a result of this interview that Kosygin appeared cool to a missile curb. See *The New York Times,* February 10, 1967, p. 1.

February 21, 1967 (p. A1), said that the State Department indicated the Soviets might be interested in a BMD moratorium. Marder said that this disclosure "was timed to offset increasing publicly expressed skepticism that the talks can succeed." The day before, Senator Henry Jackson urged that a $5 billion BMD deployment be prepared to protect the MINUTEMAN ICBM fields, in the event the talks with the Soviets failed [25].[7]

Meanwhile, an internal Soviet debate about the effectiveness of its missile defenses was revealed. The Soviets had been remarkably public in their claims about BMD progress. These claims have varied from outright claims that they had solved the BMD problem: such as Khrushchev's celebrated statement that a Soviet ABM could "hit a fly in outer space" and Marshal Malinovskii's at the 22nd Party Congress that "the problem of destroying missiles in flight . . . has been successfully solved," to more guarded statements such as Marshal Malinovskii's at the 23rd Party Congress in April 1966 that Soviet defenses could cope with some but not all enemy missiles [26]. In November 1966 Soviet Deputy Minister of Defense Marshal Nikolai Krylov declared that the Soviets were capable of midcourse interception of ICBMs [27].[8] In February 1967 General Paval F. Batitsky, a Deputy Defense Minister, said that his anti-aircraft troops could protect the country from missile attack. General Paval A. Kurachkin of the Frunze Military Academy stated, "detecting missiles in time and destroying them in flight is no problem" and missiles fired at the Soviet Union would never reach their targets [28].[9] Marshal Andrei Grechko, a First Deputy Minister of Defense, and Marshal Visily I. Chuikov, head of the Soviet civil defense program, both acknowledged that Soviet BMD *systems* could not prevent all enemy rockets from reaching their targets. These statements seemed to contradict the earlier statements of Batitsky and Kurachkin. The use of the word *systems* by Chuikov and Grechko is important because there was a debate within the U.S. intelligence community, only recently "resolved," about the purpose of the other defensive installations going up in Russia in addition to the Moscow BMD deployment. Some thought the Tallinn Line installations plus the other installations east of the Urals were missile defense systems deployed against China or a U.S. ICBM end run, while others thought the systems were air defense

---

[7] This suggestion was remarkably prophetic of President Nixon's SAFEGUARD Phase 1 proposal of March 1969.
[8] As pointed out in the Introduction, midcourse interception covers a very large area. The U.S. SAFEGUARD system with the 400-mile range of SPARTAN can be considered a midcourse intercept system, although an interceptor with a 2,000-mile range would also be considered a midcourse system.
[9] It was inferred from these statements that the Soviets were unwilling to negotiate a BMD moratorium.

installations. Today, the latter view is the accepted one. In any event, the use of the word "systems" tended to reinforce the Defense Department view that indeed two BMD systems were being deployed.[10]

On March 2, 1967, President Johnson announced at a surprise news conference that Premier Kosygin had agreed to discussion between the United States and Russia on limiting the arms race in both strategic offensive and defensive missiles. In late February 1967 it had been reported that the Soviets might be willing to broaden the talks to include offensive weapons, too [29]. The talks were to begin in Moscow, with Ambassador Thompson representing the United States. No date for these talks was set.

The reason given for the Soviet willingness to enter such talks was that they were beset with economic resource allocation problems and were not desirous of a new round in the arms race. This author believed in 1967 [11] and still believes today that the Soviet willingness to enter any such discussions was based on the expectation that the Soviet desire to talk would result in the deferment of any U.S. decision to deploy a BMD or new offensive systems and their strategic effort would soon surpass that of the United States. Meanwhile, the Soviets could continue their strategic offensive and defensive buildup, while American strength remained constant. It should be noted that, pending the outcome of SALT, the Nixon Administration has agreed to defer any major strategic offensive programs for a year [30].

In March 1967 the Senate began debate on the $21 billion Defense Authorization Bill. Senator Russell reported that the Armed Services Committee believed the start of a thin BMD system against China should be initiated, and if no agreement resulted from talks with the Soviet Union the additional funding in the Authorization Bill should be used to expand

---

[10] It is this author's contention that the Soviets rejected the McNamara nondeployment thesis and his tutoring on strategic force structure because the Soviets saw their own security enhanced by U.S. deployment of a BMD, in the event China tried to play off the United States and the Soviets or in the event of accidental or inadvertent missile firing. Moreover, with both superpowers in possession of BMD threats from third powers might be less credible. As ICBM accuracies increased, so that even small-yield ICBMs could have a hard target kill capability, lesser countries who sought hardened ICBM forces would find their forces susceptible to counterforce attacks. Without any active means of defending their forces, as they would be priced out of the BMD race, they had a choice of re-basing their forces at sea or in very hard silos (very expensive), or of contemplating a preventive, preemptive, or fire-on-warning strategy. This latter strategy could be negated if both the United States and the Soviets possessed BMD.

[11] The author took this position in his Ph.D. thesis, *The Anti-Ballistic Missile (ABM): A Study of the Effect of Strategic Weapons Technology on the Political System*, unpublished Ph.D. thesis from the University of Pennsylvania, 1968, p. 619.

the initial deployment. Both Senators Joseph Clark and Jacob Javits (R-N.Y.) opposed the inclusion of the $377-million standby production funds, believing Secretary McNamara was correct in his judgment that BMD was not needed or desirable at this time. Clark felt that the Soviet-American talks should be given a chance and recited all the same arguments against BMD that were cited in the past and would be recited in the future. A heated debate occurred between Senators Clark and Thurmond as to why Charleston, South Carolina, was on the list of the 25 initially defended cities. Later a second list of 25 was made public. The subject of this debate was precisely what Secretary McNamara and others predicted would occur if BMD were deployed in some places but not others. Clark said:

> Both Pittsburgh and Philadelphia are included on the list of 50 cities. But what do I say to my constituents in Reading, Allentown, Bethlehem, Lancaster, Scranton, Erie and Harrisburg and the other cities, as to why they must go without protection.
>
> In a democracy the suggestion that we confine protection to our major cities, letting the rest go without defense, is not politically feasible. Nor am I content to permit the Joint Chiefs of Staff or even the President to determine the cities to be protected. Moreover the war psychology which inevitably would be engendered from the installations of anti-ballistic missiles around our major urban centers and the construction of a comprehensive fallout shelter system that would be necessary to give protection, are results I hate to contemplate. [31]

Clark inferred that Charleston was included because that is where Representative Mendel Rivers (D-S.C.), Chairman of the House Armed Services Committee, comes from.[12] This inference is what precipitated the clash with Thurmond. The Senate then passed the bill 86 to 2 with Clark voting for the bill. Only Senators Ernest Gruening (D-Alaska) and Wayne Morse (D-Ore.) opposed.[13]

In the scientific and academic community, the missile defense question intensified as Dr. Teller said he believed a BMD system could be developed through underground testing, experiment, and theory. Shortly after Teller's speech, three members of the Federation of American Scientists

---

[12] Charleston is the site of the Atlantic Coast POLARIS base.
[13] During the course of early 1967, numerous statements were made for and against BMD in the Congress, with each speaker providing relevant background material and hometown editorials. Opposition was also voiced in the House to including the $377 million for NIKE-X. The opposition came from Representatives Cohelan, Otis Pike (D-N.Y.), and Lucien Nedzi (D-Mich.). Nevertheless, the bill was passed on May 9, 1967.

held an impromptu news conference to refute Teller's statement and to indicate that he misled the public on the possibility of developing a missile defense system.[14] Meanwhile, Dr. Ralph Lapp, a long-time disarmament advocate, spoke to the Midwest Conference of Political Scientists in Lafayette, Indiana. His paper, entitled "Weapons Culture," was devoted primarily to the military-industrial complex and the reasons why BMD should not be deployed.

On May 10, 1967, the Senate Disarmament Subcommittee released the heavily censored *U.S. Armament and Disarmament Problems* transcript. In this hearing, the Joint Chiefs endorsed immediate BMD deployment, while Dr. Foster of DDR&E thought any large BMD system would become rapidly obsolete. Deputy Secretary Cyrus Vance suggested that a light area missile defense against the Chinese was possible and desirable but no decision was necessary now. This point was challenged by Senator Gore, who thought the Chinese nuclear advances were ahead of the Defense Department timetable. The significance of this hearing was that the Foreign Relations Committee decided to inject itself into the strategic weapons policy issues so as not to leave this area to the Senate Armed Services Committee to mold congressional opinion. Senator J. W. Fulbright (D-Ark.) felt that the BMD issue had strong foreign policy implications and should not be discussed only in the military context [32].[15] Secretary of Defense McNamara indicated that while very little progress had been made in convincing the Soviets to hold strategic arms limitation talks, the possibility did exist that both sides would be permitted limited BMD deployments against the Chinese [33].

By late spring, the Defense Department became even more concerned over growing Soviet strategic capabilities and the lack of a decision to deploy NIKE-X [34]. With the Chinese detonation of an H-bomb in June 1967, there appeared to be even greater pressure on the Administration to deploy a missile defense around the United States [35].

---

[14] The three individuals were Marvin Kalkstein of the State University of New York at Stonybrook, outgoing chairman of FAS; Dr. J. Orear, incoming chairman of FAS from Cornell; and Leonard Rodberg, treasurer of FAS from the University of Maryland.

[15] This was a position the committee was to take more frequently in future years with respect not only to BMD but to MIRV and other strategic weapons programs. It is ironic to note that Gore and Symington took the view that a BMD should be deployed at a time when the Administration so far had refused to deploy. After September 1967, but particularly after President Nixon's SAFEGUARD announcement, these same individuals were especially active in criticizing and opposing that deployment decision. It seems these individuals and others opposed the no-deployment policy of the Johnson Administration and then turned around and opposed both the Johnson and Nixon Administrations' deployment policies when they were announced!

The *Washington Post* reported on June 26, 1967, that the Soviets had ruled out for the present any negotiations on BMD limitation. This position apparently was communicated to the President by Mr. Kosygin during the Glassboro conference in June 1967.[16] It was felt that, while Kosygin had repeated his London statement on BMD and strategic disarmament, the outstanding issues of Vietnam and the Middle East made the time inappropriate for arms limitation talks. It was reported in this same article that Soviet Foreign Minister Andrei Gromyko privately told other diplomats after the first Glassboro session the Soviets had rejected the kinds of talks proposed by the United States on the grounds that the United States wanted to negotiate on the technical level, while the Soviets wanted broad political talks on the implication of nuclear weaponry [36]. In a television interview at the United Nations following the Glassboro talks, Kosygin was asked the following question and gave the following reply:

Q. What are the prospects of an agreement between the U.S. and the Soviet Union on limiting the development of anti-ballistic missile systems? A. As regards an anti-missile system, our position is well known. We believe that the discussions should center not on merely the problem of an anti-missile defense system. Because, after all, the anti-missile system is not a weapon of aggression, of attack; it is a defensive system. And we feel therefore that what should be considered is the entire complex of armament and disarmament questions.

Because, otherwise, if—instead of building and deploying an antiballistic missile system—the money is used to build up offensive missile systems, mankind will not stand to gain anything. It will, on the contrary, face a still greater menace and will come still closer to war. And we therefore are in favor of considering the whole range of questions relating to arms and disarmament, and we're ready to discuss that question—the general question of disarmament. [37]

In textual changes to the Premier's remarks several days later, it was clearer that the Soviet position on talks had become harder [38].

A new approach to missile defense was revealed in July when the Navy indicated studies were being initiated to base ABMs at sea on large submarines and warships. The system, called SABMIS, would use POLARIS boosters or a new booster. With its potential for forward basing, the system could become a true midcourse system [39].

By summer of 1967 the lines of battle were clearly forming. The Chairman of the JCS had presented to the House Defense Appropriations Committee an argument for initiating a BMD deployment. Some of the

---

[16] See Henry Cabot Lodge. "A Citizen Looks at the ABM," *Reader's Digest,* June 1970.

more influential Senators, Stennis, Thurmond, Jackson, and Russell, along with Representatives Rivers, Mahon, Sikes, William Minshall (R-O.), and Flood, were championing the military's position; whereas Senators Young, Clark, and Javits and Representatives Bryan Dorn (D-S.C.) and Cohelan opposed BMD.[17] The Chairman of the Joint Atomic Energy Committee, Senator John Pastore (D-R.I.), urged immediate deployment; while Senator Clark, in several speeches, argued the folly of any deployment [40]. By late August, Senator Henry Jackson announced plans to hold hearings on the matter. Congressional disenchantment had increased: the Joint Atomic Energy Committee [41] and the Senate Appropriations Committee [42] had both publicly recommended deployment of NIKE-X, the former because of the rapid emergence of the Chinese threat. The House Republican Policy Committee made a similar plea [43], and Senator Joseph Clark urged the President to appoint a blue-ribbon committee to aid in his decision whether or not to deploy a BMD [44].

Since 1968 was a presidential election year, evidence indicated the Republicans intended to make the nondeployment policy a campaign issue. Governor Ronald Reagan of California and Presidential nominee Richard Nixon had both discussed the lack of BMD in political speeches [45]. And, the Public Relations Division of the Republican National Committee had published a 55-page background report entitled *The Missile Defense Question, Is LBJ Right?* [46]

On September 8, 1967, Secretary of State Rusk warned that time was running out on the Adminitsration's willingness to defer deployment of a missile defense. In effect, he warned the Soviets that if they did not agree to start talks soon the United States would be compelled to begin deployment [47]. Adding fuel to the debate was the report that the Soviets were developing some kind of multiple warhead for their large ICBMs [48]. The House Armed Services Committee released a report prepared for it by retired military officers which concluded:

> The preponderance of evidence points to a conclusion that the Soviet Union is succeeding in its massive drive toward strategic military superiority and that the United States is cooperating in this effort by slowing down its side of the arms race. [49]

These political and military pressures were forcing a reevaluation of the nondeployment policy. The reevaluation would be in terms of: is

---

[17] A debate of rather substantial size went on in the Congress in the summer of 1967 as to whether a BMD should or should not be deployed. The *Congressional Record* for the months of June, July, August, and September 1967, contains a wealth of material on this debate, which repeated all the arguments for and against deployment already noted.

now the time to begin deployment? However, the changing strategic-military-technological situation in China and in the Soviet Union by late summer of 1967 and the mounting political pressure on the President to deploy now made it imperative that the policy of nondeployment be reexamined. In retrospect it appears that the gap was widening between the President and the Secretary of Defense over the issue of deployment as well as on Vietnam. A policy statement on BMD was to be the subject of McNamara's speech to the United Press International in San Francisco on September 18, 1967. Originally, he was to argue the case for continued nondeployment. At the last moment, however, McNamara revised his speech to reflect the President's decision to begin deployment of a missile defense against China! [18]

References

[1] Text of President Johnson's State of the Union Message, *The New York Times,* January 11, 1967, p. 6.

[2] "Plea on Missiles Is Sent to Soviet," *The New York Times,* January 15, 1967, p. 23.

[3] John W. Finney, "Johnson Backed on Missile Pact," *The New York Times,* January 18, 1967, p. 92. Gore's Subcommittee eventually held closed hearings, on February 16, 1967, about the ABM and released a four-page report entitled *Status of the Development of the Anti-ballistic Missile Systems in the United States,* prepared for the Subcommittee on Disarmament of the Senate Committee on Foreign Relations, 90th Cong., 1st Sess., 1967.

[4] John W. Finney, "U.S. Says Soviet Shows Interest in Missile Curb," *The New York Times,* January 21, 1967, p. 1.

[5] William Beecher. "Johnson Wants Stand-by Fund for Nike-X System," *The New York Times,* January 25, 1967, p. 16.

[6] U.S. Department of Defense, *Statement of Secretary of Defense Robert S. McNamara Before a Joint Session of the Senate Armed Services Committee and the Senate Subcommittee on Department of Defense Appropriations on the*

---

[18] Careful reading of the speech reveals that McNamara referred to the decision to deploy BMD against China only at the very end, after having delivered nearly all (22 of 25 pages) of his speech. It is unlikely, had the *original* purpose of the speech been to announce BMD deployment, that so much time and text would have elapsed before the announcement. Neil Sheehan, writing in *The New York Times,* November 29, 1967, p. 16, indicates that McNamara was forced to change his speech from an argument against deployment to announce the President's decision. The author believes that one of the reasons McNamara may have left the Cabinet was a result of his growing isolation on the BMD issue.

Fiscal Year 1968–72 Defense Program and 1968 Defense Budget, mimeographed, January 23, 1967, p. 44, hereafter cited as *1967 Annual Posture Statement.*

[7] U.S. House of Representatives, Committee on Armed Services, *Hearings on Military Posture and H.R. 9240,* 90th Cong., 1st Sess., 1967, p. 468, hereafter cited as *House Defense Authorization for FY 1968.*

[8] *1967 Annual Posture Statement,* p. 53.

[9] *1967 Annual Posture Statement,* p. 40.

[10] U.S. Senate, Committee on Armed Services and the Subcommittee on Department of Defense of the Committee on Appropriations, *Military Procurement Authorizations for Fiscal Year 1968,* 90th Cong., 1st Sess., 1967, p. 249, hereafter cited as *Senate Defense Authorizations 1968.*

[11] *Senate Defense Authorizations 1968,* pp. 249–250.

[12] *Senate Defense Authorizations 1968,* p. 250.

[13] *Senate Defense Authorizations 1968,* p. 250.

[14] *Senate Defense Authorizations 1968,* pp. 251–252.

[15] U.S. Senate, Hearings Before the Subcommittee on Disarmament of the Committee on Foreign Relations, *United States Armament and Disarmament Problems,* 90th Cong., 1st Sess., 1967, pp. 86–87, hereafter cited as *U.S. Armament and Disarmament Problems.*

[16] U.S. House of Representatives, Hearings Before Subcommittee of the Committee on Appropriations, *Department of Defense Appropriations for 1968,* Part 2, 90th Cong., 1st Sess., p. 201, hereafter cited as *House Defense Appropriations FY 1968.*

[17] *House Defense Appropriations FY 1968,* Part 2, p. 635.

[18] *House Defense Appropriations FY 1968,* Part 2, p. 772.

[19] *House Defense Appropriations FY 1968,* Part 2, p. 773.

[20] *House Defense Appropriations FY 1968,* Part 2, p. 909.

[21] *House Defense Appropriations FY 1968,* Part 2, p. 909.

[22] *House Defense Appropriations FY 1968,* Part 2, p. 637.

[23] "Pentagon's Urgent Worry: Can U.S. Missiles Survive Russia's 'X-Ray Defenses'?" *U.S. News and World Report,* 6[1967]36.

[24] U.S. Arms Control and Disarmament Agency, *Documents on Disarmament 1967,* Publication 46, 1968, pp. 60–61, hereafter cited as *Documents on Disarmament 1967.*

[25] Murray Marder, "Soviets Seen Interested in ABM Accord," *Washington Post,* February 21, 1967, p. A1.

[26] All quotations taken from Dr. Thomas Wolfe's testimony in U.S. Senate, Hearings Before the Subcommittee on Military Applications of the Joint Com-

mittee on Atomic Energy, *Scope, Magnitude, and Implications of the United States Antiballistic Missile Program,* 90th Cong., 1st Sess., 1968, p. 66, hereafter cited as *Scope and Magnitude of U.S. ABM Program.*

[27] Henry Brandon, State of Affairs Column, "A New Missile Race?" *Saturday Review of Literature,* 4[1967]16.

[28] "Russians Say Anti-missile System Will Protect Them from Attack," *The New York Times,* February 21, 1967, p. 5.

[29] Hedrick Smith, "Soviet Would Widen Talks Asked by U.S. on Missiles," *The New York Times,* February 22, 1967, p. 1.

[30] U.S. Department of Defense, Defense Report Before a Joint Session of the Senate Armed Services and Appropriations Committee, *A Statement by Secretary of Defense Melvin R. Laird on Fiscal Year 1971 Defense Program and Budget,* February 20, 1970, mimeographed, p. 50, hereafter cited as *Laird Posture Statement.*

[31] *U.S. Congressional Record,* March 21, 1967, p. S4955.

[32] Donald C. Winston, "U.S. May Revise Timing on ABM," *Aviation Week and Space Technology,* 20[1967]22.

[33] Robert H. Phelps, "Chinese a Factor in Missile Accord," *The New York Times,* May 19, 1967, p. 1.

[34] Hanson Baldwin, "Pentagon Concern on Lack of Missile Defense Grows," *The New York Times,* May 21, 1967, p. 1.

[35] William Beecher, "Pressure in U.S. for Defense Seen," *The New York Times,* June 18, 1967, p. 2.

[36] Murray Marder, "Russia Rejects Talks on Anti-Missile Race," *Washington Post,* June 26, 1967, p. A1.

[37] *Documents on Disarmament 1967,* p. 270.

[38] Murray Marder. "Moscow Hardens Kosygin's Remarks," *Washington Post,* June 30, 1967, p. A1.

[39] William Beecher. "Antimissile Net at Sea Proposed," *The New York Times,* July 4, 1967, p. 1.

[40] *U.S. Congressional Record,* July 27, 1967, p. S10364.

[41] U.S. Congress, Joint Committee on Atomic Energy, *Impact of Chinese Communist Nuclear Weapons Progress on United States National Security,* 90th Cong., 1st Sess., 1967.

[42] U.S. Senate, Committee on Appropriations, *Department of Defense Appropriations Bill, 1968,* Report No. 494, 90th Cong., 1st Sess., 1967, p. 7.

[43] House Republican Policy Committee, *Statement on the Deployment of an Anti-Ballistic Missile System,* Washington, August 9, 1967, p. 1.

[44] John W. Finney, "Clark Urges Presidential Study of Missile Defense," *The New York Times,* July 27, 1967, p. 12. See text of speech by Joseph S.

Clark, *Anti-Ballistic Missiles and the Military Industrial Complex,* August 1967, mimeographed.

[45] "Missile Defense Is Urged by Nixon," *The New York Times,* September 15, 1967, p. 9.

[46] See also *The Missile Defense Question: Is LBJ Right?* A background report by the Republican National Committee, Washington, February 20, 1967.

[47] John W. Finney, "Rusk Urges Speed on Missile Freeze, " *The New York Times,* September 9, 1967, p. 1.

[48] William Beecher, "Soviet Reported Stressing Multiple Warhead Missile," *The New York Times,* September 10, 1967, p. 1.

[49] William Beecher, *The New York Times,* September 10, 1967, p. 20. See *The Changing Strategic Military Balance U.S.A. vs. U.S.S.R.,* a study prepared for the House Armed Services Committee by the National Strategy Committee of the American Security Council, June 1967.

CHAPTER 12

The Sentinel Decision—The End of the No-Deployment Policy

For a decade before the September 18, 1967, announcement that the United States was going to deploy a missile defense, every Administration refrained from such a decision. It can be seen that until 1965 such decisions were based on technical, economic, and military reasons. After 1965, the reason for nondeployment became political. To understand this political aspect, it is necessary to assess the events following the decision to deploy SENTINEL.

Even when the decision was announced that the United States was going to deploy a BMD against the emerging Chinese threat, McNamara qualified this decision by saying:

> . . . our decision to go ahead with *limited* ABM deployment in no way indicates that we feel an agreement with the Soviet Union on the limitation of strategic nuclear offensive and defensive forces is any the less urgent or desirable. [1]

In the case of BMD, there appears to have been a singular and deliberate lack of recognition concerning the real and immediate strategic threat from the Soviet Union; a nonexistent (so far) Chinese ICBM force has been the object and rationale for deploying BMD. The United States, by deploying BMD against the Chinese threat, maintained the position that offensive power was cheaper and more reliable for offsetting the Soviet defenses. Moreover, by notifying the Soviets that SENTINEL was not designed to affect Soviet forces, the Administration clearly indicated its pursuit of a mutual deterrence strategy. Evidence of this abounded in McNamara's speech on September 18, 1967, to the editors of United Press International in which he announced the decision.

McNamara argued that the present superiority of the United States was due more to misinformation than to planning, which "is a significant illustration of the intrinsic dynamics of the nuclear arms race." [2] Not knowing what Soviet intentions were in 1961, when they had a small ICBM force but the technological and industrial capacity to enlarge that force, the United States embarked on its massive solid-fuel ICBM building program.

Thus in the course of hedging against what was then only a theoretically possible Soviet buildup, we took decisions which have resulted in our current superiority in numbers of warheads and deliverable megatons. [3]

If the United States had had access to more information about Soviet intentions and strategic force structure, it would not have needed as large a strategic offensive force as it now has. Indeed, according to McNamara, it appeared that the United States never desired or sought nuclear superiority against the Soviets; that it came about "accidentally." Deploying BMD would certainly be inconsistent with a policy which eschewed superiority. In the case of nondeployment, BMD became a means for communicating U.S. intentions to the Soviets. McNamara said:

> What is essential to understand here is that the Soviet Union and the United States mutually influence one another's strategic plans.
>
> Whatever be their intentions, whatever be our intentions, actions—or even realistically potential actions—on either side relating to the buildup of nuclear forces, be they either offensive or defensive weapons, necessarily trigger reactions on the other side.
>
> It is precisely this action-reaction phenomenon that fuels an arms race.
>
> Now, in strategic nuclear weaponry, the arms race involves a particular irony. Unlike any other era in military history, today a substantial numerical superiority of weapons does not effectively translate into political control or diplomatic leverage.
>
> While thermonuclear power is almost inconceivably awesome, and represents virtually unlimited potential destructiveness, it has proven to be a limited diplomatic instrument. Its uniqueness lies in the fact that it is at one and the same time, an all powerful weapon—and a very inadequate weapon. [4]

Based on the logic and reasoning in his speech, it is obvious that the attempt to prevent the action-reaction phenomenon of an arms race had been a major component of foreign and military policy. It was also the primary reason why BMD was never officially authorized against any Soviet threat, even though SENTINEL could have been expanded to defend "our MINUTEMAN sites against Soviet attack." [5] It was hoped that despite Soviet efforts to improve its assured destruction and damage-limiting forces, the U.S. ability to penetrate Soviet defenses, deny them a decisive first strike, and maintain a credible assured destruction capability would obviate the need for a "destabilizing" weapon like BMD while still providing a credible deterrent. This would avert an arms race and a concomitant increase in military technological developments. It is because of the certainty of a corresponding Soviet reaction to the deployment of an American BMD, said McNamara, that four prominent presidential scientific advisors (Drs. James Killian, Kistiakowsky, Wiesner, and Donald Horning) and three directors of DDR&E (Drs. York, Brown, and Foster) "have unanimously recommended against the deployment of an ABM system designed to protect the U.S. population against a Soviet attack." [6]

Certainly, all indications from 1965 on make it appear that every decision to withhold NIKE-X production was a holding action designed to forestall the present situation; i.e., Soviet deployment of BMD. The only problem was that the Soviets did not cooperate, and, indeed, it is questionable whether they wanted to or could have done so. In announcing the decision to deploy a BMD, McNamara said "there are marginal grounds for concluding that a light deployment of U.S. ABMs against this (China) possibility is prudent." [7] The system would be relatively cheap— $5 billion—and would have a higher degree of reliability against a Chinese attack (small threat) than a larger system would have against the Soviets. McNamara stated that the system would have other advantages.

. . . it would provide an additional indication to Asians that we intend to deter China from nuclear blackmail, and thus would contribute toward our goal of discouraging nuclear weapon proliferation among the present non-nuclear countries.

. . . allowing expansion to defend MINUTEMAN against Soviet attack adding to the effectiveness of our offensive forces without having to expand them.

. . . protect the population from accidental launch of an ICBM. [8]

McNamara said that actual production would begin at the end of the year. He cautioned that there were two possible dangers in this decision. One, the United States will lapse into the old oversimplification of the adequacy of nuclear power to deter, because it possesses a defense. Two, the "small momentum intrinsic to the development of all nuclear weaponry" will lead to pressure out of all proportion to its actual need from many directions to procure and deploy the weapon.

The danger in deploying this relatively light and reliable Chinese-oriented ABM system is going to be that pressure will develop to expand it into a heavy Soviet-oriented ABM system.

We must resist that temptation firmly—not because we can for a moment afford to relax our vigilance against a possible Soviet first-strike —but precisely because our greatest deterrent against such a strike is not a massive, costly but highly penetrable ABM shield, but rather a fully credible offensive assured destruction capability.

The so-called heavy ABM shield—at the present state of technology—would in effect be no adequate shield at all against a Soviet attack, but rather a strong inducement for the Soviets to vastly increase their own offensive forces. That, as I have pointed out, would make it necessary for us to respond in turn—and so the arms race would rush hopelessly on to no sensible purpose on either side. [9]

If the BMD had such technical weaknesses that it could easily be overcome, how much would the Soviets have to increase their strategic offensive inventory to overcome a U.S. missile defense? McNamara said this inventory was greatly in excess of a credible assured destruction capability, as was ours.

At the heart of McNamara's reluctance to deploy BMD was the idea that U.S. security and that of the Soviet Union would be best served by the ability of each side to threaten and actually carry out, if necessary, the destruction of respective population and industrial centers; i.e., to hold the people on both sides as hostage.[1] It was precisely this morally and ethically reprehensible idea that led many scientists such as J. Robert Oppenheimer to object to the crash development of the H-bomb instead of provision for strategic air defenses for the United States.

In an interview in Washington given to James Mossman of the BBC on February 15, 1967, Robert S. McNamara set forth the rationale for nondeployment which appeared in the San Francisco speech. He said that he would prefer building more offense to counter any Soviet defense, arguing that, in the event deterrence failed, the United States should have the ability to limit damage to itself, but that he did not believe it could attain such a goal by building BMD. McNamara said during the interview that defense is in the Soviet psychology and in its emotional desire to protect Mother Russia. McNamara disagreed with Kosygin's statement that it is better to build defense than offense. He insisted that we must build offense if the Soviets build defense [10]. It is ironic that when the interviewer asked McNamara whether the Soviet response to the vastly superior U.S. offense should not be defense, McNamara answered:

> Well, if they are, they are responding in an erroneous way. I—in a sense, if I were they, I wouldn't consider our force vastly superior. It is superior in numbers for reasons we needn't go into, but we're quite prepared to

---

[1] McNamara assumed that both the United States and the Soviets were rational and had a common interest in preventing a nuclear war; therefore, the Soviets would accept McNamara's logic and reasoning on strategic nuclear force structure. Unfortunately, the Soviets had a different conception of the use to which military force could be put without resorting to war; i.e., nuclear weapons could be an instrument of national policy, an idea the United States has chosen not to exploit, since the Cuban Missile Crisis in 1962.

say, and I've stated publicly, that we with our force, superior as it is in numbers, do not have sufficient power to destroy them without in effect destroying ourselves in the process. [11]

In short, the Soviets do not need defense to deter the United States; the ability for each to destroy the other is sufficient.

For these reasons the Defense Secretary advised the President not to deploy a heavy BMD, as it would not contribute in the long run to U.S. security vis-à-vis the Soviet Union. While in themselves these reasons may have appeared questionable, especially to BMD proponents, within the broader context of contemporary U.S. defense policy objectives, as McNamara saw them, these reasons were valid and consistent as a result of the assumptions inherent in that policy.[2]
In essence:

As long as deterrence of a deliberate Soviet (or Red Chinese) nuclear attack upon the United States or its allies is the overriding objective of our strategic forces, the capacity for "Assured Destruction" must receive the first call on all of our resources and must be provided regardless of the costs and the difficulties involved. "Damage Limiting" programs, no matter how much we spend on them, can never substitute for an Assured Destruction Capability in the deterrent role. *It is our ability to destroy an attacker as a viable 20th Century nation that provides the deterrent, not our ability to partially limit damage to ourselves.* [12]

Those opposed to Secretary McNamara's defense policy attacked his BMD policy, which was the embodiment of his position on national security; i.e., mutual deterrence through parity. General Wheeler, Chairman of the JCS, presented the argument as follows:

We feel that they (Russians) would also be faced with the grave uncertainties associated with targeting against an ABM defended nation. We believe that the Soviet offensive and defensive buildup does increase the risk of nuclear war. Deterrence is a combination of forces in being, and state of mind.

Should the Soviets come to believe that their ballistic missile defense, coupled with a nuclear attack on the United States, would limit

---

[2] Senator Russell has pointed out that there are some defects in the Secretary's reasoning which lead to his faulty conclusions about BMD: "In trying to support his conclusions that it is expensively futile to build an ABM defense against the Soviet Union, the Department of Defense presented an involuted series of assumptions, hypotheses, and assumptions upon assumptions. . . . If one accepts every premise in this syllogism, he will arrive at the conclusion the Department desires." See *U.S. Congressional Record,* March 21, 1967, p. 4172.

damage to the Soviet Union to a level acceptable to them, whatever that level is, our forces would no longer deter. The first principle of our security policy would be gone.

I should say here that while I certainly agree—and so do the Joint Chiefs—that the basis of deterrence is the ability to destroy an attacker as a viable nation, as a part of this, there is also the ability of the nation to survive as a nation—in other words, the converse of the first point. [13]

In attempting to communicate the logic of his strategic rationale to the Soviets,[3] Secretary McNamara argued that a BMD system introduced so many uncertainties into the strategic equation that a nation is better off without it, since with it, one nation may feel it has acquired an advantage which in reality is not the case.

At the heart of the debate regarding defense policy formulation, as symbolized by BMD, is the proper role of military forces in the nuclear age. BMD opponents, although not necessarily advocates of unilateral disarmament, view strategic military force technology as a liability in the effort to achieve political stability in a deterrence environment. These individuals tried to persuade others that military force was not the solution to the security needs of either side. Since they believed it was impossible to win a nuclear war and that it would be disastrous to wage one, a solution had to be found to the contradiction of the possession and advanced development of nuclear weapons to the fact that no one wants to use them.[4] A first step is to bring about mutual deterrence while building trust and confidence; thus their interest in informal arms control and disarmament measures. In the "new outlook," which was enunciated and communicated to Moscow during the McNamara reign and which derived from the ideas of Thomas Schelling (a Harvard University Economics Professor), "weapons, however powerful, that weaken stability have a minus value; weapons that contribute to the stability have a plus value, whichever side has them." [14]

Such concepts helped to provide the Defense Department with a rationale for trying to deal with the thermo-nuclear dilemma. With both sides sharing an interest in stability, the objective was to design forces primarily to achieve stability rather than victory, and to influence the other side to do the same. [15]

---

[3] "During the last several years we have released more information of a formerly classified nature than ever before, because we wanted the Soviet Union to know our capability so that they would not misinterpret our power, and our capability to destroy them as a viable nation should they attempt to attack us." Part of Deputy Secretary of Defense Vance's testimony in the *U.S. Armament and Disarmament Problems*, p. 43.

[4] These individuals attributed these same views to the Soviets, which was a cardinal error.

The U.S. offer to refrain from deploying a weapon that was not yet operational was a significant deviation from traditional disarmament proposals. Thus far the terms of disarmament have referred only to existent or operational weapon systems. Now a system not yet deployed was being offered as a form of unilateral disarmament; i.e., the United States would refrain from deployment if the Soviets did likewise. This condition might be acceptable if both sides adhered to such an agreement. If one side did not, then a dangerously unbalanced technological strategic-political situation would occur; the violator would have the opportunity to use his military-political superiority for his own interest at the expense of the observer of the agreement.

The Johnson Administration viewed the unilateral decision not to deploy BMD as a means for building mutual trust and confidence into Soviet-American relations and also to reduce tensions between them by having parity with mutually deterring offensive retaliatory forces on both sides. The BMD deployment issue was seized upon as the means for communicating this broader objective both to the Soviets and to those in the Administration and military establishment who opposed that policy and desired a missile defense. Unfortunately, this unusual experiment in arms control and signaling intentions to the Soviets and to the U.S. military failed. What the BMD proponents feared was that the Soviets were deliberately trying to acquire strategic superiority to be used (1) if deterrence failed, (2) as part of a politico-military strategy designed to blackmail the United States, to undermine its will to resist or challenge its vital interests without necessarily going to war, or (3) deliberately to eliminate the United States as a world power by attacking her. Those favoring BMD deployment do not accept the action-reaction thesis which would necessarily cause the Soviets to expand their offense if the United States deployed BMD. The proponents believe that Soviet strategic planning and force structure reflect its own objectives, which are quite independent of U.S. objectives. Dr. Herzfeld revealed that in an attempt to convince the Soviets of the futility of their BMD effort, the argument against deployment was presented on three occasions at the Pugwash Conferences. "On the first two occasions the Russians did not understand the argument that there might be an advantage in not having a defense; the third time they said it was too late." [16]

It appeared that the decision not to deploy NIKE-X during the Kennedy and Johnson Administrations was an attempt to "persuade the Russians to accept a common view with the United States of a strategy in a nuclear-armed world." [17] Every decision concerning strategy, force structure, and research and development in a deterrent environment must be viewed from the point of international stability and the dynamic effect on the arms race. This reasoning was not illogical and not without foundation when the decision not to deploy BMD against the Soviets was considered. Yet opponents of deployment in any form understood that even a BMD against the Chinese would cause a Soviet reaction. As good strategic planners, the Soviets had to hedge against the possibility that the American BMD was better than theirs, that it could be expanded to counter their ICBM threat, or that it was actually being deployed against them, with the Chinese merely serving as an excuse. The Administration apparently believed that the Soviets would not misinterpret U.S. intentions, since they had been made aware before the decision was announced that the deployment was against a Chinese threat and not their own. It is interesting to speculate why the Russians indicated a desire to discuss strategic arms limitation shortly after the SENTINEL decision was announced.

So long as the U.S. security policy was to deter an enemy attack, and this could be accomplished by ensuring penetration of enemy defenses in order to destroy the fabric of his society, the primary requirement was for offensive weapons. Refraining from deploying BMD was consistent with this policy. Therefore, nondeployment could be viewed as presenting little risk to the United States if it presented the means of gaining a great political victory and provided the Soviets subscribed to a similar view and reciprocated.

At the heart of the Administration's defense policy was the belief that U.S. security would best be preserved and maintained if it offered up its citizens as hostages to the Soviets in return for the same. Since such a policy could not tolerate population defense, BMD was a real threat and challenge to the assured destruction defense policy of Secretary McNamara.

McNamara's attempt to control the arms race was a heroic one and only history will judge the correctness of his position. If he can be faulted, it was that he believed too long, in the face of overwhelming evidence, that the Soviets accepted his view of security and his rationale for structuring strategic forces and held a common interest with the United States in toning down the arms race.[5]

In this sense, BMD was as important a political issue as it was a strategic, economic, military, and technical one.

---

[5] In a little known and anonymously written article ("Soviet Missile Power: A 'Credible Threat' Now" by Xenophon) in the February 1967 issue of *Triumph* magazine a Catholic journal of news and opinion there appeared a very remarkable and authoritative article on the Soviet-American strategic-technological balance, the Soviet and American BMD programs, U.S. BMD deployment policy and its inconsistencies up to that time, an analysis of the then little known MIRV program and a cogent argument for deploying a missile defense system as well as developing one for area defense. This remarkable article was re-printed in the U.S. *Congressional Record*, February 17, 1967, pp. S2152–2155. It bears very careful reading.

References

[1] U.S. Department of Defense News Release No. 868–67. *Address by Honorable Robert S. McNamara, Secretary of Defense Before United Press International Editors and Publishers, San Francisco, California, September 18, 1967,* p. 24, hereafter cited as the *Sentinel Decision Speech.*

[2] *Sentinel Decision Speech,* p. 9.

[3] *Sentinel Decision Speech,* p. 9.

[4] *Sentinel Decision Speech,* p. 10.

[5] *Sentinel Decision Speech,* p. 22.

[6] *Sentinel Decision Speech,* p. 17.

[7] *Sentinel Decision Speech,* p. 22.

[8] *Sentinel Decision Speech,* p. 22.

[9] *Sentinel Decision Speech,* pp. 23–24.

[10] *U.S. Department of State Bulletin,* March 20, 1967, pp. 442–447.

[11] *U.S. Department of State Bulletin,* March 20, 1967, p. 444.

[12] U.S. Department of Defense, *Statement of Secretary of Defense Robert S. McNamara Before the Senate Armed Services Committee on the Fiscal Year 1969–73 Defense Program and 1969 Defense Budget,* January 22, 1968, pp. 47–48, hereafter cited as *1968 Posture Statement.*

[13] U.S. Congress, House, Hearings Before a Subcommittee of the Committee on Appropriations, *Department of Defense Appropriations for Fiscal Year 1968,* 90th Cong., 1st Sess., 1967, p. 178.

[14] Norman Moss, "McNamara's ABM Policy: A Failure of Communications," *The Reporter,* 4[1967]34.

[15] Moss, p. 34.

[16] "On an Anti-Ballistic Missile System," *Summary of Discussion at the Ninth Meeting of the European Study Commission,* Institute for Strategic Studies, January 14–15, 1966, p. 17.

[17] Moss, p. 34.

PART IV
Safeguard

CHAPTER 13

From Sentinel to Safeguard

With the decision to deploy a light area missile defense, round two of the missile defense controversy began. Round one was the limited and ineffectual opposition by a group of senators and representatives to halt the pre-production fund appropriations for NIKE-X beginning in the spring of 1967. The end of round two, a year and a half later, would see the entire SENTINEL deployment halted and then scrapped, only to be replaced by a "new" system—the SAFEGUARD deployment. The SENTINEL decision also ended the 10-year nondeployment period for U.S. missile defense policy.

SENTINEL deployment,[1] oriented against China, would consist of 17 sites: 15 in the continental United States and one each in Hawaii and Alaska. Six PARs, each with one northward-pointing face, would be deployed across the northern United States; each PAR would have collocated with it an MSR and SPRINTs to protect the PAR and MSR. Eleven additional MSR sites would not be defended, but deployed to provide complete coverage of the 48 continental states, Hawaii, and Alaska. The four MSRs deployed in the MINUTEMAN fields and the one at Washington, D.C., would each have four faces to provide 360-degree coverage. All the sites would be equipped with SPARTANs, except the Hawaiian site, which would have only SPRINTs [1].

One characteristic of this deployment was that 10 of the 15 continental sites were located in or near most of the major U.S. metropolitan areas, giving the impression that SENTINEL was the start of a heavy city defense against the Soviets. In fact, even before the SENTINEL decision was officially announced, several members of Congress and opponents of BMD viewed SENTINEL as the forerunner of the larger Posture A system costing between $7 billion and $15 billion. Senators Pastore and Henry Jackson (D-Wash.) of the Joint Congressional Committee on Atomic Energy, which had originally scheduled hearings on the need to deploy BMD against China, now decided to focus its hearings on the need for a Soviet BMD.

The reaction to the SENTINEL decision was varied. There were

---

[1] Known only as Model 167; the name was assigned later.

those who urged a larger and thicker defense. The British were irritated at not being consulted. They warned that the deployment would lead to a new round in the arms race and the United States would be forced to break the 1963 Nuclear Test Ban Treaty in order to perfect the system [2].[2] To counter these fears in London and elsewhere, Adrian Fisher, Deputy Director of ACDA, delivered a statement to the ENDC on September 19, 1967, about the SENTINEL deployment. He emphasized the limited nature of the system, as it was described in McNamara's speech. Fisher argued that its hard point defense provisions were less provocative than building more ICBMs. He said that a heavy urban defense was not feasible and could easily be offset by the Soviets. Fisher stated the SENTINEL deployment would not aggravate the U.S.-U.S.S.R. strategic arms race, pointing out that the Soviets had already deployed their own BMD. Moreover, he said, the Soviets never indicated that a limited U.S. BMD deployment would be provocative. Fisher concluded by saying he did not believe the SENTINEL decision posed any technical or political impediment to arms control, especially a nonproliferation treaty (NPT) or the control of strategic weapons [3].[3]

The Chinese reacted to the U.S. announcement by asserting that the system was not designed for defense but for attack and nuclear threats against them [4].

James Reston suggested the BMD deployment was really designed to prevent the Republicans from making a presidential campaign issue of missile defense. Reston said the decision represented a compromise to assume the worst from China and the best from the Soviets [5].

The Canadian Government ruled out any participation in the proposed system and Lester Pearson, the Prime Minister, said he regretted the decision [6].

In the Congress, reaction was mixed. Senators Stennis, Clinton Anderson (D-N.Mex.), John Tower (R-Tex.), and Bourke Hickenlooper (R-Ia.) unequivocally supported the decision, as did Representative Craig Hosmer (R-Calif.). Senator Jackson was unwilling to accept the Chinese rationale. Senators Frank Church (D-Idaho) and Fulbright were unhappy

---

[2] Curiously, Chalmers Roberts of the *Washington Post* reported that the Soviets were informed before it was announced that this system was Chinese-oriented and should not stand in the way of arms limitation talks. See 'U.S. Gave Russians Advance ABM Notice," *Washington Post,* September 20, 1967, p. A18.

[3] It should be noted that the successful conclusion of a nonproliferation treaty could prevent the United States from providing BMD to its allies in Europe or Asia, as has been proposed. Others argue that BMD is a device to make a nonproliferation treaty work; by providing defense to the signators against non-signing nuclear or potential nuclear powers, the threatened states would have little incentive to develop nuclear weapons of their own.

with the decision. Several weeks later, Senator Clark called it an "expensive toy" which could be neutralized if the Chinese brought nuclear weapons into the United States in a merchant ship or a suitcase.[4]

In an exclusive interview with *Life*, Secretary McNamara explained the logic behind the deployment decision, arguing that (1) it could deter the Chinese, (2) if the Chinese tried to attack, U.S. fatalities could be kept to one million or under, and (3) it was not directed against the Soviets. He said that the United States continued to have strategic superiority, that megatons were less meaningful as a measure of superiority than numbers of deliverable warheads, and that the Soviets were making a mistake in deploying BMD because they were falling into the peculiar momentum of the arms race which he discussed in his San Francisco speech [7].

Secretary McNamara discussed the decision and rationale at the NATO Nuclear Planning Group meeting in Ankara. In a separate report to the group, Dennis Healy, British Defense Minister, argued against a European BMD because of its prohibitive cost and lack of effectiveness against a Soviet attack [8].[5]

The Russians blamed pressure from Pentagon hawks and munitions makers for the decision [9].

Assistant Secretary of Defense Paul C. Warnke delivered a speech in Detroit in which he went to great lengths to explain the United States decision [10]. He said, against the small threat from China, there would be no doubt about our deterrent credibility. Warnke suggested Chinese leaders were probably no less cautious than other leaders of states with nuclear weapons. However, in a deep U.S.-China crisis, the Chinese might fear the United States would strike first. This could lead the Chinese to consider preemption (causing tens of millions of U.S. fatalities). The purpose of SENTINEL was to prevent hypothetical scenarios such as this from being carried out. Warnke made clear to his audience that the greatest period of danger was when the Chinese ICBM force was vulnerable to U.S. attack; i.e., the United States had an incentive to take these ICBMs out. Once they became invulnerable—i.e., a secure second-strike force like the Soviet's—the danger would pass. Warnke said the BMD deployment would make it easier, rather than harder, to negotiate the NPT, because it would make other Asian countries (Japan and India) more willing to sign if they knew the U.S. deterrent was credible.

He said deployment of BMD did not change the U.S. attitude toward the Soviet Union. While there were deep areas of disagreement, there was

---

[4] See "Senator Clark Calls Antimissile System an Expensive Toy," *The New York Times*, October 8, 1967, p. 36.

[5] In the spring of 1968, a plan to deploy BMD in Europe was rejected by this group.

a common interest for preventing nuclear war. In addition, both sides would like to reduce the amount of resources each was then allocating for military purposes. As a result of these two common goals, the United States was still willing to seek cooperation and agreements with the Soviets on such goals, and SENTINEL should not compromise this effort. He hoped that by parallel action or formal agreement both sides might be able to limit offensive and defensive strategic weapons.

In November 1967 the Soviets revealed a new ICBM—the SS-9—which came to play a pivotal role in the missile debate 2 years later. The House Republican Committee on NATO warned that a U.S. BMD could split NATO, because it would be viewed as a purely national defense system.

The Jackson Subcommittee, which opened hearings early in November, heard Administration witnesses back the thin BMD deployment, while civilian strategists and geopoliticians warned the committee of the growing Soviet military-technological threat. The committee, in particular Senator Jackson, raised the question after the Warnke speech on unilateral inspection and parallel action as to whether the United States was moving unilaterally to limit its strategic nuclear forces. What Jackson was concerned with was whether the United States was maintaining only the capability to deter, giving up any attempt to maintain superiority in the expectation the Soviets would recognize such efforts and reciprocate. Implicit in such a policy was the need for the Soviets to acquire parity—i.e., catch up—with the United States before the basis for mutual (formal or informal), unilateral, or parallel arrangements could be established.

It was reported that the Administration was considering expanding the SENTINEL system to protect the MINUTEMAN sites against the Soviets [11]. But Deputy Secretary of Defense Nitze said a year could pass before such a decision had to be made and that no such decision had yet been made [12].

A sharp clash over the desirability of BMD occurred at the Atoms for Peace Awards in November 1967 between members of the scientific community. Dr. Alvin Weinberg of Oak Ridge National Laboratory thought a strong defense could counter the ICBMs effectiveness and end the arms race. Dr. Isidor Rabi a Nobel Prize winner in Physics and Professor of Physics at Columbia suggested that deploying BMD was political madness and technically unsound, because BMD was ineffective, could be broken, would force an acceleration of the arms race, and result in a distortion of American society away from more essential tasks. He said Weinberg's opinion was not that of the scientific community [13].

Late in November, it was announced that Secretary of Defense McNamara would be leaving the Pentagon. It was speculated that part of the reason was over disagreement with the Administration's Vietnam policy and the decision to deploy SENTINEL [14].

Dr. Foster's revelation of the MIRV program on December 13, 1967, led to another clash within the scientific community about BMD. At the American Association for the Advancement of Science (AAAS) Convention in New York, Dr. Hans Bethe and Dr. Freeman Dyson argued over MIRV and BMD. Bethe saw MIRV as a national response to BMD and said that MIRV could lead one country to fear that its entire land-based ICBM force would be knocked out, thereby giving it an incentive to strike first. Richard Garwin director of applied research, T. J. Watson Research Center of International Business Machines and a former member of the President's Scientific Advisory Committee felt MIRV was extremely destabilizing. Bethe argued there were numerous ways to spoof BMD and that ICBM RVs could be hardened against the X-ray effect of BMD. Dyson argued BMD would lead to a détente and relaxation of tensions, since it was defensive and would not require an offensive response from the United States in the event of a Chinese attack. Dyson asserted that even if BMD were less than 100 percent effective, many people in some cities could be saved in the event of attack. Bethe countered by saying that the central task was not to reduce casualties but to avoid nuclear war [15].

Beginning in 1968, the BMD issue entered a new phase as concerted opposition to it arose in Congress, in the academic/scientific community, and from the public in areas where SENTINEL was to be deployed. The Administration continued to explain its deployment decision on the basis of an irrational Chinese attack, saying that it was not directed against the Soviets and that a heavy Soviet defense was infeasible and undesirable.

Secretary McNamara, in his farewell Posture Statement, made it quite clear there was no advantage to superiority and that any attempt to attain it would be easily countered by the Soviets. He stressed the importance of maintaining an assured destruction capability in the face of the Soviet strategic buildup and said that steps were being taken to improve this capability. He reasserted that it was U.S. ability to destroy the Soviets and/or the Chinese as a society and the ability of the Soviets to do the same to the United States that would provide U.S. security, not BMD. He continued to argue that a terminal defense of MINUTEMAN would offer only a partial substitute compared to expanding the force should the "Greater-than-Expected Soviet Threat" emerge.

In a chart showing the futility of city defense, McNamara was very careful to show that SENTINEL would not reduce U.S. fatalities below 100 million unless the United States struck first. Again, as it had done on numerous occasions since the SENTINEL deployment was announced, the Administration was reassuring the Soviets not to be disturbed by SENTI-

NEL. McNamara recommended that $651 million plus $229 million from fiscal 1968 be used for SENTINEL deployment; $313 million for SENTINEL development; $165 million for NIKE-X; and $103 million for Defender [16].

Former President Dwight Eisenhower, in an interview, said he doubted the success of a thin ABM, saying the best defense was a good offense, and we had that [17].

The Defense Department hearings in Congress provided very little insight on the missile defense program, except that the Army provided a point-by-point refutation of the article in the March 1968 *Scientific American* in which Garwin and Bethe had said that the SENTINEL was unnecessary and explained in great technical detail how it might easily be defeated [18].

To understand what happened to BMD in 1968, the reader must bear in mind the political climate in the United States at the time. There were the growing concern of the Soviet strategic threat, MIRV, BMD, the Tet Offensive, the campus unrest, attacks on the military-industrial complex, military research, and the $6-billion-budget cut which would affect many domestic programs. There appeared to be growing disillusionment with the military, foreign involvement, defense spending, and Vietnam. All of this made the SENTINEL deployment a logical focus of attention by those opposed to BMD and by those who saw it as a readily grasped issue symbolic of what was wrong in America. In addition, the Secretary of Defense indicated that the Chinese ICBM threat had slipped a year. Therefore, the urgency for SENTINEL decreased.

The opposition to SENTINEL revolved about seven issues: (1) the validity of the rationale, (2) its impact on international affairs and the cold war, (3) the effect on arms control, (4) its cost, (5) the implications for the Administration's domestic programs, (6) its effect on U.S. national security, and (7) the system's effectiveness and feasibility. The author does not intend to go into the arguments for or against BMD any more than is necessary, as he feels that by 1968 all the arguments which could be stated had been.

On April 18, 1968, the Senate resumed consideration of the military authorization bill. Senator Margaret Chase Smith (R-Me.) asked that the SENTINEL decision be reconsidered. Senator Clark proposed eliminating all expenditures or authorizations for BMD which, he said, every competent scientist and military expert knew was worthless [19]. Senator Gaylord Nelson (D-Wis.) offered an amendment that would delete $342.7 million for SENTINEL from the total $956.1 million authorization for procuring Army missiles. Nelson's amendment was defeated 17 to 41. Senator Cooper next offered an amendment prohibiting the use of funds for the deployment of any BMD until the Secretary of Defense certified in writing that research had proved the system practical and that the cost of such a system was reasonably accurate [20]. Again, the merits of the system were argued, and the amendment was defeated 28 to 31.

By mid-May, the Defense budget and U.S. defense policy were coming under broad attack in the Senate. Adding more fuel to the fire, a top-level Republican Party paper charged the Democrats with seriously weakening U.S. strategic superiority in particular by not exploiting new concepts in science and technology. On June 13, 1968, Senator Cooper offered two amendments, one to the military procurement appropriation and one to the military construction bill, to strike all funds for BMD deployment. The amendment originally proposed by Senator Cooper, now called the Cooper-Hart Amendment, was designed only to delay deployment by not expending any funds for SENTINEL in fiscal 1969. To support the amendment, Senator Philip Hart (D-Mich.) introduced a letter he received from Assistant Secretary of Defense Warnke indicating that the Chinese ICBM test flight would be delayed a full year [21]. Senator Jackson introduced a letter from Secretary of Defense Clark Clifford which stated that it would be a mistake to eliminate construction and procurement funds for SENTINEL during fiscal 1969. Continuing his defense of deployment, Jackson argued that such an amendment, if passed, would delay the BMD effort two years and would restrict the current research and development program [22]. The debate on SENTINEL continued for over a week, but on June 24, 1968, the Cooper-Hart Amendment was defeated 34 to 52. The same day, Senator Young offered an amendment to strike the $227.3 million for constructing SENTINEL facilities. Young's amendment was defeated 12 to 72.

During the debate on SENTINEL, Dr. Wiesner published a letter June 23, 1968, in *The New York Times,* in which he termed BMD wasteful. The *Times* editorial for June 23, 1968, likewise urged postponement of the SENTINEL deployment, as did that of the *Washington Post*. On June 23, 1968, the Senate approved the $1.8 billion military construction bill which included $227.3 million for SENTINEL. One of the key points in the transcript in the *Congressional Record* of the debate on SENTINEL was that the SENTINEL system was really considered a forerunner of a large anti-Soviet ABM deployment [23]. Both *The New York Times* and *Washington Post* thought the vote for SENTINEL was regrettable. On June 27, 1968, the Soviet Union affirmed its willingness to open discussions on mutual limitation of BMD deployment [24]. Could the Senate vote have spurred them in this direction?

At signing ceremonies for the NPT on July 1, 1968, President Johnson announced that agreement had been reached with the Soviets to begin talks in the near future to limit both offensive and defensive nuclear weapons [25].

The need to cut $6 billion from the fiscal 1969 budget in return for a 10-percent tax surcharge indicated the defense budget was likely to come under careful scrutiny by both the Administration and Congress. Many opponents of BMD suggested SENTINEL as a prime candidate for a budget cut now that the Chinese threat was pushed back a year and the Soviets had indicated a willingness to discuss a strategic-weapons moratorium.

Senator Eugene McCarthy (D-Minn.), a 1968 Presidential candidate, on July 10, 1968, released a position paper on arms control authored by Doctors Jerome Wiesner and George Kistiakowsky. This paper suggested an immediate unilateral freeze on the U.S. deployment of SENTINEL, POSEIDON, and MINUTEMAN II [26].

During this period, from about July 1, 1968, the Senate Preparedness Investigating Subcommittee was releasing testimony on the magnitude of the Soviet threat [27]. The committee's report issued in late September made no recommendations on missile defense but did reveal that the Secretary of Defense turned down the JCS recommendation to proceed with NIKE-X for defense of U.S. cities against a Soviet attack. The Committee Panel felt that funding for SENTINEL in fiscal 1969 was adequate as a first step toward the JCS-recommended full city defense [28]. This is further confirmation of the real purpose of the SENTINEL deployment.

On July 11, 1968, Representative Robert Leggett (D-Calif.) proposed an amendment to strike more than $525 million from the Military Procurement Authorization Bill for SENTINEL deployment. This would have the effect of cutting $227 million for SENTINEL. Representative Brock Adams (D-Wash.) introduced a report asserting that SENTINEL would be of doubtful effectiveness, would cause an increase in Soviet military preparedness, could not replace deterrence as a strategy because BMD was imperfect and would not work. This report was prepared by the ABM Committee of the Seattle Association of Scientists of the Federation of American Scientists and was dated May 29, 1969 [29]. Leggett's amendment was rejected 17 to 40. On July 25, 1968, Representative Cohelan indicated he would offer amendments to the Defense and Military Construction Appropriations Bills to delete funds for SENTINEL. After intense debate, the Cohelan amendment was defeated 37 to 106 [30].

On August 1, 1968, the Senate deliberated the Military Construction Appropriations Bill. The bill as reported out of the committee contained four dissenting views on BMD. Again a debate ensued as Senator Nelson introduced an amendment to delete SENTINEL construction funds. His argument was based on the need for a reorientation of American priorities from military to domestic. This amendment was defeated 27 to 46 [31].

Much of the month of August was devoted to attacking the MIRV development program, which was linked to BMD, by pointing out the insanity of and consequences of the nuclear arms race. It was reported that Soviet BMD work had slowed [32].

On September 6, 1968, Defense Secretary Clifford exempted SENTINEL from any Pentagon budget cuts. He also indicated the Soviet-American arms limitations talks would be delayed because of the invasion of Czechoslovakia [33].

The House began debate on the Defense Appropriations Bill for Fiscal 1969, and Representative Cohelan indicated he again would offer amendments to halt SENTINEL deployment but not development. Representative Mahon opposed the amendment. As the debate continued, Representative Thomas Pelly (R-Wash.) reported that, contrary to earlier assurances from the Army, not all SENTINEL sites would be away from population centers; the Army now wanted to put a site within one mile of downtown Seattle. He said the Army denied his request for a hearing. Pelly said the people of Seattle found the site quite objectionable and that they had organized opposition against it [34]. This was the first sign that grass-roots opposition was building up against SENTINEL deployment. In the ensuing debate, the House shouted down the SENTINEL amendment with only Cohelan speaking and went on to pass a $72.2 billion Defense Appropriations Bill.

On October 2, 1968, the Senate began consideration of the Defense Appropriations Bill. Senator Cooper again introduced his amendment, along with Senators Hart, Clifford Case (R-N.J.), Clark, McCarthy, George McGovern (D-S.Dak.), Lee Metcalf (D-Mont.), Walter Mondale (D-Minn.), Nelson, and Young, to delete $387.4 million for SENTINEL deployment. At the request of Senator Cooper, the Senate went into closed session [6] so he could ask certain questions about the SENTINEL system. The questions revolved about the effectiveness of the system, whether it was to be deployed before sufficient tests were conducted, and whether SENTINEL was intended as a city defense against Soviet attack.

One very interesting point to emerge was Senator Russell's admission to Senator Fulbright that the Defense Appropriations Subcommittee and Armed Services Committee called no one opposed to SENTINEL to testify. The only testimony was given by Administration witnesses. Senator Hart introduced a telegram signed by Wiesner, Gilpatric, Kistiakowsky, Carl Kaysen the Director of the Institute for Advanced Study at Princeton, N.J., and Hans Bethe, among others, supporting the Cooper-Hart Amend-

---

[6] The nature of this debate became evident later when the proceedings of that session were published in the November 1, 1968, *Congressional Record,* pp. E9638–9650.

ment. In their telegram, they said important domestic priorities were being sacrificed for the deployment of a BMD which would not add to U.S. security. They expressed concern, too, that Clark Clifford rejected a Soviet offer to begin talks in Geneva on a missile freeze, justifying it by saying the time was inappropriate because of the invasion of Czechoslovakia. They believed the talks were necessary to halt the arms race, and deploying SENTINEL to present a position of strength avoided the central issue [35]. Entered into the record, too, was a series of technical questions to be asked in the closed session. The content of the questions indicated they were prepared by a scientist with a knowledge of missile defense. Later, it was revealed Dr. Inglis of the Argonne National Laboratory had prepared them [36].[7] Then, in the open session, a telegram signed by York, Wiesner, Bethe, and Kistiakowsky urged that SENTINEL deployment be delayed one year. The vote on the Cooper-Hart amendment defeated it 25 to 45. This was the last congressional attempt in 1968 to defeat SENTINEL. But the defeat was in the making from a completely unexpected source.

The debates in Congress over SENTINEL, as well as the other aspects of military spending, were a dress rehearsal for what followed in 1969. The arguments offered against SENTINEL were political judgments about its feasibility and its desirability in light of its fueling the arms race and because of domestic needs of the country. The opposition contended defense was at a disadvantage compared to offense in that the former could not tolerate a single warhead's getting through, while the offense did not have to be perfect.

As the presidential election drew near, charges, assertions, and denials of security gaps filled the press as did the need for military superiority, the loss of superiority, and the value of superiority. BMD did not figure in the campaign as much as the idea of superiority and arms races and where would it all lead and where would it end.

After Richard Nixon's election, the SENTINEL issue returned to the news, as five scientists (including Dr. David Inglis, former FAS Chairman, from the Argonne National Laboratory in Chicago) formed the "West Suburban Concerned Scientists Group" committed to stopping SENTINEL site construction in Chicago and its suburbs. This group's effort began on November 15 when it learned the Army had started test drilling at 5 sites in Chicago. This new effort to stop BMD deployment raised the specter of a defending missile's accidentally blowing up at its site or at too low an altitude above the city it was protecting, thereby destroying the city. Inglis

---

[7] See John Finney. "Halt of Sentinel Is Traced to a 10-Month Old Memo," *The New York Times,* February 9, 1969, p. 1.

suggested that deploying BMD in Chicago would make the city a target for Soviet ICBMs [37]. (*Note:* According to the assured destruction strategy, all population centers should be targeted regardless of whether BMD is present.) The issue of an accidental detonation, denied by the Army, had also been raised by Senator Cooper during the closed Senate session of October 11, 1968. The five scientists were asking the Army to hold hearings before acquiring any more land for test drilling so that concerned individuals could state their reservations on proposed sites. The Chicago scientists were being joined by the FAS to alert congressmen, scientists, and the public to Army BMD activities near urban areas.

At a BMD debate in New York, sponsored by the Center for the Study of Democratic Institutions, Senator George McGovern saw the $5 billion SENTINEL system as a blunder second only to the Vietnam escalation. Supporting the SENTINEL decision, Dr. Donald G. Brennan of the Hudson Institute suggested the offense might no longer count on easily and economically penetrating a missile defense system [38].

Science magazine revealed that Representative Sidney Yates (D-Ill.) reported heavy opposition to SENTINEL sites close to Chicago. In a letter to Mendel Rivers, Yates called for a congressional investigation of proposed SENTINEL sites near urban areas and for the Army to hold open public hearings on the matter [39].

Norman Cousins, editor of the *Saturday Review,* writing in the December 14, 1968, issue urged a full-scale national debate on the correct priorities for American society, pointing out there was no defense against nuclear warfare except peace and that BMD was but another step pushing the world arms race past the point of no return. A year earlier, shortly after the SENTINEL decision announcement, Marvin Kalkstein of FAS in a letter to *The New York Times* (October 8, 1967, p. E11) had called for a public debate on BMD so the pressure from small segments and vested interests could be countered.[8]

On December 17, 1968, the Army, under mounting congressional

---

[8] Kalkstein suggested in his letter that if people understood that strategic *sufficiency* rather than superiority was all that was required of the U.S. and Russia, then progress toward arms reduction and a rational approach to national and world security could be made. President Nixon in 1969 was to replace his campaign pledge for superiority with the term sufficiency. See *The New York Times,* January 30, 1969, p. 6. In this same article in *The New York Times* it was reported that a study by Dr. George W. Rathjens, a former director of the Weapons Systems Evaluation Division of the Institute for Defense Analyses, currently a professor of Political Science at Massachusetts Institute of Technology and a leading BMD opponent, suggested the current balance between Russia and the United States as "one of sufficiency in strategic forces." The study sponsored by the Carnegie Endowment for International Peace was entitled *The Future of the Strategic Arms Race: Options for the 1970's.*

pressure, gave Detroit area congressmen a classified briefing on the deployment of missile defense sites near urban areas. The Army then consented to give an open hearing to the public on the Chicago site. Another Detroit area representative, John Conyers (D-Mich.), said he had doubts about going ahead with SENTINEL because it might reduce the chances of reaching an arms control agreement with the Soviets. Conyers said he was asking scientists in his area to advise him and the public about the risks of BMD [40]. With the support of local congressmen and of Senator Hart, additional protests over BMD sites were raised by several Detroit area scientists, especially regarding safety features against accidental explosion.

With swelling public opposition and rising congressional concern over the urban site preparations for SENTINEL, the year came to an end.

On January 15, 1969, Clark Clifford presented the outgoing Administration's defense program [41]. Clifford discussed: continued expansion of the Soviet strategic effort, the slowdown in their GALOSH BMD deployment around Moscow, the Johnson Administration's desire to open the strategic arms limitation talks (SALT)[9] with the Soviets now that the Czechoslovakian crisis had passed, and the NPT would be ratified.

Clifford reiterated the need to maintain the assured destruction capability and saw the SENTINEL as technically and economically feasible against the Chinese threat through the mid-1980s. He said that SENTINEL, of course, could be used against a Soviet ICBM attack but it would have little effect on the outcome of such an attack. In discussing BMD, Clifford said that after 15 years of research and development efforts worth $4 billion, the Defense Department and its contractors were fully convinced BMD was technically feasible; i.e., under certain conditions, it would identify, track, and destroy an incoming RV. "How effective such a system would be against actual attack is quite another matter. That would depend upon the purpose the system is intended to serve."[10] [42] He indicated the SENTINEL program would be pressed and, until a workable agreement with the Soviets on arms limitation occurred, the option to deploy a BMD against the Soviet Union would be kept open. For SENTINEL in fiscal 1970, there was $335 million for R&D; $736 million for procurement; $647 million for construction; and $70 million for operations—this was in addition to the fiscal 1969 budget item for $962 million. For advanced ABM concepts for NIKE-X $175 million was budgeted and for SABMIS $3 million. The Soviets indicated on the day of Mr. Nixon's inauguration

---

[9] However, the Soviets indicated they would prefer to wait until the Nixon Administration took office to reopen the matter.

[10] Clifford conceded there could be questions regarding the worth of SENTINEL if one did not believe the original rationale for deployment.

that they were ready to initiate serious discussions on control of strategic weapons.

On January 15, 1969, the House Appropriations Committee was briefed on the SENTINEL system with particular emphasis on the status of construction and the method of selecting sites. The briefing was prompted by questions from their constituents raised by Representatives Pelly, Roman Pucinski (D-Ill.), Yates, and Robert McClory (R-Ill.). Yates wanted to know why the sites were near or in cities when he was led originally to believe they would not be so placed. Yates was concerned whether there would be an accidental launch of SPARTAN or detonation of its warhead, if the system was effective, and could the attacker use penaids or beta-patch blackout? Yates's questions were the same as those submitted into the *Congressional Record* by Senator Case in October 1968 during the closed session of the Senate.

Representative Pelly said he was told by Representative Sikes the criteria for selection involved remoteness from populated areas, use of Government land, and arriving at a satisfactory decision with the local officials on a site which was least objectionable to the people near the site [43]. Pelly, unlike Yates, was not opposed to the SENTINEL but only to its siting so close to Seattle. Representative Pucinski ardently supported the SENTINEL deployment, arguing that range and coverage requirements for the missiles made the particular sites chosen necessary. Pucinski also argued that, since the objective of SENTINEL was to protect cities and urban areas, the SPRINT in the city areas was necessary.

Representative McClory said that while there was substantial opposition to the Libertyville site near Chicago, the bulk of the objections he received was from people against SENTINEL, not the site. Indeed, McClory said he received no official objections from anyone about the Libertyville site. Later, however, a letter was inserted in the *Record* from the City Council of Highland Park, asking the Army to reconsider the Libertyville site.

General Alfred D. Starbird's (Director of the SENTINEL program) testimony explained why the sites were chosen as they were—to provide the means for countering the expected Chinese threat; he outlined chances of an accident and what SENTINEL was designed to do. The site selection criteria, he said, fell into three major areas: (1) engineering and economic feasibility, (2) the kind of impact on civilians in the area, and (3) the location for tactical effectiveness [44].

The political climate in the United States in early 1969 was one of continued frustration, fear that the arms race was accelerating as the rush to deploy BMD and MIRVs on both sides diminished hopes of curbing the race. The Nixon Administration seemed in no hurry to get started with

SALT or have the NPT ratified. In fact, Secretary of Defense-designate Melvin Laird suggested it would not be until the summer or fall of 1969 before the new Administration would be willing to enter into talks with the Russians. There were additional concerns within the Congress and country at large about inflation, Vietnam, the cost of the war, the so-called misuse of science for defense, the few dollar resources that might become available for domestic purposes after the war was phased down, the enormous cost of weapons, the cost-overruns, and the need for new strategic weapons which had been deferred because of Vietnam. The social unrest, the unrest on campuses, and the concern about the so-called military-industrial complex all pointed to a thorough scrutiny of defense expenditures in 1969 by Congress, the mass media, and the public.

In February 1969, a major bipartisan campaign was begun to halt SENTINEL.[11] The impetus for the movement coincided with indications by Nixon Administration officials that they held some reservations about SENTINEL. Similar reservations were stated by a staunch proponent of SENTINEL, Senator Stennis [45]. John Finney of *The New York Times* described how opposition to SENTINEL began 10 months earlier with a memorandum to Senator Cooper suggesting that the SENTINEL program ought to be questioned as it had not yet been proved. The campaign to win support for his opposition was slow but steady. It was reinforced late in 1968 by the many labor unions, civic and religious groups, city councils, conservationists, real estate developers, concerned individuals, peace groups, and scientists who protested the placement of nuclear armed missiles in their backyards. The Senators consulted with and were advised by scientists opposed to the system. While Cooper led the open battle, Senator Charles Percy (R-Ill.) worked behind the scenes, speaking to President Nixon about his opposition to SENTINEL.

Meanwhile, the "New England Citizens Committee on ABM," formed by Abram Chayes, a former State Department legal adviser, indicated it would sponsor a national conference on BMD. The opposition forces grew stronger as they became informed. They put the Senate Armed Services Committee on the defensive by the questions they asked, questions the committee neither understood nor could answer. Their efforts were reinforced by a bombardment of letters to senators and congressmen from people near the cities where deployment sites were being prepared.

Senator Edward Kennedy (D-Mass.) was drawn into the controversy when, at a town meeting in Reading, Massachusetts, the site of a SENTI-

---

[11] The remainder of this chapter is based on the daily issues of the *Congressional Record, The New York Times,* and the *Washington Post.* Events are placed in their order of occurrence whenever possible regardless of when they were actually reported or revealed.

NEL base, the Army ran into well-organized opposition from Drs. Wiesner and George Rathjens and Mr. Richard Goodwin the latter an ex-Kennedy organization man and speech writer. They promptly called Senator Kennedy and implored him to enter the fight [46]. This resulted in a letter [12] from Senator Kennedy to U.S. Secretary of Defense Melvin Laird urging that a freeze on the deployment be made, pending an investigation and review of the SENTINEL program. Kennedy said in his letter that a very thorough and extensive examination of the wisdom of authorizing and appropriating money for SENTINEL would be made in fiscal 1970 by the Congress. He cited five reasons against deployment: (1) technical questions on its effectiveness, capability, and feasibility; (2) its impact on the Soviet strategic force structure by heightening the arms race and making arms limitation talks more difficult; (3) site locations near urban areas, chances of accidents, and possibility of the site itself becoming an attractive target; (4) costs, inflation, and overruns, as well as the compulsion to expand the system to a thick one; and (5) distortion of federal funding priorities.

During this period, too, there were conflicting reports on whether the Administration would go ahead with the deployment on the basis of its original rationale—against China—or whether a deployment was being used as a bargaining card in the upcoming SALT.

On February 4, 1969, Senate critics of SENTINEL asked a delay, fearing it would start a new arms race. Senator McGovern argued that SENTINEL would be ineffective and overpowered in a Soviet attack, which was precisely the idea to be conveyed to the Soviets by the Adminitsration's decision to deploy it against China.

On February 6, 1969 Secretary Laird ordered a halt to the SENTINEL system, all land acquisition, and site surveys, and cessation of construction pending a month-long review of the situation. At the President's news conference that day, he indicated SENTINEL was substantially more than a thin Chinese defense, that it had considerable damage-limiting capability.

The same day FAS issued a statement urging the scrapping of SENTINEL.

Representative Mendel Rivers, by ordering hearings on further site acquisitions for SENTINEL, temporarily blocked continued deployment of SENTINEL. By law, the military is required to inform the House and Senate Armed Services Committees when and for what purpose they want to acquire land. If the committees raise no objections within 30 days, the

---

[12] The text can be found in *U.S. Congressional Record*, February 4, 1969, pp. H669–670.

military can proceed. In this case, Rivers decided to hold hearings on the matter.

Shortly after Laird made his SENTINEL freeze announcement, there were indications that work would be resumed soon after tempers had time to quiet down. Laird expressed concern over the Chinese threat, while pointing also to the Soviet expenditures for strategic defense as being three times that of the United States in the previous two years. This, he said, made it imperative to deploy BMD so the United States could obtain the knowledge the Soviets had on BMD.

Five alternatives seemed to be emerging as a result of the SENTINEL halt: (1) no BMD deployment until SALT began, (2) defend the ICBMs, (3) move the sites away from urban areas, (4) build a thick system, and (5) deploy a very thin system of about 100 SPARTANs. There seemed to be little doubt that some form of BMD was seen as necessary by the Administration, for whatever reasons.

In a reversal of its earlier role urging a Chinese BMD as the beginning of a heavy Soviet one, the Joint Atomic Energy Committee was circulating a paper "What's Wrong with SENTINEL." The Committee (based on this paper) was prepared to oppose any type of city defense, preferring rather a hard point terminal defense of the ICBM sites using many SPRINTs and some SPARTANs [47].

The *Washington Post* revealed in mid-February the existence of an Army public relations plan to sell SENTINEL to the American public with the Army remaining in the background. Part of the plan called for countering the objections of scientists such as Bethe, Wiesner, and Rathjens to SENTINEL by the use of nongovernment scientists. Deliberate revelation of this document at the time served to heighten public and congressional opposition, not so much to BMD as to the pervasiveness of the military in the daily lives of the U.S. public and in the domestic and foreign policy of the United States.

Senator Kennedy announced on February 20, 1969, he had hired a private panel headed by Dr. Jerome Wiesner and Mr. Abram Chayes to prepare a report on the BMD deployment. Kennedy felt the report was necessary for him, the Senate, and the public, since it appeared that the Defense Department review would only result in the resumption of the SENTINEL deployment, albeit in a modified form designed to mollify the Senate critics. A split in the Administration on the desirability and timing of BMD deployment appeared to be evident during the Foreign Relations Committee Hearings on the NPT. Secretary of State Rogers seemed more anxious to get talks started than was Laird, who wanted BMD started. The NPT was hardly discussed as the committee expounded its arguments against SENTINEL and fought the Defense Department position on deployment in favor of talking with the Soviets. The committee also questioned the consistency of the Administration position: wanting to talk and deploy at the same time.

On February 24, 1969, Representative Cohelan asked the House to schedule a special order on the 26th to discuss BMD. To focus on the relevant issues, the discussion and material introduced covered 70 pages of the February 20, 1969, *Congressional Record*.

On February 28, 1969, the Senate Foreign Relations Committee under the auspices of Senator Gore's Disarmament Subcommittee announced the decision to hold educational and informational hearings on the "Strategic and Foreign Policy Implications of the ABM." The real purpose was to provide a means to counter the influence of the Armed Services Committee and to oppose BMD.

In March a Pentagon plan for a revised deployment was revealed. It was designed to facilitate arms limitation talks while providing a defense against the growing Soviet strategic threat which included a BMD around Moscow and indications that the Soviets were developing and testing a more advanced BMD system. The new plan would: move long-range SPARTANs away from urban areas, add SPRINTs at the MINUTEMAN sites, increase coastal radar coverage against SLBMs, delay construction starts until proper land surveys were made, and delay missile emplacement until 1972, although the radars and computers would be deployed [48].

Senator Hart asked that a letter dated February 25, 1969, be printed in the March 4, 1969, *Congressional Record* stating the opposition to SENTINEL (with all of the same arguments) of 39 members of the University of Michigan Physics Department.

Norman Cousins editorialized in the March 8, 1969, *Saturday Review*, that the ABM was going to be President Nixon's Vietnam and that the time had come to stop the juggernaut.[13]

March 4, 1969, was the day of the national strike against the misuse of science, originally planned to be held only on the Massachusetts Institute of Technology (MIT) campus. It spread across the nation's colleges and universities. Figuring prominently in this protest were dozens of panels devoted to arguing the BMD issue and opposing such deployment.

At the President's news conference of March 4, 1969, he said he would make and announce a decision on BMD early the following week. At the Gore Subcommittee Hearings, Gerard Smith, Director of ACDA, stated that the BMD was no bar to starting SALT with the Russians. Dr. Hans Bethe and Dr. J. P. Ruina stated at these hearings that U.S. ICBMs were

[13] The editorial was reprinted as a full-page advertisement in *The New York Times*, March 11, 1969, p. 19.

so secure the Soviets could not eliminate them in a devastating attack. Therefore, there was no need for defending them with BMD. Bethe conceded, however, that the Soviet introduction of MIRV could make a BMD defense necessary, but how urgent a hard point defense was now was debatable [49]. Dr. Ruina, Dr. Bethe, and Dr. Daniel Fink, former Deputy Director of DDR&E and now the General Manager of General Electric's Space Division, felt the SENTINEL deployment could be delayed without any danger.

The Russians entered the BMD debate by suggesting the deployment of SENTINEL could set back any chances of successful U.S.-U.S.S.R. arms control talks. Drs. Killian and Kistiakowsky, and H. York, Director of Defense Research during the Eisenhower Administration, said BMD would decrease U.S. security and contribute to the action-reaction cycle (reference to McNamara's San Francisco speech); moreover, as Dr. York argued, *firing* an ABM would require such a swift decision that only computers and junior officers could be involved [50]. He thought this was the ultimate in absurdity, pointing out that at least with an ICBM there would be presidential control, whereas because of the time constraints involved with BMD, presidential control would inevitably be lacking.[14] Additional witnesses at the Gore Hearings echoed the theme that deployment of BMD would result in decreased security, hamper arms control talks, and retard progress toward a peaceful, stable world. It should be noted that some BMD opponents conceded that hard point defenses of ICBM sites might be necessary and possibly beneficial but only if the need arose. The argument (Dr. Kistiakowsky and Dr. Wolfgang Panofsky, Director of the Stanford Linear Accelerator Center, were two of these individuals) rested on the ability to defend hardened targets with cheaper and simpler interceptors and radars, which would make the system more effective and less costly. BMD, when used to protect retaliatory forces, they argued, was not destabilizing but contributed to assured destruction. This argument, which accepted the need for BMD under certain circumstances, but not SENTINEL, was in contrast to those who categorically opposed any BMD of any sort for any purpose.

On March 14, 1969, President Nixon announced his new BMD plan— later to be called SAFEGUARD.

---

[14] How can firing a "city-busting ICBM" with presidential authority be compared to firing a *defensive weapon* like an ABM, even without such authority? York elaborates on his thesis in his *Race to Oblivion: A Participants View of the Arms Race,* Simon and Schuster, 1970.

References

[1] U.S. House of Representatives, Hearings Before Subcommittees of the Committee on Appropriations, *Safeguard Antiballistic Missile System,* 91st Cong., 1st Sess., 1969, p. 24.

[2] John Hess, "NATO Is Studying Antimissile Plan," *The New York Times,* September 20, 1969, p. 9.

[3] *Documents on Disarmament 1967,* pp. 402–404.

[4] "Peking Accuses U.S. on Antimissile Plan," *The New York Times,* September 22, 1967, p. 10.

[5] James Reston, "Washington: The Anti-Republican Missile," *The New York Times,* September 22, 1967, p. 46.

[6] Gerald Waring, "Canada Won't Join U.S. in ABM System," *Washington Post,* September 23, 1967, p. A3.

[7] *Life,* 13[1967]28A.

[8] Terrence Smith, "NATO Unit Orders Atom-Mine Plan," *The New York Times,* September 30, 1967, p. 6.

[9] "ABM System Blamed on Hawks' Pressure," *Washington Post,* October 4, 1967, p. A16.

[10] Warnke speech, in *Documents on Disarmament 1967,* pp. 454–459, note from p. 459.

[11] John W. Finney, "White House Weighs Expanding Sentinel Defense," *The New York Times,* November 13, 1967, p. 10.

[12] *Scope and Magnitude of U.S. ABM Program,* p. 36.

[13] "Experts Disagree on Missile 'Role,' " *The New York Times,* November 15, 1967, p. 25.

[14] Neil Sheehan, "Shift of McNamara Brings Speculation of War Policy Shift," *The New York Times,* November 29, 1967, p. 1.

[15] Walter Sullivan, "Merits of Ballistic Missile Defenses Debated at Science Parley," *The New York Times,* December 27, 1967, p. 6.

[16] *1968 Annual Posture Statement,* p. 75.

[17] "Eisenhower Doubts 'Thin' Missile Plan Can Be Successful," *The New York Times,* January 16, 1968, p. 13.

[18] U.S. House, Committee on Armed Services, *Hearings on Military Posture and S. 3293,* 90th Cong., 2nd Sess., No. 56, pp. 9022–9046, hereafter cited as *House Military Posture FY 1969.*

[19] *U.S. Congressional Record,* April 18, 1968, p. 54192.

[20] *U.S. Congressional Record,* April 18, 1968, p. 4259.

[21] *U.S. Congressional Record,* June 19, 1968, p. 7463.

[22] *U.S. Congressional Record,* June 19, 1968, p. 7469.

[23] *U.S. Congressional Record,* July 11, 1968, p. H6376.

[24] Raymond Anderson. "Gromyko Offers To Start Talks on Missile Curbs," *The New York Times,* June 28, 1968, p. 1.

[25] Carroll Kilpatrick, "U.S., Russia Plan Talks on Restricting Missiles," *Washington Post,* July 2, 1968, p. A1.

[26] William Chapman, "McCarthy Asks A-Freeze," *Washington Post,* July 11, 1968, p. A1.

[27] See U.S. Senate, Hearings Before the Preparedness Investigating Subcommittee of the Committee on Armed Services, *Status of U.S. Strategic Power,* Parts I and II, 90th Cong., 2nd Sess., 1968.

[28] U.S. Senate, Report by the Preparedness Investigating Subcommittee of the Committee on Armed Services, *Status of U.S. Strategic Power,* 90th Cong., 2nd Sess., 1968.

[29] *U.S. Congressional Record,* July 11, 1968, pp. 46335–40 for Seattle Report.

[30] *U.S. Congressional Record,* July 29, 1968, p. H7734.

[31] *U.S. Congressional Record,* August 1, 1968, p. S9990.

[32] George Wilson, "Russians Slow Work on Anti-Missile Sites," *Washington Post,* August 11, 1968, p. A1.

[33] Peter Grose, "Clifford Exempts Missile Defense from Budget Cut," *The New York Times,* September 6, 1968, p. 1.

[34] *U.S. Congressional Record,* September 12, 1968, p. H8555.

[35] *U.S. Congressional Record,* November 1, 1968, p. E9645.

[36] *U.S. Congressional Record,* November 1, 1968, p. E9649.

[37] George C. Wilson, "Foes Picture ABM Risk to Defended City," *Washington Post,* November 22, 1968, p. A8.

[38] *Anti-Ballistic Missile: Yes or No,* a Special Report from the Center for the Study of Democratic Institutions, Hill and Wang, 1968.

[39] Marti Mueller, "Proposed ABM Sites Protested," *Science,* December 6, 1968, p. 1107.

[40] George C. Wilson, "Public Hearing Is Set on ABM Site," *Washington Post,* December 17, 1968, p. A8.

[41] U.S. Department of Defense, *A Statement by Secretary of Defense Clark M. Clifford on the 1970 Defense Budget and Defense Program for Fiscal Years 1970–74,* January 15, 1969, hereafter cited as *1969 Annual Posture Statement.*

[42] *1969 Annual Posture Statement,* p. 53.

[43] U.S. House, Briefing Before the Committee on Appropriations, *Sentinel Anti-Ballistic Missile System,* 91st Cong., 1st Sess., 1969.

[44] *Sentinel Anti-Ballistic Missile System,* p. 28.

[45] *U.S. Congressional Record,* February 4, 1969, pp. S1367–1368.

[46] John W. Finney, "Halt of Sentinel Is Traced to a 10-Month-Old Memo," *The New York Times,* February 9, 1969, p. 1.

[47] John W. Finney, "Congressional Panel May Oppose Nixon if He Pushes for Sentinel Deployment," *The New York Times,* February 16, 1969, p. 26.

[48] William Beecher, "Pentagon Drafts Revised Proposal on Missile Shield," *The New York Times,* March 2, 1969, p. 1.

[49] U.S. Congress, Senate, Hearings Before the Subcommittee on International Organization and Disarmament Affairs of the Committee on Foreign Relations, *Strategic and Foreign Policy Implications of ABM Systems,* Part I, 91st Cong., 1st Sess., 1969, hereafter cited as *Implications of ABM.*

[50] *Implications of ABM,* p. 95.

CHAPTER 14

Safeguard

President Nixon in announcing his decision to reorient the SENTINEL deployment explained his alternatives:

1. A deployment which would attempt to defend U.S. cities against an attack by the Soviet Union
2. A continuation of the SENTINEL program approved by the previous Administration
3. An indefinite postponement of deployment while continuing research and development [1]

Secretary Laird, in explaining the basis for the President's decision several months later in House Defense Appropriations Hearings, added:

Terminate all work on the Sentinel system as such, and continue only research and development in more advanced ABM technology . . . Reorient and rephase the entire SENTINEL program. [2]

The President rejected the three options because of the growing Soviet threat: it was still not feasible or practical (politically, militarily, or economically) to defend against a heavy Soviet attack; there were too many risks in halting all work; and only operational experience could provide answers to certain problems which R&D could not.

Continuing, the President said he thought the SENTINEL program had to be modified; that the country's security demanded a carefully phased and deployed BMD; and said any new program would be reviewed annually from the technical, threat, deployment, and arms control viewpoints.

The purpose of the new system was:

1. Protection of U.S. land-based retaliating forces against a direct attack by the Soviet Union
2. Defense of the American people against the kind of nuclear attack which Communist China is likely to be able to mount within the decade

3. Protection against the possibility of accidental attacks from any source [3]

The President said the deployment would start with two ICBM sites and be implemented from there by the periodic analysis of the threat.

Mr. Laird later suggested three major and two minor reasons for deploying BMD. The major reasons were to:

1. Protect cities and population from heavy Soviet attack
2. Protect retaliatory forces as a substitute to their further expansion in the event the Soviets threaten their survival
3. Protect cities and population from a Chinese attack

The minor reasons were to:

1. Protect against accidental launch of an ICBM
2. Protect from a "demonstration-launch" [4]

Note that Laird places population defense first.

In light of the foregoing, the President concluded that protection of U.S. deterrent forces was the most critical so they would not become vulnerable to a Soviet attack. He pointed out that to protect them he could increase their number, but he felt this would appear to the Soviets to threaten their deterrent force and stimulate an arms race. These forces could be hardened, but by itself hardening would not afford adequate protection against foreseeable Soviet advances in accuracy. A third alternative was to protect the deterrent forces with a missile defense system, which is what he chose.

The system he proposed would not require installations near major cities, the cost would be between $6 billion and $7 billion, and the initial cost would be less than the Johnson Administration's fiscal 1970 request for SENTINEL; the system would be closely related to the actual threat development, would not be provocative, would reduce the chance of surprise attack against the U.S. deterrent, and would not complicate or hamper arriving at an agreement with the Soviets on offensive or defensive arms limitation.

The JCS, while affirming the SAFEGUARD decision, still continued to believe that the foremost requirement for U.S. security was a heavy BMD for city defense against the Soviet Union.[1] It was toward this objective they

---

[1] It was reported several days after the SAFEGUARD announcement, that Admiral Thomas Moorer, now Chairman of the U.S. Joint Chiefs of Staff and General McConnell decided to support only the SAFEGUARD deployment, thus breaking ranks with their colleagues. See *New York Times,* March 18, 1969, p. 1.

had accepted SENTINEL [5]. The House seemed to accept the President's decision; the Senate was divided. Conservative Republicans and many members of the Armed Services and Defense Appropriations Committees agreed with it, while most liberals and members of the Foreign Relations Committee did not [6]. The *Washington Post* thought the decision a reasonable compromise [7]. *The New York Times* thought the decision wrong and the rationale—to protect the ICBM force—hollow [8].

The SAFEGUARD system incorporates both an area and terminal defense capability, using the same components as SENTINEL but deployed with a different ordering of priorities. Whereas SENTINEL had the option for ICBM force defense, it was primarily configured to protect cities. SAFEGUARD would be initiated to protect two MINUTEMAN sites and later, if needed, SAC bomber bases. If it became necessary to defend the bomber force, the additional sites would permit a truly thin anti-Chinese ICBM area defense, too. The only city to be defended would be Washington, D.C., the control center of the National Command Authority.

The total SAFEGUARD deployment would have 12 sites. To provide all-around coverage, especially from SLBM attack, there would be 7 PARs with 11 faces. Two additional sites beyond the 12, 1 each in Alaska and Hawaii, could be added to give area defense to all 50 states. It was proposed to begin the initial deployment with a single-faced PAR and one four-faced MSR at each of two ICBM sites, Malmstrom Air Force Base (AFB) in Montana and Grand Forks AFB in North Dakota. This first phase would cost about $2.1 billion with $800 million already available. These figures did not include the Atomic Energy Commisison (AEC) warhead costs or Research, Development, Test and Evaluation (RDT&E) costs. A Phase 2 option with 3 alternatives was included in the proposal. Phase 2A, if the Soviet ICBM threat grew, included adding 2 more SAFEGUARD sites at Whiteman and Warren AFBs, adding additional SPRINTs and beginning defense of Washington, D.C. Phase 2B, if the Soviet SLBM threat to SAC bombers increased, would include activating all 12 sites. Phase 2C would involve activating 12 sites, also, with fewer missile interceptors, PARs and MSRs, to meet a Chinese threat. In contrast to SENTINEL, which moved on a fixed basis, SAFEGUARD deployment could be adjusted according to need.

A week later Secretary Laird was to go before the Gore Subcommittee to testify on SAFEGUARD, and several days later before the Senate Armed Services Committee to do the same. Both of these committees were engaged in a jurisdictional fight over military and foreign policy, with each holding hearings in what the other thought was its purview. The Gore Subcommittee was determined to fight the SAFEGUARD decision: wanting to know how the retaliatory force was imperiled by the recent Soviet strategic buildup; why BMD was the best way to protect them; whether defending the ICBM force was a provocative act likely to trigger a spiral in the arms race; and by deploying BMD and MIRVs, might not the United States and the Soviet Union be throwing away the last opportunity to limit the strategic arms race.

A quiet campaign began to gain acceptance for SAFEGUARD. The President met with the Presidential Scientific Advisory Council (PSAC) to discuss the program with the members who opposed it. The White House released a letter from Dr. Lee Dubridge, the President's science advisor, indicating his support for SAFEGUARD, and Vice President Agnew talked with six freshman senators about supporting the decision when it came time for voting funds in the Senate.

Robert Semple, Jr., of *The New York Times,* described how the President reached his decision on SAFEGUARD. The decision, Semple says, was highly internalized; the President, himself, met with few proponents or opponents of SENTINEL, but his staff provided him the daily developments on the issue and the pros and cons of deployment. Apparently there were two decisions. The first was made around March 8 or 9, 1969, when the President decided to deploy BMD to protect the deterrent force. The second decision, made on March 10 after the President returned from Key Biscayne where he made the first decision, related to the speed of deployment. The factors influencing him concerned the diplomatic and arms control implications of deployment, the growing Soviet strategic threat, and, not surprisingly, the ongoing debate in the Congress. Before the President left for Europe, four options were presented to him: the thick city deployment; a thinner SENTINEL—only 15 instead of 25 cities; a modified SENTINEL deployment called Plan 1–69, which was the SAFEGUARD deployment; and no deployment at all. No recommendations were made to the President and he ordered additional studies, especially of the diplomatic consequences of each option. Lawrence Lynn, a member of the National Security Council (NSC), who worked with Deputy Secretary of Defense David Packard on the various options, was to write a paper against each option. Meanwhile, Henry Kissinger, the President's national security advisor, consulted with groups of scientists and asked some of his friends in Cambridge to provide him with papers on the technical feasibility of the project and the sentiment of the scientific community at MIT and Harvard. The President, during his European trip, became attracted to Plan 1-69 because of its nonprovocative and small-economic-outlay characteristics. On March 5, 1969, he decided on Plan 1-69 at an NSC meeting. On March 7, 1969, Senator Javits, Percy, and Cooper told Kissinger of the congressional opposition to SENTINEL and why they opposed it. A briefing book was made up for the President on all this material plus

Lynn's dissenting arguments. The next step after the President decided on Plan 1-69 was to determine how best to implement it. Again, there were several options: move SENTINEL from the cities to the bases or begin deploying it at the bases the following spring. Each of these options would occasion work simultaneously on 12 to 15 sites, which would involve a sizable expenditure. Such an effort would be rather inflexible for diplomatic, arms control, or military reasons. Another option was to continue R&D, which was considered the most politically attractive. This option had been urged by many in Congress and in the scientific/academic community. This was rejected because the system had come to the end of the R&D road, and further system improvements could only come from tests carried out at the actual sites. A year's delay could have meant a two-year operational delay, too. So a fourth option, the phased-deployment plan, was chosen. In his announcement, the President said that his Foreign Intelligence Advisory Board would review annually the need for further deployment. Semple reported that this was added to the speech as a result of Dr. Killian's (former science advisor to President Eisenhower) suggestion that any deployment decision be withheld until an independent council of private citizens could review the country's strategic requirements. While this did not impress the President, the idea of an independent review and assessment of the country's BMD requirements did [9].

A week after the decision, the BMD debate continued unabated in Congress as more and more opposition was raised to SAFEGUARD, its feasibility, effectiveness, rationale, and the desirability and wisdom of deploying it. Again BMD came under criticism as a symbol of the military-industrial complex and the tremendous resources it consumed. A dispute erupted in Canada over SAFEGUARD when it was learned that the Canadian Government was never consulted for permission by the United States to fire defensive warheads over Canadian soil [10]. Despite the President's decision to make the deployment he thought necessary palatable to its many critics, the proposed deployment was headed for a difficult fight in the Senate. On March 20, 1969, the fight for SAFEGUARD began.

Secretary Laird revealed in open hearings [2] of the Senate Armed

---

[2] The open session was unusual for the Senate Armed Services Committee but was forced on it by the Foreign Relations Committee in their long-simmering battle over BMD and military policy in general. The latter intended to hold open hearings when Secretary Laird testified on March 21, 1969, about the BMD. So the Armed Services Committee was forced to do likewise. However, the Administration, by presenting its position first, was able to attack BMD opponents and rebut their arguments against SAFEGUARD. The impetus for the open session also came from Senator Russell's earlier confession that no opponents of BMD were heard. The Gore Subcommittee, capitalizing on this, planned to have some BMD proponents testify, forcing the Armed Services Committee to include opponents of BMD, who then would have a second chance before the public.

Services Committee that the extent of the Soviet strategic buildup included a Fractional Orbital Bombardment System (FOBS), POLARIS-type submarines, and an ICBM (the SS-9) capable of delivering a 25-megaton warhead or three 5-megaton multiple warheads. In addition, there was evidence of a new BMD being tested. On the basis of this evidence, especially the existence of the SS-9,[3] Laird predicted that the Soviet Union would acquire a first-strike capability by the mid-1970s if the United States did not take steps to protect MINUTEMAN [11]. This contention by Laird, backed by Packard, Foster, and Wheeler, that the Soviets were going for a first strike became the real issue in the so-called Great BMD Debate of 1969. For in fact, the debate was less over SAFEGUARD, although all the old arguments and questions of desirability, feasibility, effectiveness, and capability would continue to be raised, than over the Administration's credibility, MIRVs, and a Soviet first-strike strategy.

The debate over BMD was only the surface manifestation of deeper rooted causes about the military-industrial complex, pervasiveness of military influence, distorted priorities, Vietnam, social unrest, cost overruns, etc. The BMD in 1969 also became symbolic of Congress' efforts to reassert some of its authority and control over the Executive Branch.

The day after his testimony before the friendly Armed Services Committee, Laird testified before Senate Foreign Relations Committee, where the hard-core opposition to BMD existed. He repeated his testimony from the day before. Instead of his qualified statement that the Soviets appeared intent on attaining a first-strike capability, he said "the Soviets are going for a first-strike capability, and there is no question about it."[4] [12] The Committee questioned the Secretary on why all of a sudden the Russians had "become 10 feet tall" and were ready to overwhelm the United States, and then accused him of using fear techniques to precipitate congressional approval of the program [13]. Senator Symington asked why MINUTEMAN could not be used rather than SPARTAN. Dr. Foster, who accompanied Secretary Laird and answered the question, misunderstood the intent of Symington's question. In so doing, Foster inadvertently revealed the existence of another BMD concept using MINUTEMAN as an interceptor. He said the present MINUTEMAN did not have the capability to receive radar instructions to guide it to an impact point in space. Moreover, while the system could be made to function as such, it would

---

[3] The SS-9 was to become a major issue in the BMD debate because Laird based his prediction of a first-strike capability on this weapon. The SS-9 debate revolved about its accuracy, rate of deployment, purpose, size of warhead, and whether the system had some form of multiple warhead.

[4] Laird was, later in the year, to retract this assertion.

take MINUTEMAN away from its primary deterrent role.[5] Laird repeated his earlier assertion that a threat to POLARIS existed, but refused to speak openly about it.

Dr. Foster testified that the SPARTAN warhead still had to undergo further testing and would not be ready until 1973. When Senator Claiborne Pell (D-R.I.) asked how that comported with arriving at an underground test ban, Laird replied he was more concerned with maintaining the deterrent than a complete test ban. Senator Fulbright asked Laird to provide him with a list of witnesses who were not in the contracting business, working with BMD contractors, or Defense Department employees who would testify in favor of BMD. Such a list was supplied [14].

One of the most interesting exchanges which occurred concerned how any defense could complicate the offense. Laird revealed that at least 2 MINUTEMAN warheads were targeted on each of the 64 GALOSH sites around Moscow. Aside from indicating MINUTEMAN's probable overall reliability, this statement indicated that just targeting the systems' radar was not sufficient to neutralize the system at least for the offensive planner. If this were so, then the opponents of SAFEGUARD who contended the PAR or MSR was vulnerable to attack were refuted. The question of whether Canada had been consulted on the deployment was raised as a result of *The New York Times* article several days earlier. Laird said as far back as 1967 an understanding on SENTINEL had been reached. This was contrary to Prime Minister Trudeau's impression. Laird stated, too, that Canada should not be given a veto over U.S. BMD firings. Even after Trudeau visited the United States and spoke with the President he was not convinced of the moral and political aspects and implications.

Throughout the remainder of the spring Appropriations and Authorization Hearings, Laird and Packard, accompanied by General Wheeler and Dr. Foster, stated the Administration's case for SAFEGUARD, which rested primarily on the Soviet threat. The first-strike threat rationale was continually questioned and the Senate divided on the question of SAFEGUARD. Of additional concern to the senators were whether BMD and MIRV were part of the action-reaction cycle and whether MIRV could neutralize BMD. In either case these new deployments were leading to a new arms race which the SAFEGUARD opponents stated had to be

---

[5] The system Senator Symington referred to was the dual-role MINUTEMAN, it is discussed at length, is compared with SPARTAN, and its capabilities are described in U.S. House of Representatives, Committee on Armed Services, *Hearings on Military Posture*, 91st Cong., 1st. Sess., Part I, 1969, pp. 2055–2078. An excellent description of the SABMIS system is given on pp. 2031–2053. It turned out later that Symington was not talking about using MINUTEMAN as an ABM, but rather employing the tactic of "launch-on-warning."

stopped. Added to these considerations were 7 issues which are presented in Table 3. The remainder of this chapter deals with the developments on both sides leading to the vote on authorization and appropriations.

The "Battle of the Charts" and the "Panofsky Affair" occurred on March 26, 1969. Deputy Secretary of Defense David Packard presented a series of charts to the Gore Subcommittee showing that the Soviets were attaining equality with the United States in ICBMs and SLBMs. Packard inferred the Soviets were seeking to attain a first-strike capability. Senator Gore then produced his own charts showing, in terms of deliverable warheads, that the United States was so strong it need not fear a Soviet first strike. The committee obtained a commitment from Packard that the Defense Department would not proceed with SAFEGUARD, using leftover funds, until it had been authorized to do so by Congress.

The committee asked Packard whether the Administration had consulted any nondefense scientists in its review of SENTINEL. Packard replied he discussed it with Dr. Wolfgang Panofsky. Panofsky, who was present, said he had only a casual conversation with Packard at an airport and had some serious engineering criticism of the system [15].

Panofsky questioned the urgency for SAFEGUARD, was considerably skeptical of the Defense Department's first-strike rationale (a position taken by other witnesses, including Dr. Rathjens), and objected to the need for defending bombers with BMD. His major criticism was that an economical defense of hard targets such as missile silos had different technical requirements than defense of soft targets like cities. The SENTINEL was originally intended to defend cities, but the same components were being used for hard point defense. Panofsky thought a policy decision—going from SENTINEL to SAFEGUARD—which used the same components for different purposes was a very poor engineering decision. His argument is quite illuminating of the missile defense problem and is worth the reader's consideration.

A city defense requires intercept at high altitude, a long flyout range for the interceptor, soft or slightly hardened radars, decoy discrimination at high altitutde, and perfect defense (100-percent kill); it also involves the high cost of a missile interceptor. Furthermore, the number of ABMs needed is related to the size of the attacking force. A hard point defense could have low-altitude intercepts and short flyout range; needs very hard radars; uses atmospheric filtering (a city defense with a terminal component, such as SPRINT, relies on atmospheric filtering, too); could be less than perfect; and should be inexpensive. The number of ABMs needed should be related to the number of targets being protected. From this comparison Panofsky drew a number of conclusions. A hard point defense (HPD) radar can be simple and cheaper than a city defense radar and requires

TABLE 3

Pro's and Con's of BMD—1969

Pro	Con
Will the BMD Slow the Arms Race?	
The BMD is defensive, requires no Soviet reaction, is not provocative.	It will force Soviets to react and expand their offensive forces.
Does It Encourage Arms Talks?	
It strengthens U.S. bargaining power; gives Soviets, who have a BMD, the incentive to reach an agreement.	It will complicate and obstruct arms limitations.
Does It Enhance National Security?	
It protects the deterrent from a surprise first strike.	It is superfluous, because of U.S. present deterrent; could leave U.S. worse off, since the Soviets must react offensively; will degrade U.S. security because of its presence and negative influence on arms control.
Can It Forestall Countermeasures?	
An airtight defense is not needed for defending ICBM sites, forces enemy to allocate more offensive resources, reduces his payload as he makes room for decoys and penaids, complicates his plans.	The system can be spoofed, saturated, and attacked directly; the radar can be blinded and is vulnerable.
Is It Feasible?	
Current component tests have been successful, should work as planned.	Insufficient testing has been covered; combat environment can not be replicated; too complex compared to any system yet devised, especially computer programs.

TABLE 3—Continued

Is SAFEGUARD an Improvement for Defending Cities?	
Can not defend cities, and at present it is not desirable to do so.	How will citizens accept the protection of ICBMs before themselves; city defense is provocative and destabilizing.

Is It Essential for the Chinese Threat?	
Eventually, yes.	China has yet to fire an ICBM.

less traffic handling capacity. An HPD radar must be at least as hard as the target it is protecting or the enemy will target the vulnerable radar first and render an effective defense impossible. Missiles for HPD could be smaller, simpler, cheaper, and shorter range than is the SPRINT missile. HPD missiles should be cheap in relation to the target defended if HPD is to have more advantage than just increasing the deterrent force to gain additional protection. Panofsky concluded that SAFEGUARD is a very imperfect and expensive system for the mission to which it is assigned [16].

The next day, U.S. Secretary of State William Rogers told the Gore Subcommittee that the Administration could end any BMD deployment if and when the Soviets did, and the SAFEGUARD proposal would have no adverse effects on the SALT. He thought, too, BMD was not a particularly good bargaining point in any negotiations. These remarks seemed to undercut the Administration's rationale for SAFEGUARD's immediate need [17].

The Soviets meanwhile accused the United States of stepping up the arms race by the Administration's initiating deployment of a BMD and asserting a Soviet first-strike threat [18].

Donald Brennan of the Hudson Institute, a national security research organization appeared before Gore's Committee and, while he did not argue the case for SAFEGUARD, he did argue the case for BMD of cities. He said that BMD, for reasonable cost, could reduce U.S. fatalities in the event of war. It would cost the Soviets as much or more to nullify such a defense than the cost of the defense (he is talking of a large-scale city defense). No cheap or reliable penaids have been developed which will work effectively against a good defense. The deterrent requirement does not preclude defending. Since BMD cannot reduce fatalities to such a level as to make war likely, defense seems to reduce the likelihood of war by complicating the attacker's plans. Brennan said the United States and the Soviet Union had a common interest in reducing the scale of damage likely to occur from a nuclear war. Therefore, both should favor and deploy defenses. Defense, he said, can be used as an umbrella under which to reduce offensive forces and could tone down the offensive arms race [19].[6]

By the early spring it was apparent that a public debate on BMD

TABLE 4

A Partial List of Organizations Opposed to SAFEGUARD—1969 [a]

University of Michigan Physics Department—39 members (*CR*, 3/4/69, S2243)

National Academy of Scientists (*Washington Post*, 3/22/69, p. A4).

Stanford University—342 scientists and engineers (*CR*, 4/16/69, E3006)

Union of Concerned Scientists (*CR*, 4/28/69, E3434)

University of Minnesota—400 students and faculty (*CR* 4/2/69, E216)

National Religious Committee Opposing ABM [*The New York Times* (NYT), 4/30/69]

United Auto Workers International Executive Board (*CR*, 5/1/69, S4388)

National Council of Jewish Women, Inc. (*CR*, 5/5/69, S4563)

International Longshoremen's and Warehousemen's Union (*CR*, 5/2/69, E3714)

Federation of American Scientists (*CR*, 5/2/69, E3714)

Amalgamated Meat Cutters and Butcher Workmen (*CR*, 5/8/69, S4743)

The University of California, Berkeley, Physics Department—124 members (*CR*, 5/28/69, E4442)

National Council of the Churches of Christ in USA (*CR*, 6/5/69, E4655)

National Science Advisory Committee on the ABM (*CR*, 6/12/69, S6343)

Computer Professionals Against ABM (*CR*, 7/7/69, S7583)

University of Texas, Austin, Department of Physics—13 members (*CR*, 6/20/69, E5125)

Texas A. & M., Physics Department—14 members (*CR*, 6/20/69, E5125)

University of Texas, Austin—1,000 signatures of members and students (*CR*, 6/20/69, E5125)

American Veterans Committee (*CR*, 7/15/69, E5975)

Diocesan Council of the Episcopal Diocese of Long Island (*CR*, 7/24/69, E6280)

---

[6] The reader should bear in mind that the arguments for and against SAFEGUARD and/or BMD presented by individual witnesses were repeated two, three, and four times during the spring and summer of 1969. Many of the witnesses appeared before several committees which conducted hearings into the BMD matter.

TABLE 4—Continued

Council for Humanist and Ethical Concerns		(p. 1350)
Friends Committee on National Legislation		(p. 1356)
SANE	(Senate Defense Authorization Hearings, FY 1970, Part 2)	(p. 1378)
United World Federalists		(p. 1423)
Universities Committee on Problems of War and Peace		(p. 1425)
Women's International League for Peace and Freedom		(p. 1435)
Women's Strike for Peace		(p. 1443)

Ad Hoc Committee to Stop ABM (*Washington Post* (WP), 7/23/69, p. C3)

Educational Committee to Halt Atomic Weapons Spread, U. N. Association, U.S.A. (*WP*, 7/22/69, p. C26)

Americans for Democratic Action	
Anti-Pollution League	
New Democratic Coalition	
GRIPE	(*The New York Times*, 6/19/69, p. 12)
Student World Federalists	
Union of American Hebrew Congregations	
Unitarian Universalist Association	
United Methodist Church, Division of Peace and World Order	

Universities Committee Against ABM (*NYT*, 3/23/69, p. 7E)

Ad Hoc Committee of New Yorkers Against ABM (*CR*, 3/17/69, E2088)

University of Hawaii, Department of Physics and Astronomy—15 members (*CR*, 3/13/69, H1761)

[a] Taken from the *Congressional Record* (*CR*) January through August 7, 1969, and from House and Senate hearings.

was shaping up across the nation. Ad hoc groups were forming at the grassroots level. For example, a group called the Ad Hoc Committee of New Yorkers against ABM was formed by Representative Jonathan Bingham (D-N.Y.). Another group was headed by Sanford Gottlieb, executive director of SANE a long time nuclear disarmament committee for a sane nuclear policy. It consisted of 25 peace, liberal, and disarmament groups and met in late February in Washington. A third group was headed by ex-Kennedy-organization men Richard Goodwin and William Vanden Neuvel. In addition to the ad hoc groups, newspaper editorials, individuals, students, universities, peace groups, religious organizations, labor unions, and faculty departments submitted petitions, studies, and statements to local and national newspapers, to their congressmen, and to the White House, all opposing BMD. (See Table 4 for some of the organizations opposed to SAFEGUARD.) Daily, congressmen were making speeches, reading into or having printed in the *Congressional Record* voluminous material on both sides of the issue. The ground swell of opposition to BMD from the academic/intellectual/scientific community precipitated a reaction within that same community from those in favor of deployment. Individuals spoke out and groups were formed to defend SAFEGUARD. In the subsequent months these competitive groups carried on a lively and heated debate publicly through the newspapers, their congressmen, or those congressmen sympathetic to their respective views. They provided analytic material (see Table 5 for a list of some of this material as printed in the *Congressional Record*), spoke publicly, published books and articles, and furnished speakers at public meetings to prevent the views of one side from going unopposed. They conducted seminars, counseled congressmen, consulted, and advised.

Since the Administration's case for SAFEGUARD apparently rested on the existence of this missile and what it could do against MINUTEMAN sites, much of the then current controversy centered on the SS-9, its capabilities, characteristics, and payload. Dr. Ralph Lapp, the long-time disarmament advocate acting as an informal consultant to SAFEGUARD congressional opponents, produced a paper purporting to show that even by using Defense Department calculations on the SS-9 the MINUTEMAN force could not be eliminated as an assured destruction force; consequently, SAFEGUARD was not necessary.

A number of large city mayors opposed the SAFEGUARD because of the funds it would divert from domestic programs.

In mid-April BMD opponents sought to tie SAFEGUARD deployment to an overall freeze on the deployment of all offensive and defensive weapons.

In mid-April the opponents broadened their attack from the issue of

TABLE 5

A Partial List of Studies and Analysis Regarding SAFEGUARD
Printed in the *Congressional Record* to August 7, 1969

Boston Based Union of Concerned Scientists. *Report on ABM*, (4/28/30, p. E3434)

AEC Statement on SAFEGUARD Warhead Costs (5/8/69, S4766)

Report of National Citizens Committee Concerned About Deployment of ABM (5/14/69, E3937)

The Shifting Balance of Nuclear Power (6/4/69, E4606)

Ripon Society Report (6/12/69, S6333)

American Security Council Report. *The ABM and the Changed Strategic Balance: U.S.S.R. vs. U.S.A.* (6/19/69, E5119); Rebuttal to this study (8/5/69, S9219)

ABM Democratic Study Group, House of Representatives, 1969 (6/20/69, S6871)

Critique by Dr. Rathjens of House Armed Services Committee Hearing on SAFEGUARD ABM (7/2/69, S7550)

Union of Concerned Scientists. *Report on MIRV* (7/8/69; E5691)

Unsigned/Unidentified Rebuttal to White House Question-and-Answer Fact Sheet on SAFEGUARD (5/8/69, S4679)

A Report of the Cost of SAFEGUARD and Alternative Proposals, University of Michigan (7/9/69, S7776)

American Enterprise Institute. *SAFEGUARD ABM* (7/14/69, S8032)

Ballistic Missile Defense and the Alliance (7/17/69, S8220)

P. Peckarsky. *Computerized Cost-Effectiveness Study of Assured Destruction Capability Defense Alternatives,* (MIT Study, 7/17/69, S8224)

Dr. C. K. Manacher, President, Institute for Computer Research, University of Chicago (7/22/69, E6143)

The Starbird Memorandum: Public Affairs Plan for the SENTINEL System (7/25/69, S8605)

Committee to Maintain a Prudent Defense Policy (CMPDP). Paper #2—*SAFEGUARD: Does the Supposed "Softness" of the Radars Render SAFEGUARD Vulnerable?* (7/29/69, S8722)

American Security Council Evaluation of the Wiesner-Chayes Study (7/31/69, S8895)

Good Guys, Bad Guys and the ABM (8/4/69, S9063)

TABLE 5—Continued

CMPDP. *The Problem of Coordinating a Surprise Attack—Can Our Deterrence Depend on It?* (8/5/69, S9168)

CMPDP. *Instead of Deploying SAFEGUARD, Could We Not Wait and See Whether the Soviet SS-9 Threat Continues to Develop, Since We Could Deploy More Offensive Missiles if It Does* (8/5/69, S9168)

J. F. Anderson. *The Case Against SAFEGUARD,* University of Minnesota (8/5/69, S9103)

CMPDP. *Will SAFEGUARD Precipitate an Arms Race?* (8/6/69, S9307)

Report of the Citizens Panel on Washington Area Citizens Against ABM (8/6/69, S9313)

Significant Dates in Atomic Weapons Development and Subsequent Test Ban and Nonproliferation Negotiations (8/6/69, S9257)

---

missile defense to an attack on the Pentagon: its pervasive influence, budget size, mismanagement, procurement mistakes; and its influence on the arms race because of its demand for more and newer weapons. This attack culminated in an attempt to slash $5 billion from the Defense budget. At the same time the BMD opponents challenged the Administration's rationale, assumptions about SS-9 deployment rates, and the Soviet capability to launch a surprise attack to wipe out simultaneously the entire U.S. deterrent force, and questioned how much the SS-9 really threatened the deterrent.

To avoid a complete break with the Administration, several Republican opponents suggested to the Administration that it announce its willingness to enter into a strategic moratorium with the Soviets. Part of this offer would include the suspension of the SAFEGUARD deployment.

As the debate progressed, it appeared that the President's prestige was at stake on this issue and the Administration was determined to fight rather than compromise. Indeed, the way the opponents were gaining support, it might be only the prestige of the President and the Office which could win the day.

As a result of his opposition to BMD, the White House vetoed the appointment of Dr. Franklin A. Long of Cornell as the Director of National Science Foundation (NSF). Long had argued in the December 1968 *Bulletin of the Atomic Scientists* that BMD would accelerate the arms race, although he never criticized BMD publicly or openly [20].

Arthur Goldberg announced the formation on April 18 of the National Citizens Committee Concerned About the Deployment of the ABM.

The President at his April 18 news conference said he had no plans to go to the country for support of SAFEGUARD but pledged a fight for it. He did not think the issue was partisan, as he made his decision on the basis of what was best for the nation. He expected that the upcoming debate in Congress would be fought on the basis of what each congressman felt was best for the nation. The President tried to soften Mr. Laird's assertion about Soviet first-strike intentions by saying he did not know what their intentions were, why they were moving so fast on the SS-9 deployment, or how they intended to use that missile [21].

The Soviets interjected themselves into the BMD debate by saying the SAFEGUARD system was really the prelude to a larger deployment, even though Phase 1 was not too big or aggressive. The Soviets also contended they were no more eager for SALT than was the United States (a reference to the fact that the Soviets were making overtures for the talks, but the United States was taking its time) [22].

A coalition of 37 Washington, D.C., area groups (the Washington Area Citizens against ABM) opposed to SAFEGUARD demanded that the City Council hold hearings on the Administration's decision to deploy a defense around Washington [23].

A Harris poll survey late in April indicated that 47 percent of the sample favored deploying a BMD, while 26 percent did not, and 27 percent was undecided. Those favoring deployment held some doubts as to the system's effectiveness and cost.

At the American Physical Society meeting in Washington a technical panel session on BMD was held and the issue debated by Drs. Rathjens, Bethe, Brennan, and Dr. Eugene Wigner, a Nobel prize winner and professor of mathematical physics at Princeton, who in recent years has participated in several civil defense studies. A poll of the attendees at the meetings showed that 76 percent opposed and 21 percent favored deployment. All over the country anti-BMD organizations were being formed; the April 25, 1969, *New Republic* published a list of some of them. Federal government employees collected 1,500 signatures from other government workers asking Congress to reject the SAFEGUARD system.

At Senate Armed Services Hearings, proponents of deployment Paul Nitze and Dr. William McMillan argued SAFEGUARD was needed to parry a potential Soviet move to acquire a first strike and to provide a strong bargaining hand in any SALT meetings. The opponents attacked SAFEGUARD on the basis that its radars were vulnerable and that too many interceptors—almost as many as were planned to protect the MINUTEMAN—would be required just to defend the radar. Dr. Frederick Seitz defended the deployment as a means for gaining practical knowledge for future missile defense systems. He was sure the system would work and the warning the system would provide might prevent a surprise attack. The Soviets, who were deploying BMD, should have no reason to assume U.S. deployment was anything but defensive, too [24].

The debate by mid-May had shifted from scientific argument to political debate as the Pentagon was accused of changing its figures, withholding data from Congress, making worst-case assumptions, and misstating intelligence. The Kennedy-sponsored study appeared early in May attacking the need, feasibility, desirability, effectiveness, and wisdom of deploying SAFEGUARD. The release of the study brought a prompt rebuttal from the Pentagon, which found numerous errors, faulty conclusions, and inadequate methodology. Dr. Foster questioned whether the editors had time to prepare a paper which met the standards of the scientific profession [25].

The Administration's hope of having the SAFEGUARD deployment voted on in the House first was set back on May 20, when Speaker of the House of Representatives John McCormack (D-Mass.) decided the Senate should vote on the issue first.

In renewed Senate Armed Services Hearings, Dr. Albert Wohlstetter, professor of Political Science at the University of Chicago and a Senior Staff Member of The RAND Corporation, attacked the Kennedy-sponsored study, Dr. Lapp's calculations on the SS-9,[7] and Dr. Rathjens [8] for overestimating the MINUTEMAN silo hardness, underestimating the projected size of the SS-9 inventory, and not giving the SS-9 three 5-megaton warheads. (Rathjens gave them four 1-megaton warheads.) Wohlstetter also accused BMD opponents of favoring an increase in offensive systems, which is more likely to produce an arms race than deploying BMD is to defend the offense [26].

Dean Acheson, the former Secretary of State under President Truman, formed the Committee to Maintain a Prudent Defense Policy. Acheson formed the Committee to provide a more balanced and reasoned debate on BMD, as the current situation had been rather one-sided. The committee, it was envisioned, would serve as a counterweight to the group of scientists and scholars who authored the Wiesner-Chayes book and to other scholarly and scientific/academic opponents of BMD.

A so-called nonpartisan group, the Citizens Committee for Peace with Security, reportedly with no ties to the Administration, released the results

---

[7] See p. 210 in this chapter.
[8] Wohlstetter and Rathjens later engaged in an open debate on their respective calculations and assumptions through the letters to the editor column of *The New York Times.* See "Letters to Editor," *New York Times,* June 15, 1969, p. E17 for both letters. The *U.S. Congressional Record,* June 18, 1969, p. S6668 reprinted both letters.

of a survey which showed that 84 percent of all Americans thought the United States should have a BMD. The Commitee was, in fact, top-heavy with Nixon supporters, friends, and Republican Party contributors.[9]

In early June the Soviets voiced displeasure with the Administration's defense policies, which could upset the current arms balance, and with its failure to set a date for the start of SALT [27].

During June the SAFEGUARD debate seemed to lose momentum as the MIRV program became the focus of attention. Senator Edward Brooke (R-Mass.) was sponsoring a resolution urging the President to seek an agreement with the Soviets to halt multiple warhead tests. In retrospect, the reader should realize that the real evil genie was MIRV, not BMD. In fact, with the likely deployment of the first MIRVs scheduled for June 1970, the BMD issue, after the crucial August votes, was considered of secondary importance compared to MIRV.

It was reported by *The New York Times* that the U.S. Intelligence Board which is presided over by the Director of Central Intelligence did not agree with Laird that the Soviets were seeking a first-strike capability. Such a conclusion was in contradiction to the Administration's position on which it based its missile defense case [28]. To clear up the first-strike matter, testimony was given June 23, 1969, in a top secret session before the Senate Foreign Relations Committee by Secretary Laird and CIA Director Richard Helms. Helms' testimony and introductory statement were deleted in their entirety [29]. However, it was revealed several weeks later, when the Senate SAFEGUARD debate opened, that both were in agreement over the long-term strategic threat; although Helms did not endorse Laird's position, he did not disagree with it. The difference of opinion between the Pentagon and the intelligence community was over the Soviets' intent to continue their strategic buildup into the 1970s and whether they had the capability to do all the things which Secretary Laird suggested they would do [30].

On June 27, 1969, the Senate Armed Services Committee approved the deployment of SAFEGUARD by a 10 to 7 vote. The majority felt that the President with SAFEGUARD would be in a better negotiating position in SALT than he would be if the program continued in R&D. The Phase 1 procurement was not viewed as escalating the arms race or jeopardizing the arms talks with Russia. The majority of the Committee felt Congress had control of the program and could review it annually. They did not feel that any of the possible alternatives to SAFEGUARD was the prudent course to follow—feeling the technical problems would be solved in order to make the system operationally effective. Their report

---

[9] See *Congressional Record*, p. 5909, June 5, 1969, for poll and its results.

stated that the system would provide sufficient protection of MINUTEMAN and reduce its vulnerability, but the system could be saturated [31].

The minority view signed by Senators Symington, Young, and Daniel Inouye (D-Hawaii) favored continued R&D, but held that the system would not add to U.S. security; the radars were vulnerable; it could be easily overcome by the Soviets; it was the wrong system for protecting the deterrent; and the money for this doubtful system could be better put to use in domestic programs than in military ones [32].

Senator Thomas J. McIntyre (D-N.H.) proposed a third alternative to no deployment and deployment. His proposal would:

1. Authorize a concentrated developmental testing program of the radar, computer, and related electronic components of the SAFEGUARD system at the North Dakota and Montana locations suggested by the President

2. Authorize production engineering and continued developmental testing of the system's missiles

3. Preclude the deployment or production of operational SPRINTs or SPARTANs, the construction of missile launch facilities, and the acquisition of land at other than the two locations

4. Require full congressional review and approval before any such deployment or production of weapons, silo construction, or further land acquisition. [33]

He said his proposal would retain the option to deploy on the President's schedule if Congress decided the following year to authorize full deployment. It would allow another year for intelligence to be gathered about the Soviet threat. It would allow the most difficult technical problems to be solved. It would aid SALT and symbolize the nation's desire to de-fuse the arms race and establish a fresh set of priorities [34].

As the BMD debate entered its final month, the lines were firmly drawn for the showdown on SAFEGUARD. The Administration maintained its position on the Soviet threat, rationale, the vulnerability of MINUTEMAN and the need to reduce the vulnerability with active missile defenses, and SAFEGUARD's bargaining advantage at SALT.

The opposition contended there was insufficient evidence the Soviet strategic buildup and threat would continue as the Administration predicted. Consequently, the United States could delay deployment and thereby not provoke the Soviets to react. In addition, SAFEGUARD would not escalate the arms race and not give SALT a chance. The opponents also argued that the Soviets could build ICBMs much more cheaply and quickly than the United States could deploy SAFEGUARD, thereby negating its value. Furthermore, the Soviets could overwhelm SAFEGUARD with saturation tactics. A targeting of the "vulnerable" radars of SAFEGUARD could mean that SAFEGUARD would be forced to defend itself rather than the intended MINUTEMAN targets. In short, the opponents said the system would not work, was not needed, and was undesirable.

The debate opened on July 9, 1969, as the Senate began consideration of the Defense Authorization Bill for fiscal 1970. Senator Stennis began the fight for deployment, asking for a closed session of the Senate, but was thwarted by opponents. When Stennis proposed a time limit to debate, Majority Leader Mike Mansfield (D-Mont.) argued that the debate should run its course. Senators Cooper and Hart announced introduction of an amendment which would not oppose the Administration's $759.1 million request for SAFEGUARD, but would prevent any of the money's being spent for deployment.

After Senator Stennis' defense of SAFEGUARD, Senators Thurmond and Jackson fought the opening round in the Senate for the Administration.

Another amendment and possible compromise was the McIntyre Plan —to go ahead with Phase 1 site deployment but withhold production and deployment of the SPARTAN and SPRINT interceptors.

Meanwhile BMD proponents Dr. William R. Kintner, Director of the Foreign Policy Research Institute, and Mr. Herman Kahn, of Hudson Institute, each planned books supporting the deployment of SAFEGUARD. The Kintner book, *SAFEGUARD: Why the ABM Makes Sense,* was a direct rebuttal of the Kennedy (Wiesner-Chayes) book plus a collection of official and unofficial statements and articles. The Holst-Schneider book from Hudson Institute, *Why ABM: Policy Issues in the Missile Defense Controversy,* was a collection of technical and historical papers dealing with BMD and a series of well-written analytic papers looking at the issues affected by BMD deployment [35]. Senator Kennedy charged, on hearing of the Hudson Institute book, that the Defense Department was supporting its publication, because Hudson then held some $873,000 in research contracts (about 75 percent of its total) from the Defense Department between July 1968 and March 1969. He suggested that some of the defense money was for a study on the strategic implications of SAFEGUARD from which the book derived [36].

With Senator George Aiken's (R-Vt.) opposition (it was believed he held the key vote of the 10 uncommitted ones, because he was the ranking Republican), supporters of SAFEGUARD began looking for a compromise plan involving radar site deployment or a program which was clearly an R&D deployment rather than a full Phase 1 deployment. Only Senator

Tower rose to defend the deployment during the July 11, 1969, Senate debate.

One of the problems faced by the Administration was the bipartisan nature of the opposition, which included such prominent Republicans as Cooper, Aiken, Javits, and Smith, along with many Democrats [37]. The Administration was clearly opposed to a compromise plan which suggested deployment of a radar on Eniwetok as an R&D facility with missiles on Kwajalein [38].

In a surprise move, Senator Winston Prouty (R-Vt.) announced his support for SAFEGUARD, although a year earlier he had opposed SENTINEL. His reason for switching was his belief that SAFEGUARD would defend ICBMs, not cities, as SENTINEL did. Moreover, he felt SAFEGUARD strengthened the hand of the United States at SALT. Prouty said he felt many BMD opponents were using SAFEGUARD as a vehicle to attack the Pentagon [39].

Meanwhile, a new argument was introduced by Drs. Ruina and York, who contended SAFEGUARD would be deployed to protect an ICBM force which would be made obsolete by the eventual Soviet introduction of more accurate multiple warheads. The growing vulnerability of MINUTEMAN led both York and Ruina to suggest either giving up reliance on MINUTEMAN as the main element of the U.S. deterrent or obtaining a mutual moratorium on multiple re-entry vehicle/multiple independent re-entry vehicle (MRV/MIRV) testing with the Soviets [40]. The Senate finally met in secret session on July 17, 1969, to discuss SAFEGUARD.[10] The session was called by opponents in order to show a secret Pentagon chart illustrating, so they contended, that the Soviets could easily add a few more SS-9s to their inventory and nullify any advantage SAFEGUARD might have had [41].

A Gallup poll released in late July indicated that 58 percent of the sample was uninformed or undecided on the issue. Those in favor of deployment had dropped from 25 percent to 23 percent since March. The reasons given for supporting deployment were: we need the protection, we should trust the President's judgment, and we should keep pace with the Russians. Those opposed felt it was unworkable, cost too much, and would escalate the arms race [42].

The Senate debate was entering its fourth week. The opponents thought the momentum was shifting in their favor. Tempers were running high as proponents of deployment threatened to bring the Cooper-Hart amendment to a vote, while the opponents charged the Administration was

---

[10] A censored transcript of this session can be found in *U.S. Congressional Record*, November 20, 1969, pp. E9908–9934.

providing the proponents with last minute intelligence and withholding secret material and data critical of SAFEGUARD from them. As the debate continued the opponents showed a General Electric film (originally produced to show how MIRV worked) submitted to show how a BMD system could be overwhelmed.

Senator Gore returned to the "unsuitability for hard point defense" argument in the closing round of the debate. Gore submitted three reports: (1) from the Institute for Defense Analyses Jason Panel on HPD, (2) from an Aerospace Corporation report, and (3) from an ARPA BMD Conference held in the fall of 1968 at Cape Kennedy. All purported to show that the radars needed for HPD required different characteristics than did the MSRs, more were needed than one per site, and they had to be hardened much more than did the SAFEGUARD radars. The proponents submitted a one-page report from the Defense Science Board task force meeting of the previous March, which stated the "systems design appeared to be adequate and would meet the stated objectives for the SAFEGUARD system." [43] According to Senate sources, a later meeting of the task force in the summer of 1969 raised many of the objections in the three reports introduced by Senator Gore [44].[11]

Senator Warren Magnuson (D-Wash.) announced he would vote against SAFEGUARD. The opponents believed they now had 50 of 51 votes necessary to win the vote on the Cooper-Hart amendment.[12]

On the eve of the Senate vote, *The New York Times* reported that in the June Opinion Research Corporation poll, published as a full-page ad in several newspapers, which indicated that 84 percent of those interviewed supported BMD, 55 of 344 signers were connected with defense industries, and some were directly involved in SAFEGUARD work. More-

---

[11] This task force was named the Goldberger Panel after its head, Dr. M. L. Goldberger, a professor of physics at Princeton, and was convened under the auspices of the White House Science Advisory Committee to consider the technical feasibility of BMD but not whether it should be deployed. A year later in the spring of 1970 Goldberger and Dr. Sidney Drell, Deputy Director of the Stanford Linear Accelerator Center, served on a BMD advisory panel for the Defense Department headed by Lawrence H. O'Neill of Columbia University. Both Drell and Goldberger took exception to Dr. Foster's assertion based on the findings of the O'Neill Panel Report that SAFEGUARD would do the job it was intended to do. Drell and Goldberger claimed the report did not reach such a conclusion and Drell, like Dr. Panofsky a year earlier, expressed concern over the wisdom of adopting the components of essentially a city defense BMD system to hard point defense. See U.S. Senate Hearings before the Subcommittee on Arms Control, International Law and Organization of the Committee on Foreign Relations, *ABM, MIRV, SALT, and the Nuclear Arms Race*. 91st Cong., 2nd Sess., 1970, pp. 525–526; 534–538, hereafter cited as *ABM, MIRV, SALT, and the Arms Race*.

[12] By Senate rules, a tie vote on an amendment defeats the amendment.

over, the *Times* reported that rumors persisted that the White House had encouraged the formation of the committee sponsoring the poll [45].

On August 5, 1969, Senator Smith (R-Me.) said she would offer an amendment to prohibit use of military funds for any aspect of missile defense development and construction. The Smith amendment was in addition to the Cooper-Hart amendment and the McIntyre amendment, none of which would reduce the authorization of $759.1 million but only restrict the purpose for which the money could be spent.

The House approved a $1.5 billion military construction bill which contained $2.5 million for a BMD communications installation at the North American Aerospace Defense Command (NORAD) headquarters. True to his promise to wait until the Senate voted on SAFEGUARD, Representative Rivers offered an amendment to delete the $2.5 million, but by voice vote the House killed the amendment and proceeded to vote the $1.5 billion bill [46].

On August 6, 1969, the voting began. Senator Smith's first amendment to bar all spending on SAFEGUARD was defeated 11 to 89. Her second amendment, which would have barred the SAFEGUARD system but would have permitted other BMD research, was defeated 50 to 51, Vice President Agnew casting the 101st vote. The Cooper-Hart amendment was defeated 49 to 51, with Mrs. Smith voting against it. This amendment would have banned deployment of SAFEGUARD but permitted R&D to continue [47].

Apparently, the second Smith amendment was worked out as a compromise by the opponents and Mrs. Smith to allow the Cooper-Hart supporters to get Mrs. Smith's vote for their amendment. Earlier in the day she had said she would not support R&D on a system which she disapproved of in the first place. She held to this position and voted against the Cooper-Hart amendment which provided R&D for SAFEGUARD because she opposed SAFEGUARD whether for deployment or R&D [48].

The vote and issue, as the author pointed out earlier, were symbolic of the frustrations and rebellion brewing in Congress with the military and Executive Branch, respectively. The vote put both the Defense Department and the White House on notice that military budgets were going to get the closest and most careful attention possible in the future. With the vote,[13]

---

[13] Since both houses of Congress must approve both Authorization and Appropriations Bills, this gave the BMD opponents four chances to halt deployment. Should either of the two bills reported out of one house be different from the bills reported out of the other, then a conference committee is convened to iron out differences. This could give the opponents another two chances for a total of six opportunities to halt deployment. So, in theory, this one vote did not mean victory for the Administration, but in reality it did, as this was the opponents' high watermark.

the Administration "got" its bargaining card for SALT and the first installment of the ICBM missile defense deployment it contended it needed. On August 7, 1969, the McIntyre amendment was defeated 27 to 70 [49].

On September 18, 1969, the Senate finally approved the $20 billion Military Authorization Bill. After the SAFEGUARD votes in August, the bipartisan coalition against defense spending steadily lost ground as it challenged and opposed major Pentagon programs. The first three days of October saw a miniature repetition of the Senate BMD debate in the House. The debate included all of the same arguments for and against deployment. Representative Charles H. Wilson (D-Calif.) introduced an amendment to reduce SAFEGUARD authorization by $345.5 million. Meeting as a Committee of the Whole, the House, after a 4-hour debate, defeated the amendment 105 to 209 [50]. The next day, October 3, 1969, the House defeated a motion to recommit the bill to committee because of objections to the amounts authorized, including money for SAFEGUARD. An amendment to remove all SAFEGUARD authorization money was also defeated 93 to 270 [51].

The Soviets accepted President Nixon's invitation to discuss arms limitations on October 25, 1969, and BMD was formally linked to SALT. The talks were to open on November 17, 1969, in Helsinki. Meanwhile, the Soviet strategic arms buildup continued unabated [52].

By agreement, the SALT was to be shrouded in secrecy. The talks in Helsinki were really preliminaries for more substantive matters to be discussed in 1970. The Helsinki talks apparently were to be devoted to developing procedures and the agenda for later discussions [53].

On November 12, 1969, the House Defense Appropriations Committee approved $2.5 million for a SAFEGUARD Command Center and $14.1 million for SAFEGUARD R&D and construction of a Kwajalein missile range. Before floor consideration of the Defense Appropriations Bill, 10 members of the House Committee questioned the value of SAFEGUARD and the $359.5 million appropriated for its deployment.[14]

On December 8, 1969, the House approved a $69.9 billion Defense Appropriations Bill after having defeated 25 to 78 a series of amendments offered by Representative Yates to eliminate all SAFEGUARD deployment [54].

Meanwhile a renewed fight against SAFEGUARD was brewing in the Senate where the $69.9 billion Defense Appropriations Bill, just passed by the House, was being considered. Senator Smith offered an amendment to strike all funds for the SAFEGUARD system. A short debate ensued and the amendment was rejected 36 to 49 [55].

---

[14] See House Appropriations Committee, Defense Subcommittee Report No. 91-698.

Late in December, *The New York Times* reported the Administration was weighing the question of expanding the Phase 1 SAFEGUARD deployment. Part of the problem was whether to risk another fight in Congress, whether an expansion could hurt the SALT, and where the money would come from—nondefense or defense monies, or by raising the ceiling imposed by the White House on the defense budget. The proponents of expansion favored the complete Phase 2 proposal because of the rapidly growing SS-9 deployment and Soviet strategic threat and the steady progress in the Chinese threat. The proponents feared failure to expand would result in key manufacturers' laying off personnel, a delay of 2 years beyond 1976 before full operational capability, and less incentive for the Soviets to negotiate seriously at SALT. The opponents were concerned about increased expenditures and whether an expansion would be viewed by the Soviets as an act of bad faith [56].

The new year opened with the Administration's deciding to seek an expansion of the Phase 1 deployment. How much of an expansion was an open question. Part of the impetus for expansion was the faster-than-expected deployment rate of Soviet SS-9 ICBMs [57]. Secretary Laird indicated the SAFEGUARD deployment was already six months behind schedule because of the delay in getting final congressional approval. A new battle appeared to be shaping up on BMD as Senator Gore said he was considering a thorough review of the BMD program and deployment issue to determine if an expansion would hurt SALT, if the threat really demanded new defensive measures, and if the Administration had a case for expansion or if SAFEGUARD is a "weapon in search of a mission."

The President announced at his news conference the decision to proceed with an expansion of SAFEGUARD, but the details would not be announced for a month [58]. Part of the delay stemmed from the Defense Department's proposal to add additional protection for MINUTEMAN and to start a nationwide missile defense. Arms control officials at a National Security Council meeting objected that the Soviets would misconstrue a thin area deployment as the start of a heavy one directed toward them. This could only provoke them into building more ICBMs and undermining the hopes of a strategic weapons freeze at the SALT, which was due to resume on April 16 in Vienna. These reservations caused the President to order a review. Apparently McNamara's heavy defense legacy still was with the government. The Pentagon proposal included (1) two new sites: one at Whiteman AFB and one in upper Washington State, the former to protect additional MINUTEMAN missiles and the latter to defend against a Chinese ICBM; (2) site acquisition and preparation around Washington, D.C.; and (3) two additional sites in southern

New England and in the Michigan-Ohio area as protection against a Chinese attack [59]. So the BMD rationale had come full circle—back to the Chinese threat! And they had not yet tested an ICBM. In response to the President's plan, Senate Majority Leader Mansfield asked, "Where the hell is it going to end." [60] Both the *Washington Post* and *The New York Times* decried the announcement in editorials on February 1, 1970, p. B6, and February 2, 1970, p. 30, respectively.

The budget for fiscal 1970 included $1.5 billion for SAFEGUARD. On February 4, 1970, Mansfield attacked the decision, the rationale, and the Administration's credibility [61].

George Kennan former U.S. Ambassador to the Soviet Union testified during a Senate Foreign Relations Committee Hearing that a U.S. BMD deployment would lead the Soviets to doubt whether the United States really wanted strategic arms limitation. Rather than representing a stronger hand for the President at SALT and an incentive for the Soviets to reach agreement, the expansion of SAFEGUARD could raise doubt and uncertainty in the Soviet Union about U.S. goals and intentions. Kennan argued some unilateral restraint was necessary. He warned, too, that the United States had a knack for undertaking great programs to be used as instruments of foreign policy, but invariably they soon became vested interests which could no longer be bargained away [62].

On February 18, 1970, President Nixon delivered his Foreign Policy Message to Congress. In it he described the growing Soviet strategic threat as approaching and, in some categories, exceeding ours in numbers and capability. The President expressed serious concern about Soviet intentions. He asked whether assured destruction (holding Soviet and American cities hostage) was sufficient to deter war or did the offense need to be complemented with defense. While asking his questions, he indicated that a long, hard review was under way to obtain answers to some of those questions and that any additional BMD deployment would be consistent with his statement of the year before [63].

On February 29, 1970, Secretary Laird delivered his Annual Posture Statement to Congress. Laird said if the Soviet strategic buildup continued, the United States could find itself a second-rate power by the mid-1970s. Without a SALT agreement, the United States would be compelled to rush into development and production of a new series of offensive systems. However, the proposed SAFEGUARD expansion program could allow the Administration to postpone for a year any decisions for increasing and improving strategic offensive forces. By expanding SAFEGUARD to hedge against a moderate threat and the option to meet a heavy threat, the United States would also be able to pursue SALT without exacerbating the arms race.

Laird also suggested the Soviet threat might turn out to be considerably larger than the present SAFEGUARD could handle. In this case the Defense Department was pursuing several courses to reduce the vulnerability of MINUTEMAN other than expanding SAFEGUARD to meet a highest threat level. He said:

> We have further decided to continue deployment of SAFEGUARD because the additional cost needed to defend a portion of MINUTEMAN is small if the full area defense is bought. [64]

Laird said if MINUTEMAN defense had to be expanded, a new and smaller radar which would be less costly than the MSRs could be placed in the ICBM fields. A program to determine the optimum radar for such a defense was provided for in the fiscal 1971 budget.

He concluded his discussion on SAFEGUARD by pointing out that many possible arms control agreements could emerge which would allow BMD on both sides "which would be consistent with our national security objectives and the legitimate security interests of the Soviet Union." [65] Laird indicated that an orderly, measured, flexible BMD deployment would help maintain a relative positive position for the United States at SALT and improve its chances for success. Laird pointed out, also, the BMD program was flexible and could be modified in many ways as a result of an arms control agreement and unilateral action on the part of the Soviets. The SAFEGUARD program was budgeted for $1.49 billion in fiscal 1971. The Administration in contrast to the opponents of SAFEGUARD saw no inconsistency with expansion of SAFEGUARD and the chances of success at the SALT. While the Administration's proposed expansion had not been announced, it was apparent that a policy shift in the rationale for deployment had taken place. Now SAFEGUARD was viewed as a positive influence on SALT with a concomitant playing down of the Soviet strategic threat.

By the end of February the Administration's expension plan was expected to include a proposal for two more sites at the other MINUTEMAN fields and site preparation for a thin area defense. The Administration's plans were dealt a setback when Senator Jackson said he did not think he could go along with a thin area defense, and Senator Pastore said he would not go along with any expansion beyond the present two. Both Jackson and Pastore were prime movers for the SENTINEL deployment. Jackson was a senior member of the Armed Services Committee and the Joint Congressional Committee on Atomic Energy. Pastore was a vice chairman of the Joint Atomic Energy Committee [66].

On February 24, 1970, Secretary Laird outlined the Administration's proposed expansion of SAFEGUARD. The request was to defend one more MINUTEMAN site—Whiteman AFB—and to begin site acquisition and preparation at four other sites including Washington, D.C. Four of these sites were the start of a thin anti-Chinese area defense, while the fifth site was to protect another MINUTEMAN field at Warren AFB, Wyoming. This program, he said, would stretch out the SAFEGUARD program about two more years. His rationale included the growing Soviet and continuing Chinese threat and the necessity of preserving a strong bargaining hand at the SALT.

Dr. Foster indicated that an improved SPARTAN, with much higher velocities and a smaller warhead, was being developed to deal with SLBMs and low-trajectory ICBMs. It would be ready in 1976. Development of a new and smaller radar dedicated to hard point defense was initiated, in order to provide a cheaper alternative to the MSR, in case the need to expand the hard point defense portion of SAFEGUARD became necessary because of a growing Soviet threat. Laird indicated the full program increased in cost by $1.6 billion to $11.9 billion. The increase was due to inflation; $395 million stretched out for the whole program to $575 million, design changes rose to $650 million [67].

In the hearings during the spring of 1970, the Administration maintained its rationale for SAFEGUARD, contended it would not harm the chances of SALT, and indicated the deployment of MIRVs and BMD was not irreversible. Editorials in the *Washington Post* (February 27, p. A18) and *The New York Times* (March 1, p. 16E) disapproved of the Modified Phase 2 deployment, as it was called, and suggested Congress should ask some very serious questions about this deployment and its effect on the arms race.

The prevailing climate in the United States during the early part of the year was one of concern with MIRV, SALT, military spending and influence, and Vietnam. Except for the few days before and after the Modified Phase 2 decision, BMD was of less importance than these other issues. Indications were that Congress was willing to fight any further expansion, especially on cost and the thin area deployment rationale. Perhaps to encourage the U.S. opponents of the military and critics in and out of Congress on defense spending, the Soviets broke a prolonged silence on BMD.

They proclaimed they could hit attacking missiles of any speed at great distances from the defended target [68]. Whether this statement by Defense Minister Grechko was intended for a Soviet audience as a counter to the U.S. claim of a virtually infallible area defense provided by SAFEGUARD or as a gambit or bargaining move in SALT was not clear. In any event, a week later on March 7 the Soviets reacted to the U.S. BMD effort by criticizing U.S. weapons development and deployment plans as potentially damaging to the chances of reaching an arms control accord.

The Soviets, the *Pravda* article said, had now attained parity and were willing to accept this new balance and were not seeking superiority, but certain American officials were still seeking superiority over the Soviets. The article also rebutted Administration assertions that the Soviet buildup was mounting at a dangerous pace [69]. The *Pravda* article was quite clearly aimed at the U.S. BMD program and at influencing the U.S. bargaining strategy for the second round of SALT starting in Vienna in April.

Throughout the period from December 1969 to the spring of 1970, rumors were reported in articles in both the *Times* and the *Post* that missile defense was the one subject discussed in all its implications at Helsinki. It was reported in these articles that a BMD limitation or moratorium on deployment could be the subject of an agreement between both sides. It was reported the military was opposed to any MIRV or BMD curb below the level of the full SAFEGUARD program [70].

The American Assembly met at Arden House to discuss the subject of arms control. The Assembly issued a report calling for a six-month moratorium on MIRV deployment and postponement of the Modified Phase 2 SAFEGUARD deployment [71]. A similar recommendation was made by an Administration advisory committee appointed by President Nixon to advise ACDA on policy [72]. At the Gore Subcommittee, a similar initiative was urged by McGeorge Bundy the former national security advisor to President's Kennedy and Johnson. The Senate voted a resolution 72 to 6 for an ABM/MIRV freeze [73].

In a repeat performance from the year before, the Gore Subcommittee continued to parade the same BMD opponents as witnesses: York, Rathjens, Panofsky, Wiesner, etc. Many of the BMD opponents objected to the thin area deployment against China as compromising any improvement in United States-China relations.

On April 16, 1970, the House Armed Services Committee approved a $20.2 billion Defense Authorization Bill and in the process defeated 3 amendments to slash funds for SAFEGUARD. Representative Leggett moved to strike out $660.4 million for all SAFEGUARD deployment. This amendment was defeated 7 to 31. He then moved to strike out the $203 million for the modified Phase 2 deployment. This lost 7 to 31, also. Representative Charles Gubser (R-Calif.) moved to delete $25 million for advance site preparation of the 5 additional sites to be added to SAFEGUARD under Phase 2. This was defeated 11 to 28 [74].

On April 16, 1970, it was reported that President Nixon had decided the United States should push at SALT for a comprehensive limitation on strategic weapons rather than on a weapon-by-weapon basis. [75]

On April 30, 1970, the House defeated Representative Leggett's two amendments, the same as those he offered to the House Armed Services

Committee, to delete funds for SAFEGUARD and for the Modified Phase 2 deployment by votes of 85 to 131 and 86 to 128. A short debate preceded each vote [76]. An amendment by Leggett to the Military Construction Bill to cut SAFEGUARD funds was defeated 5 to 31 on May 14, 1970.

As the spring ended, the Administration was pressing its case in Congress for SAFEGUARD, while a battle similar to last year's but of much less intensity and public involvement was shaping up in the Senate to defeat SAFEGUARD.

Chalmers Roberts of the *Washington Post* reported that the shape of a possible arms accord could be a freeze at present levels of sea- and land-based missiles, plus the acceptance of BMD systems to protect Washington and Moscow. According to Roberts, the United States introduced three SALT proposals: (1) no BMD or MIRVs, but requiring on-site inspection; (2) a joint offensive weapons launcher freeze—no on-site inspection, and the freedom within agreed numbers to switch at will from land to sea or sea to land launchers; and (3) a current level freeze on ICBMs and SLBMs without regard to MIRVs.[15] The Soviets proposed either to have a total BMD ban or allow BMD around the national capitals with a freeze on the current numbers of ICBM launchers. The Soviets have argued that a curb on the arms race will only occur if no area BMD is deployed. The Soviets contended the U.S. BMD deployment would lead to an area defense and they would have no choice but to deploy more SS-9s. Apparently, SAFEGUARD was the prime target of the Soviets at SALT [77]. The United States, according to an article by John Finney in *The New York Times* (May 22, 1970), was put on the defensive when the Soviets proposed the BMD ban except for a Moscow-Washington deployment. However, it appeared from statements in congressional hearings that the Administration would be willing to scrap the system if need be. The State Department denied Roberts' story in the *Post,* pointing out it was speculative and could jeopardize the prospects of the talks and their success, as both sides wanted secrecy [78]. By the beginning of summer, the Senate had not voted on SAFEGUARD, although the Foreign Relations and Armed Services Committees continued their hearings. The House, on June 11, 1970, defeated an amendment to the Military Construction Bill to delete $353.8 million for BMD sites by a vote of 26 to 98.[16] On June 17,

---

[15] John Finney in *The New York Times,* May 22, 1970, p. 5, reported a U.S. offer to switch from land-based to sea-based deterrent forces.

[16] Besides repeating the usual arguments of the Administration, a new argument appeared in the House during the spring of 1970. In opposing Representative Yates' amendment to block SAFEGUARD construction funds, Representative Rivers argued the Nation's security was at stake. Representative Sikes wanted to know "What's wrong with defending America?"

1970, the Senate Armed Services Committee voted 11 to 6 to proceed with the SAFEGUARD Phase 1 deployment including adding additional SPRINTs at Grand Forks and Malmstrom; full deployment at a third MINUTEMAN site, Whiteman AFB; and advanced site preparation at a fourth MINUTEMAN site, Warren AFB; but eliminated $10 million to start preliminary work on the four sites designed to provide a thin defense against China [79].

The Cambodian debate in the Senate, SALT, and campus unrest largely replaced BMD as an issue in the spring and summer of 1970. However, with the end of the Cambodian debate the SAFEGUARD BMD system again became a major issue as the Senate prepared to take up the Military Authorization Bill. The testimony given before the Senate Armed Services Committee in the spring of 1970 centered not on preventing deployment but on alternative hard point BMD systems to replace SAFEGUARD. Additional issues raised in the spring hearings included ability of the radar to withstand attack and the vulnerability of the PAR to high-altitude ionization effects.[17] The impact of these effects, the critics contend, is to create target location errors for the MSR as it receives the PAR data, hence to reduce the effectiveness and utility of SAFEGUARD [80]. The Senate Armed Services Committee adopted an interesting procedure for questioning BMD witnesses. First, many of the Senators opposed to SAFEGUARD submitted very precise and technical questions about SAFEGUARD, the answers to which were included in the released hearings. Second, to simplify the testimony and reduce the number of witnesses, the proponents and opponents of SAFEGUARD were asked to agree on two witnesses each to present their respective views before the Senate Committee [81]. The opponents chose Drs. Panofsky and Dr. Donald Hornig, the latter a former Presidential science advisor, then vice-president of Eastman-Kodak and now president of Brown University. The proponents were represented by Drs. Wohlstetter and Lawrence H. O'Neill, professor of electrical engineering at Columbia and president of the Riverside Institute of Columbia. Third, on May 19, 1970, an open session was held in the morning. A closed session was held in the afternoon and lasted until 6:00 p.m. Fourth, Dr. Panofsky, who had to leave early, was asked by Senator Symington to answer the Defense Department's comments on Dr. Panofsky's earlier testimony before the Gore Subcommittee on April 13, 1970. All of this Panofsky material was included in the printed hearings [82].

By midsummer 1970, the Administration had come to view the

---

[17] These effects include attenuation of radar signals, refraction (bending) of the radar beam, and reflection of the radar beam from the ionized region.

deployment of SAFEGUARD as necessary for ensuring progress at the arms limitation talks in Vienna. The opponents of SAFEGUARD viewed this argument as the least credible and convincing of the many arguments used in the past to justify BMD. As BMD came more and more to be linked with SALT, as a negotiating point and as part of the Administration's BMD rationale, it was inevitable that the MIRV issue—moratorium on testing, developing, and/or deploying—would reemerge and also be linked to BMD; i.e., if no BMD, then no need for MIRV.

Meanwhile, a bipartisan coalition of Senate liberals and moderates— Members of Congress for Peace Through Law (MCPL)—issued a 250-page report on military weapons programs. One of the systems they were highly critical of was SAFEGUARD. The MCPL proposed four alternatives, in the form of amendments, to the continued deployment of SAFEGUARD. These alternatives include: (1) keep SAFEGUARD at the R&D level with no deployment; (2) restrict deployment to the two sites approved in 1969; (3) end the SAFEGUARD program, diverting the research funding request for SAFEGUARD into an advanced BMD system; (4) and, most interesting, create an "escrow fund" in which SAFEGUARD, as well as MIRV, appropriations would be placed pending the results of SALT [83]. While the intensity, duration, and public involvement in the 1970 BMD debate was far shorter and less than in 1969, a sharp clash nevertheless shaped up in the Senate over SAFEGUARD in 1970.

The 1970 BMD debate reached a climax in mid-August in the Senate as 2 of 3 proposed amendments to restrict SAFEGUARD were defeated. The third amendment (the Brooke Amendment, which provided that funds earmarked for SAFEGUARD expansion at Warren and Whiteman AFBs could only be used to expand the SPRINTs and MSRs at Grand Forks and Malmstrom) was defeated 45–53.

The first amendment, sponsored by Senator Harold Hughes (D-Ia.) would strike out all funds for procurement of ABMs for SAFEGUARD and would prohibit the expenditure of any funds for its deployment, but would not reduce the funding of R&D for SAFEGUARD. This amendment was defeated 33–62 [84]. The second amendment, offered by Senators Cooper and Hart, would have permitted construction at the two original sites, Grand Forks and Malmstrom, but would have halted the expansion at Warren and Whiteman. This amendment (the Cooper-Hart amendment, which received the most publicity)[18] was defeated 47–52 [85].

Apparently as part of the Administration's strategy to salvage the

---

[18] Neither the *Washington Post* nor *The New York Times* reported the introduction or defeat of the Hughes amendment.

hard point defense portion of its Modified Phase 2 expansion, Gerard Smith, head of the U.S. SALT delegation, was asked to send a telegram to certain Senators urging that SAFEGUARD was necessary as a bargaining chip for the successful conclusion of an arms control agreement. This top secret telegram was then shown to the several senators on the Senate floor before the SAFEGUARD vote. Earlier, Senator McIntyre had called Gerard Smith in Vienna and was assured that SAFEGUARD was vital to the SALT. As a result of the telegram and telephone call, Senators Marlow Cook (R-Ky.), McIntyre, James Pearson (R-Kan.), and Clinton Anderson (D-N.M.) switched their support for the Cooper-Hart Amendment to opposing it. *The New York Times* editorial of August 13 deplored the vote on the Cooper-Hart Amendment and urged passage of the Brooke Amendment [86].

With the ending of the Vienna phase of SALT, the United States indicated a willingness to scrap its BMD system entirely if the Soviets agreed to a limitation on the numbers of SS-9 ICBMs and scrapped their BMD around Moscow. As a fallback position, the United States was willing to accept BMD around the national capitals, Moscow and Washington [87]. These positions were part of a larger and comprehensive U.S. proposal.

In the space of a year the public involvement in the BMD debate diminished to zero. Only the Senate Foreign Relations Committee and its familiar witnesses against BMD remained as the hard-core opposition to SAFEGUARD, although the Senate Armed Services Committee, in a compromise decision, eliminated funds for the thin area defense component of SAFEGUARD. MIRV, SALT, Cambodia, and Vietnam had become the latest issues. In the space of three years from the first positive deployment decision, the rationale had come full circle, back to an area defense, albeit a thin one. Then this rationale was eliminated by the Senate Armed Services Committee and the secondary mission of BMD—hard point defense came to replace its primary mission which all the BMD components were developed for—urban defense. If by mid-1970 there were any questions about BMD policy, they were related more to SALT and to providing a strong bargaining position for the United States than with the Soviet threat, which continues to increase beyond the point of parity with the United States.

Meanwhile missile defense had come to affect the SALT positions of both sides. In December 1970 the Soviets proposed a separate agreement to limit the deployment of BMD to an unspecified number of interceptors an unspecified radius from the centers of Moscow and Washington, D.C. This was rejected by the U.S. This proposal came almost four years from the day that the U.S. had proposed a BMD only limitation. This 1966 U.S. proposal was rejected by the Soviets because it did not include offensive systems. It was this impasse created by the inability for both sides to agree on the scope of the discussions which held up the initiation of SALT. Later the U.S. agreed to include offensive weapons as well. In 1970, the Soviets attempted to decouple defensive systems from the offensive ones with their proposal of a separate agreement. During this same time the U.S. BMD deployment policy and the August 4, 1970 SALT Proposal were in contradiction. Under the terms of the latter, the U.S. was committed to either eliminating all BMD or confining its deployment to 100 interceptors around the national capitals. However the U.S. BMD system was being deployed around the Minuteman ICBM sites. Such a deployment for which more money was being asked in the FY 1972 federal budget would be ruled out by the U.S. SALT Proposal and would have to be scrapped if that or any similar BMD limiting agreement were negotiated. However, in the absence of any reduction in the Soviet ICBM threat, especially in the SS-9s, the continued deployment of Safeguard would serve as an incentive to the Soviets to negotiate an offense-defense agreement.

It is ironic that the very reason for withholding BMD deployment during the Johnson Administration—to bring about a reduction in tension and de-escalation of the arms race—may very well have been accomplished only by having begun the deployment of a missile defense rather than withholding it!

References

[1] "Text of President Nixon's Announcement on Revised Proposals for Sentinel Antiballistic Missile Program," *The New York Times*, March 15, 1969, p. 17, hereafter cited as "Text of . . ."

[2] *Safeguard ABM System*, p. 20.

[3] "Text of . . .," p. 17.

[4] *Safeguard ABM System*, pp. 16–17.

[5] *Safeguard ABM System*, p. 2.

[6] Warren Unna, "Hill Divided on Missile Plan," *Washington Post*, March 15, 1969, p. A1. See *U.S. Congressional Record* for the latter half of March for additional views.

[7] "Compromise on the SENTINEL," editorial, *Washington Post*, March 15, 1969, p. A10.

[8] "The Useless SAFEGUARD," editorial, *The New York Times*, March 15, 1969, p. 32.

[9] Robert B. Semple, "Nixon Staff Had Central Role in Missile Decision," *The New York Times*, March 19, 1969, p. 22.

[10] Jay Walz, "Missile Dispute Erupts in Canada," *The New York Times*, March 20, 1969, p. 8.

[11] U.S. Senate, Hearings Before the Committee on Armed Services, *Authorization for Military Procurement, Research and Development FY 1970 and Reserve Strength*, Part I, 91st Cong., 1st Sess., 1969, pp. 119–242, hereafter cited as *Senate Defense Authorizations FY 1970*.

[12] *Implications of ABM System*, Part I, p. 183.

[13] *Implications of ABM System*, Part I, p. 203.

[14] *Implications of ABM System*, Part I, p. 205.

[15] *Implications of ABM System*, Part I, pp. 257–265.

[16] *Implications of ABM System*, Part I, pp. 326–334.

[17] U.S. Senate, Hearings Before the Committee on Foreign Relations, *Briefing by Secretary of State William P. Rogers*, 91st Cong., 1st Sess., March 27, 1969

[18] Bernard Gwertzman, "Nixon's ABM Plans Arouse Soviet Press Critics," *The New York Times*, March 28, 1969, p. 15.

[19] *Implications of ABM Systems*, pp. 348–355.

[20] Robert B. Semple. "White House Reported to Reject ABM Opponent as Science Head," *The New York Times*, April 17, 1969, p. 1.

[21] "Transcript of the President's News Conference on Foreign and Domestic Affairs," *The New York Times*, April 19, 1969, p. 14.

[22] Henry Kamm, "Moscow Scores Arms-Talk Foes," *The New York Times*, April 20, 1969, p. 27.

[23] Irna Moore, "Coalition Asks ABM Hearing," *Washington Post*, April 22, 1969, p. C1. This article lists some of the constituent groups comprising the coalition.

[24] *Senate Defense Authorizations FY 1970*, pp. 1109–1456.

[25] John W. Finney, "Kennedy Sponsored Study of ABM Upsets Pentagon," *The New York Times*, May 7, 1969, p. 1.

[26] *Senate Defense Authorizations FY 1970*, pp. 1258–1286, 1446–1456.

[27] Bernard Gwertzman, "Pravda Voices Soviet Displeasure with U.S. over Missile Policies and Delay on Arms Control Talks," *The New York Times*, June 11, 1969, p. 11.

[28] Peter Grose, "U.S. Intelligence Doubts Soviet Has First-Strike Goal," *The New York Times*, June 18, 1969, p. 1.

[29] U.S. Congress, Senate, Hearings Before the Committee on Foreign Relations, *Intelligence and the ABM*, 91st Cong., 1st Sess., June 23, 1969, printed on July 9, 1969.

[30] *U.S. Congressional Record*, July 10, 1969, pp. 7864–7865.

[31] U.S. Congress, Senate, *Report of the Committee on Armed Services Together with Minority and Supplemental Views Authorizing Appropriations for FY 1970,* Report No. 91-920, 91st Cong., 1st Sess., July 3, 1969, pp. 28-31, hereafter cited as *Senate Armed Services Committee Report.*

[32] *Senate Armed Services Committee Report,* pp. 63-65.

[33] *Senate Armed Services Committee Report,* p. 66.

[34] *Senate Armed Services Committee Report,* pp. 66-67.

[35] Henry Raymont, "ABM Supporters Planning 2 Books," *The New York Times,* July 11, 1969, p. 5.

[36] Neil Sheehan, "Kennedy Says Pro-ABM Book Is Aided by Pentagon," *The New York Times,* July 8, 1969, p. 13. See also William Beecher, "Institute's Book Upholds The ABM," July 6, 1969, p. 1.

[37] John W. Finney, "Politics of ABM: A Tough Struggle That Cuts Across Party Lines," *The New York Times,* July 18, 1969, p. E1.

[38] Jack Bell, "Revision of ABM Studied," *Washington Post,* July 14, 1969, p. A1.

[39] John W. Finney. "ABM Foes Setback as Prouty Shifts to Support Nixon," *The New York Times,* July 15, 1969, p. 1.

[40] *Implications of ABM System,* Part III, *passim.*

[41] John W. Finney, "Secret ABM Data Heard by Senate in Closed Session," *The New York Times,* July 18, 1969, p. 9.

[42] "Poll Finds Most Uncertain on ABM," *The New York Times,* July 27, 1969, p. 27.

[43] John W. Finney, "Senate Panel, with Film and Reports, Rests Case Against ABM," *The New York Times,* July 31, 1969, p. 8, hereafter cited as *Senate Panel Rests Case.*

[44] *Senate Panel Rests Case,* p. 8.

[45] Neil Sheehan, "Industries Linked to an Ad for ABM," *The New York Times,* August 4, 1969, p. 1.

[46] Spencer Rich, "House Approves Funds for ABM," *Washington Post,* August 6, 1969, p. A1.

[47] *U.S. Congressional Record,* August 6, 1969, pp. S9253, S9282.

[48] Warren Weaver, "Nixon Missile Plan Wins in Senate by a 51-50 Vote," *The New York Times,* August 7, 1969, pp. 1, 22.

[49] *U.S. Congressional Record,* August 7, 1969, p. S9341.

[50] *U.S. Congressional Record,* October 2, 1969, pp. H8847-8892.

[51] *U.S. Congressional Record,* October 3, 1969, p. H9016.

[52] William Beecher, "Soviet Arms Gain Detected by U.S.," *The New York Times*, October 28, 1969, p. 1.

[53] John W. Finney, "Compromise Plan Is Adopted by U.S. for Arms Parley," *The New York Times*, November 11, 1969, p. 1.

[54] *U.S. Congressional Record*, December 8, 1969, pp. H11894–11897.

[55] *U.S. Congressional Record*, December 15, 1969, pp. S16773–16782.

[56] "White House Debates Whether To Expand ABM in Budget Due in January," *The New York Times*, December 21, 1969, p. 43.

[57] William Beecher, "Laird Says Soviet Speeds Up Threat," *The New York Times*, January 8, 1970, p. 1.

[58] "Transcript of the President's News Conference on Foreign and Domestic Matters," *The New York Times*, January 31, 1970, p. 14.

[59] William Beecher, "President Seeks Expansion of ABM but Plans Review," *The New York Times*, January 30, 1970, p. 1.

[60] "ABM Plan Challenged by Mansfield," *Washington Post*, February 1, 1970, p. A2.

[61] *U.S. Congressional Record*, February 4, 1970, pp. S1145–1150.

[62] U.S. Senate, Hearings Before the Committee on Foreign Relations, *Exchanges of U.S.-U.S.S.R. Officials*, 91st Cong., 2nd Sess., 1970, pp. 38–42.

[63] U.S. President, *United States Foreign Policy for the 1970's: A New Strategy for Peace*, GPO, February 18, 1970.

[64] *Laird Posture Statement*, pp. 46–50.

[65] *Laird Posture Statement*, p. 50.

[66] John W. Finney, "2 Key Democrats Express Doubts on Expanded ABM," *The New York Times*, February 24, 1970, p. 1.

[67] U.S. House, Hearings Before a Subcommittee of the Committee on Appropriations, *Department of Defense Appropriations for 1971*, Part 1, 91st Cong., 2nd Sess., 1970, pp. 318–338, 385–409. See Robert Keatley, "Laird Presents Modified ABM Expansion Requesting Only One More Site Now" *Wall Street Journal*, February 25, 1970, p. 3, and William Beecher, "Expansion of ABM to 3rd Missile Site is Sought by Laird" *The New York Times*, February 25, 1970, p. 1, for additional material on the Modified Phase 2 deployment.

[68] "How Good Are the Kremlin's Weapons," *The New York Times*, March 1, 1970, p. 3E; Bernard Gwertzman, "Soviet Says Its ABM Can 'Reliably Hit' Attacking Missiles," *The New York Times*, February 24, 1970, p. 1.

[69] William Beecher, "Soviet Criticism on Arms Dismays Top U.S. Aides," *The New York Times*, March 9, 1970, p. 1.

[70] Chalmers Roberts, "Military Chiefs Oppose Curbs on MIRV, ABM," *Washington Post*, March 27, 1970, p. A6.

[71] *U.S. Congressional Record,* April 20, 1970, pp. S5975–5976.

[72] John W. Finney, "Nixon Panel Asks Moratorium Now in Missiles Race," *The New York Times,* April 8, 1970, p. 1.

[73] *U.S. Congressional Record,* April 9, 1970, p. 5509. The debate on pp. 5478–5509; the Assembly's final report, *U.S. Congressional Record,* April 20, 1970, pp. S5975–5987.

[74] Spencer Rich, "House Unit Rejects Cut in ABM Funds," *Washington Post,* April 17, 1970, p. A2.

[75] John W. Finney, "Nixon Sets Goal of Broad Accord on Nuclear Arms," *The New York Times,* April 17, 1970, p. 1.

[76] *U.S. Congressional Record,* April 30, 1970, pp. H3721–3740.

[77] Chalmers Roberts, "Shape of Arms Pact Emerges, with 50–50 Chance of Accord," *Washington Post,* May 21, 1970, p. A1.

[78] "State Hits Post Story on SALT," *Washington Post,* May 22, 1970, p. A2.

[79] U.S. Congress, Senate, Committee on Armed Services. *Report Together with Individual Views Authorizing Appropriations for FY 1971 for Military Procurement, Research and Development, for the Construction of Facilities for the Safeguard Anti-Ballistic Missile System, Reserve Component Strength, and for Other Purposes,* 91st Cong., 2nd Sess., Report No. 91–1016, July 14, 1970, pp. 18–23.

[80] "Opponents Cite ABM Vulnerability to High-Altitude Nuclear Bursts," *Aviation Week and Space Technology,* 3[1970]20.

[81] U.S. Congress, Senate, Hearings Before the Committee on Armed Services. *Authorization for Military Procurement, Research and Development, FY 1971, and Reserve Strength,* Part 3, 91st Cong., 2nd Sess., 1970, p. 2147, hereafter cited as *Senate Military Authorizations FY 1971.*

[82] *Senate Military Authorizations FY 1971,* pp. 2313–2378.

[83] U.S. *Congressional Record.* July 31, 1970, p. S12561.

[84] U.S. *Congressional Record.* August 12, 1970, pp. S13277–13281.

[85] *U.S. Congressional Record.* August 12, 1970, pp. S13282–13304.

[86] John Finney, "Senators Tell of ABM Telegram from Arms Envoy," *The New York Times,* August 14, 1970, p. 2.

[87] Hedrick Smith, "U.S. Makes Offer to Give Up ABMs If Soviet Does So." *The New York Times,* August 17, 1970, p. 1.

PART V
Analysis and Conclusions

CHAPTER 15

U.S. Missile Defense Policy in Retrospect

It should be clear to the reader that the single most critical question pervading U.S. missile defense policy since its inception has been whether or not to deploy BMD.

U.S. missile defense policy can be divided into two periods: the period of nondeployment (1957 to September 18, 1967) and, from the latter date to the present, the period of deployment. Within these two periods, missile defense policy underwent several changes in direction resulting from technological and political considerations.

BMD: A Recapitulation

A defense against missiles was sought by the United States as early as 1944 as a means to counter the German V-2. Conceptually, a number of ideas, technical descriptions of defense systems, and problems of missile defense were advanced, although little actual work was done on BMD until 1955. It has become equally apparent that Soviet BMD efforts go back to the late 1940s or early 1950s.

Work actually started on ZEUS in 1956, 3 years after an American ICBM was given top priority and several months before the first American ICBM was flight-tested successfully. In 1959, with Congress backing an Army request to begin deployment of ZEUS, Congress and the Administration found themselves in conflict for the first time over missile defense. In 1960 the Army repeated its request. This time, however, Congress supported the JCS and the President's recommendation that ZEUS be kept in R&D. The question of deploying BMD was not raised again in the Congress until the closed session of 1963.

The missile defense program in this country was born in conflict and continued in conflict into 1970. Both the Air Force and the Army had BMD concepts under development in 1957, as they do in 1970. The Army's belief was that a mixture of strategic offensive and defensive forces was necessary to maintain the deterrent. The Air Force still feels the best deterrent is a qualitatively and quantitatively superior offensive force, but circumstances today demand that the deterrent force be defended against ICBM attack.

Simultaneously with the efforts to perfect a missile defense, which many thought was infeasible or even impossible at the time, the movement to limit development and deployment was initiated. Dr. Wiesner at the Sixth Pugwash Conference in Moscow in 1960 proposed a comprehensive arms limitation program, which was quite similar to the U.S. GCD Program offered to the General Assembly in 1961 and later to the ENDC in Geneva. The U.S. arms control policy proposed a halt to development and deployment of BMD. These proposals remained a consistent part of U.S. missile defense policy. During this time, 1958–1961, a technical debate raged over ZEUS's ability to (1) discriminate warheads from decoys, (2) function in a saturation attack, and (3) survive a deliberate attack against its vulnerable radar. Because these questions remained unanswered and the Army's confidence in the system was not shared by the Defense Department, ZEUS was not deployed. It was kept in the R&D state while other BMD concepts were studied. This policy—continued R&D but no deployment—remained a fixture of U.S. BMD policy until September 1967. The result of the R&D part of this policy was to provide a technological base for developing a whole class of BMDs. After that, continued R&D was an integral part of the deployment policy and represented the fall-back position of those opposed to deployment; i.e., continue the R&D.

In 1961–62, the ZEUS testing program resulted in 10 hits out of 14 attempted ICBM intercepts, yet the Defense Department refused to authorize some form of deployment because the tests had not been conducted under combat conditions and therefore were not conclusive. Despite the frequent technological improvements made to ZEUS, the Army was unable to convince critics (including the Administration) that the system could be effective. The ability of ZEUS to shoot down an ICBM, which was the original objective of the weapon at its inception five years earlier, sounded the death knell for ZEUS. Now the offense would be compelled to use decoys and penaids to keep ahead of the defense, even though these devices were nonexistent during the life of ZEUS, but the argument they would exist was used against any ZEUS deployment.

Despite the urgings of Senator Thurmond, the Senate, in its closed session of 1963, voted against procuring the NIKE-ZEUS pending the results of a new program called NIKE-X. The NIKE-X system, consisting of phased-array radar, the ZEUS missile for long-range intercept, and SPRINT for endo-atmospheric intercept, was initiated as a means of coping with the new strides made by the offense and the inherent limitations of ZEUS. Arguing that NIKE-X was not ready for deployment in 1964 and fallout shelters were more important, the Administration postponed for another year any decision to deploy a missile defense. In 1965 the same arguments were repeated.

Despite the existence of two urban defense BMD systems, NIKE-ZEUS and NIKE-X, the lack of a positive deployment decision from 1957 to 1965 is attributable to the need to solve certain technical problems and answer certain technical and economic questions. The period 1957 to 1964 marks the end of one phase of U.S. BMD policy; from 1965 to September 1967 marks a second, within the nondeployment period.

During the period 1965 to September 1967 the Administration was under considerable pressure to deploy some form of NIKE-X and to gain operational experience with the system. These pressures were resisted by the Administration for several reasons, discussed below.

Another explanation may exist for the reason the United States did not initiate the deployment of NIKE-X, and it explains to a degree the circumstance which led, in September 1967, to the deployment of SENTINEL.

By December 1965 there was considerable evidence (believed to be true by the Administration) that China would become a major nuclear power by the middle or late 1970s, at which time the Chinese would be capable of attacking the United States with a limited number of first-generation ICBMs. Simultaneously, a breakthrough had been made in missile defense. Since the range of ZEUS had been doubled and a new family of phased-array radars had been developed, it would now be possible to tailor an area defense BMD deployment against a light and unsophisticated attack such as the Chinese might be capable of launching at some date. This kind of deployment would reduce BMD cost, since it was possible now to deploy a "cheap" and effective defense. Until late 1965 the high cost and uncertain capabilities of NIKE-X, and its potential destabilizing effect on the Soviet-American balance of power made its deployment singularly unattractive to American decisionmakers. With the new developments in BMD, the system's political attractiveness increased. This change in attitude toward the desirability and political acceptability of missile defense was caused by the advent of the Chinese nuclear threat, the length of time it would take to become significant, and the idea that the Chinese might be able to launch only 50 ICBMs without decoys or penetration aids against the United States. Since the Chinese threat was expected to emerge slowly, sufficient time, it was believed, would be available to deploy NIKE-X if the need arose while the system continued in development; thus the Soviets would not be antagonized by a BMD deployment. Since the Chinese threat would permit a postponement of a deployment decision, additional ways for bringing about a continued relaxation of tensions between the United States and the Soviet Union might still be found and given time to work.

Before the development of this building block or modular BMD and the "emergence of the Chinese threat," [1] which made missile defense attractive, it was thought that deployment would be addressed against the Soviet Union. However, for a number of political, technological, strategic, and economic reasons the Administration refrained from deploying BMD against the Soviets. The Administration, especially Secretary McNamara,[2] believed deployment of BMD against the Soviet Union would be provocative and destabilizing, would accomplish little for its cost, could not handle a sophisticated attack, would jeopardize the chances of improving the fragile relations between the two countries, would cause the Soviets to deploy more offense to counter the BMD at a lesser cost than the cost to the United States to deploy BMD,[3] was vulnerable and ineffective, could not handle MIRVs, and would accelerate the arms race to higher levels with little additional security gain for either side. The considerations involved in the Administration's decision of whether to deploy BMD against the Soviet Union derived from the likelihood of a continuing détente and of the Soviets' interpreting a NIKE-X deployment as a threat to its strategic position vis-à-vis the United States. Several conditions were offered to explain this development. First, the advent of a détente in Europe had lessened the chances of a direct Soviet-American confrontation in that part of the world. Second, the arms race appeared to have slowed down; neither side was thought to be increasing or altering its strategic balance. (Subsequent evidence in 1966 and to the present indicated, however, the Soviets were not only deploying BMD but were also expanding and improving their

---

[1] After six years, the Chinese have yet to test an ICBM. The author finds it difficult to believe a hypothetical threat from China, rather than a real and immediate threat from the Soviet Union, would provide the impetus and rationale for deploying BMD. While the Administration may have desired to placate the BMD deployment proponents by suggesting a deployment against China and also not to provoke the Soviet Union, the credibility then as well as now of the Chinese deployment rationale seems rather weak. Indeed, it was later admitted, the SENTINEL deployment was the forerunner of a thicker Soviet-oriented defense.

[2] According to Phil Goulding, Assistant Secretary of Defense for Public Affairs under McNamara, in his book *Confirm or Deny,* Harper and Row 1970, McNamara never spoke out publicly on BMD "until every word he wanted to say had been approved in full both by the Department of State and by the White House," p. 214.

[3] While a U.S. defensive system might force the Soviets to undertake steps to penetrate the U.S. BMD, the cost of such a program is considerable, if the U.S. program to penetrate Soviet defense is any indication. Because the cost of the penetration program is so high, under certain circumstances the defense is favored. The expectation that a missile defense might be deployed, or its actual presence, has exacted a high price from the offense.

ICBM force and developing a space bombardment system and a satellite interceptor.) A third explanation for this apparent stability in Soviet-American relations derived from the second condition: namely, a technological plateau was believed to have been reached, which would reduce the prospects for further advances in strategic arms development. The technological-plateau thesis originated with the BMD opponents and was first described in the Wiesner-York article in the October 1964 *Scientific American*. Since the Johnson Administration accepted the mutual deterrence thesis, there was little question that BMD deployment would upset the balance.

In early 1966 the Administration found itself able to deploy a BMD, if it chose to do so, which might have some chance of success against a light and unsophisticated threat. The BMD controversy had now passed from the question of development to the question of deployment. The irony of this situation was that the threat to which BMD should have been addressed—i.e., the Soviet Union—was considered "impractical" and politically undesirable to defend against, while the effective and cheap version of NIKE-X could cope best with a potential ICBM attack from China, which still had not tested an ICBM. As a result, the Defense Department felt a decision to deploy NIKE-X could safely be deferred until early 1967.[4]

Behind the nondeployment policy was a subjective belief on the part of the Administration that by not deploying new strategic weapons it was possible Soviet-American tensions could be reduced and the intensity of the nuclear arms race curbed. The theory behind the unilateral U.S. decision not to deploy BMD was that mutual trust and confidence could be introduced into Soviet-American relations. In turn, it was expected the Soviets would reciprocate by not deploying BMD, although reaching parity in offensive weapons with the United States was considered by the Administration as acceptable. It was thought that Soviet-American trust might be enhanced to the extent that a lasting détente between the two countries would ensue as a result of the U.S. unilateral action in withholding deployment of a BMD. The BMD policy of nondeployment (extending from 1965 through September 1967) was an example of unilateral arms control. However, reciprocal Soviet responses were not forthcoming. Why the Soviets did not respond is a matter of speculation. They may not have understood the subtleties of the U.S. approach and proposal. They did not desire an inferior strategic position or one of parity. Maybe they saw a chance to gain the strategic advantage. Or maybe there were internal

---

[4] It should be remembered that the Administration never publicly admitted that BMD deployment would be directed against the Soviet Union. When the possibility of deploying BMD arose, the Chinese threat was always mentioned.

political pressures which did not allow them to grasp the opportunity for arms control and improved relations.

By December 1966 it was clear the development program policy was successful, but the arms control policy was a failure. For the first time since the no-deployment policy had been in effect, the alternative of beginning a deployment appeared attractive, but not directly against the Soviet Union but indirectly through a Chinese-oriented deployment which later could be expanded against the Soviet Union threat. By December 1966 the Soviet technological strategic threat had developed to the point it could no longer be ignored.

By September 1967 the Administration had exhausted every political, strategic, and technological argument against deployment, including offering to negotiate a BMD moratorium with the Soviets. The failure of the Administrations' nondeployment policy can be attributed, in part, to the fact that strategic weapons technology had passed the point of no return—i.e., there was more danger in not having BMD than in continuing the nondeployment policy—and to the Soviet reluctance to subscribe to this unilateral and informal means of arms control. By continuing the nondeployment policy, President Johnson faced the prospect of: (1) increasing political criticism from Congress over defense issues, (2) providing the Republicans with a ready-made 1968 Presidential campaign issue (why did the President hesitate to protect the American people from attack?), (3) growing military disenchantment with Secretary McNamara already aggravated by the Vietnam war, and (4) damaging effects to U.S. foreign policy and the strategic deterrent. At this juncture, the President stood to lose more by nondeployment than he did if he commenced deployment.[5] Accordingly, the President decided in early September 1967 to begin BMD deployment. This decision is not as clear cut as it might appear, since the form the deployment might take was critical to the decision to deploy, as the Administration still hoped to prevent a Soviet reaction and an escalation in the arms race. The opponents of BMD were responsible for influencing the form of BMD deployment.

For 6 years the whole purpose of nondeployment was to prevent an increase in the Soviet ICBM force. The SENTINEL system, however, was thought most likely to minimize the Soviet provocation, even though it was a city defense deployment.

The problem facing the President was to choose a course of action which preserved the greatest latitude of action without foreclosing the

---

[5] The author bases this estimate on the fact, as reported, that Secretary McNamara was compelled at the last minute to change his BMD speech in accordance with the President's decision. See also Phil Goulding, *Confirm or Deny*, pp. 214–248.

greatest number of alternatives and risking a new arms race with the Soviets. The President as national decisionmaker and chief administrator of the government competes with the President as a party leader and politician, but sometimes it is difficult to separate these roles. However, some of the political pressures and problems facing the President as party leader and politician were likely to be eased by a decision to deploy BMD. In other words, any deployment was bound to be politically advantageous to the President as it would (1) thwart a Republican effort to make the lack of a missile defense a 1968 Presidential campaign issue, (2) take some of the sting out of Senator Henry Jackson's committee hearings as to why no decision had been made up until 1967 to deploy BMD, (3) satisfy his critics the United States was making an effort to counter the growing Soviet strategic threat, and (4) placate the politically potent Joint Chiefs of Staff, who were becoming more and more disenchanted and dissatisfied with Secretary McNamara's conduct of military affairs. The SENTINEL decision was another in a long line of political compromises which have marked the BMD program from its inception.

In retrospect, the SENTINEL suffered from the fundamental weakness of any urban defense; i.e., it was to be the forerunner of a defense directed solely against the Soviets and therefore was provocative. Ironically, the opposition to SENTINEL, even when it was revealed to be Soviet oriented, was not from the Soviets but from the U.S. public.

The SENTINEL system, as originally explained, was an area defense weapon that could function over a wide area against a light and/or unsophisticated attack of the kind the Chinese could be capable of launching by 1975. However, this deployment would not be capable of handling a heavy Soviet attack. The SENTINEL, however, could provide an effective defense against accidental ICBM firings or Nth-country threats. It had a secondary mission of protecting the hardened ICBM sites. Its low cost made it a low-investment, low-risk system in the event it became technologically obsolete or unnecessary, but it was also expandable to a larger deployment. For the President, the political, economic, strategic, and psychological benefits of deploying BMD made SENTINEL a logical political choice. So the unilateral arms control policy of the United States, using BMD as a gambit, came to an end in September 1967.

With the SENTINEL decision, U.S. missile defense policy entered its second period. The first phase of this period lasted about 16 months as preparations were begun to deploy SENTINEL. Grassroot opposition to the deployment started as local citizenry became alarmed over the placement of nuclear-tipped missiles in or around large urban areas. This public opposition began quite independently of earlier efforts in Congress to prevent BMD deployment. The local opposition in Seattle, Chicago,

Detroit, and Boston was given authoritative support by many scientists, some of whom had long been opposed to BMD deployment and whose views prevailed within the Government until the SENTINEL decision. Once their influence had waned, the SENTINEL decision made, and the public concern with Vietnam and the problem of domestic priorities pushed to the fore, these opponents of BMD had to look for other means to present their views and seek support. It has been shown during the course of this review that newspapers and members of Congress opposed to BMD have urged public debate of the BMD deployment issue. The *Bulletin of the Atomic Scientists* and its editor, Dr. Rabinowitch, have suggested active political participation by scientists to prevent the use of nuclear weapons and to curb the arms race. Dr. Wiesner wrote in the June 1967 *Bulletin of the Atomic Scientists,* in an article entitled "The Cold War Is Dead," that the technologically uninformed public might be willing to participate in debating the important issues associated with BMD deployment if "more comprehensible technological information were available to them." He suggested more scientists and engineers unite and speak on the broad range of issues involved in making decisions on national security. This is precisely what happened toward the end of 1968 and in early 1969.

The public outcry supported by opponents of BMD from the scientific/academic/intellectual community succeeded in creating enough pressure to halt the SENTINEL deployment in February 1969. A month later, with President Nixon's SAFEGUARD announcement, U.S. missile defense policy was again reversed. Phase 1 of SAFEGUARD, while eschewing any city defense, was clearly oriented toward a Soviet attack. The difference between SENTINEL and SAFEGUARD was the emphasis of the latter on hard point defense and protection of the deterrent force rather than the former's concern with population defense. This decision by the Nixon Administration was clearly designed for its political acceptability and to meet the immediate threat. The decision to halt SENTINEL in 1969 did not mean a reversal but merely a reorientation in the purpose of the system.

The debate which ensued during the spring and summer of 1969 was not a popular debate in the sense of mass public participation. To be sure there were statements and petitions by concerned citizens and organizations, but by and large it was the scientific/academic community, in particular a small group of scientists who had been involved in national security affairs since the end of the Second World War, who fought on both sides of the battle—lecturing, writing, speaking, debating, and testifying. In the Congress, especially in the Senate, there were hard-core opponents and proponents of deployment around whom coalesced support from those who were tutored, studied the issues, or listened to the numerous rounds of testimony, but were not members of the Defense or Foreign Affairs Committees. Despite all the seriousness attached to the "Great BMD Debate" in the scientific/academic community and the Congress, as well as in the Executive Branch whose BMD proposal hung in the balance, the author believes the BMD debate was only symbolic, except to the long-time opponents of deployment, of a mood then prevalent in the country. That mood was one of despair and frustration with the military, its influence, military spending overruns and costs, the war in Vietnam, the belief that U.S. priorities were mistakenly reversed and dislocated, inflation, and the arms race. Missile defense was something to grasp. If it could be defeated, then it was a start to altering the mood, the milieu, and the priorities. Indeed, much of the opposition to SAFEGUARD revolved around the Administration's rationale, the SS-9's capabilities, and whether the Soviets were seeking a first-strike rather than a BMD deployment. After the crucial votes in August on SAFEGUARD, the coalition which came within one vote of defeating BMD deployment, fell in strength as the margin increased by which opponents lost votes in trying to halt the spending on large weapon systems. The Senate attempt in 1969 to defeat SAFEGUARD, while a failure, would not stem later congressional opposition to BMD, to the military, and to the Executive Branch's prerogative in defense and foreign affairs.

SAFEGUARD was viewed by Congress not only from its role as representing the people but in its role as an institution and in its continuing struggle with the Executive Branch (which started over Vietnam) over constitutional power and shared responsibility and prerogatives in foreign and defense matters.

Another interesting facet of this debate was the preponderant, aggressive, and vociferous opposition from the scientific/academic community to BMD as compared to BMD proponents from this same community. Research into missile defense policy indicates the opposition from the very beginning (1959–1960) has been well organized and articulate, with the ratio of literature on BMD running by 1969 almost 8 to 10 to 1 in opposition. Unfortunately, the technical questions the opponents raise about BMD feasibility and effectiveness have not been answered officially in public, because of security considerations. Attempts to answer the opponents' technical questions have been made publicly by unofficial spokesmen like Wohlstetter, Teller, Brennan, and others. Unfortunately, the government made little attempt to refute the technical arguments by declassifying information the same way they did to state the magnitude of the Soviet threat. As in previous national security debates, the government's necessity for security, secrecy, and classification and selected release of such information has done the credibility of the government more harm than good.

Current opponents to BMD labor under several handicaps: they opposed the Nixon Administration's BMD policy; they were fighting to reverse a decision already made by the President of the United States; their attempt to influence that decision before it was made depended on access to the highest levels of Government and, in many cases, either they no longer had that access or what access they had was filtered through other ex-officials or the present Administration.

After the August 1969 votes which ensured Phase 1 deployment, the focus shifted to MIRV and SALT. Then late in that year and early in 1970 the focus shifted back to BMD as the President and Secretary of Defense indicated expansion of SAFEGUARD was necessary and likely. A disturbing feature of this contemplated expansion was its orientation, which signified another change in missile defense policy—to a light area city defense deployment. And, in fact, when the modified Phase 2 deployment was announced, it included preparation for 5 sites toward the total of 12 which made up SAFEGUARD at that time. Thus, in the space of 2½ years, BMD deployment and its rationale had come full cycle, back to a thin area population defense. Moreover, in 1970 the Nixon Administration argument for SAFEGUARD put more emphasis on the value of BMD for strengthening America's bargaining position at SALT than it did on the Soviet threat. The use of BMD as a bargaining ploy for arms control was reminiscent of the McNamara effort to use BMD in a similar manner, although McNamara refused to deploy BMD to achieve his aim, while President Nixon used deployment.

An interesting contrast in policy styles is evident between the SENTINEL deployment decision and the two SAFEGUARD decisions. During the Kennedy and Johnson Administrations, Secretary of Defense McNamara was the chief architect of BMD policy. That policy obviously was concurred in and approved by the President at least until early September 1967. Very little information is available on how, when, and with whom President Johnson consulted on his decision to begin BMD deployment, compared to the Nixon decision. However, the President, after making the decision, continued to remain in the background on the BMD issue and let Secretary McNamara make the announcement and provide the rationale within the framework of a lecture on the peculiarities of nuclear warfare. With the Nixon Administration, the President himself has taken a major role in the issue by announcing and explaining his first decision on nationwide television. While the actual nature of the deployment of Phase 2 was announced by Secretary of Defense Laird, the President had prepared the country for it by announcing an expansion would take place. Curiously, it fell to Secretary Laird to defend before Congress the Administration's rationale based on the Soviet threat, while David Packard,

U.S. Missile Defense Policy in Retrospect 249

Deputy to Secretary Laird, appeared to play a much greater role in the first decision than did Laird.

Another aspect of the BMD deployment policy issue which raises questions is the rationale used by the Johnson and Nixon Administrations to justify deployment. For the Johnson Administration, China was the threat to be defended against and the country had to be protected. The Nixon Administration said it was the Soviet threat which must be countered and ICBMs must be defended. Then in 1970 the Nixon Administration reminded the nation about the Soviet threat and strengthened the ICBM defense but also raised the Chinese threat again. But, it appears to the author upon analysis the real emphasis for continuing the SAFEGUARD deployment and expanding it was to strengthen the U.S. position at SALT and contribute to SALT's success. The use of a "to-be-deployed" BMD to achieve a formal arms control agreement contrasts with the McNamara policy of withholding BMD to arrive at an informal one. McNamara failed, and the returns are not in on the Nixon efforts. Aside from the question of which is the "real" threat which prompted the SENTINEL, SAFEGUARD Phase 1, and SAFEGUARD Phase 2 deployments, the dominant role that U.S. missile defense policy has played in the last 6 years seems to have been in arms control rather than in a military role. It is ironic too that BMD rather than MIRV has been considered the culprit in the so-called arms race.

On the other hand, for the author, the issue of whether to deploy a BMD system was less a debate about the merits of a weapon system than it was an internal governmental policy debate on what was to be the future direction and objectives of American nuclear strategy. The central issue in this debate was whether strategic superiority and a damage limiting capability was still achievable against the Soviet Union in the coming era of parity or whether something else was required. The international and domestic conditions and attitudes toward national security surrounding this debate bear a remarkable resemblance to similar circumstances which prevailed in the West during the 1920's and 1930's.

Bibliography

Official Documents

U.S. Arms Control and Disarmament Agency. *Documents on Disarmament 1961*. Publication 5. Washington: GPO, 1962.

U.S. Arms Control and Disarmament Agency. *Documents on Disarmament 1962*. Vol. 1. Publication 19. Washington: GPO, 1963.

U.S. Arms Control and Disarmament Agency. *Documents on Disarmament 1963*. Publication 24. Washington: GPO, 1964.

U.S. Arms Control and Disarmament Agency. *Documents on Disarmament 1964*. Publication 27. Washington: GPO, 1965.

U.S. Arms Control and Disarmament Agency. *Documents on Disarmament 1966*. Publication 43. Washington: GPO, 1967.

U.S. Arms Control and Disarmament Agency. *Documents on Disarmament 1967*. Publication 46. Washington: GPO, 1968.

U.S. Congress. Hearings before the Joint Committee on Atomic Energy. *Developments in Technical Capabilities for Detecting and Identifying Nuclear Weapons Tests*. 88th Cong., 1st Sess., 1963.

U.S. Congress, Senate. Hearings before the Preparedness Investigating Subcommittee of the Committee on Armed Services. *Military Aspect and Implications of Nuclear Test Ban Proposals and Related Matters*. 2 Parts, 88th Cong., 1st Sess., 1964.

U.S. Congress, Senate. Hearings before the Subcommittee on Military Applications of the Joint Committee on Atomic Energy. *Scope, Magnitude, and Implications of the United States Antiballistic Missile Program*. 90th Cong., 1st Sess., 1968.

U.S. Congress. Joint Committee on Atomic Energy. *Impact of Chinese Communist Nuclear Weapons Progress on United States National Security*. 90th Cong., 1st Sess., 1967.

U.S. *Congressional Record*. 87th Cong., 1st Sess., February 2, 1961.

U.S. *Congressional Record*. 87th Cong., 1st Sess., February 13, 1961.

U.S. *Congressional Record*. 87th Cong., 1st Sess., March 13, 1961.

U.S. *Congressional Record*. 87th Cong., 2nd Sess., April 25, 1962.

U.S. *Congressional Record*. 88th Cong., 1st Sess., April 11, 1963.

U.S. *Congressional Record*. 89th Cong., 2nd Sess., June 14, 1966.

Bibliography

U.S. *Congressional Record.* 89th Cong., 2nd Sess., July 20, 1966.
U.S. *Congressional Record.* 89th Cong., 2nd Sess., August 18, 1966.
U.S. *Congressional Record.* 90th Cong., 1st Sess., March 21, 1967.
U.S. *Congressional Record.* 90th Cong., 1st Sess., July 27, 1967.
U.S. *Congressional Record.* 90th Cong., 2nd Sess., April 18, 1968.
U.S. *Congressional Record.* 90th Cong., 2nd Sess., June 19, 1968.
U.S. *Congressional Record.* 90th Cong., 2nd Sess., July 11, 1968.
U.S. *Congressional Record.* 90th Cong., 2nd Sess., July 29, 1968.
U.S. *Congressional Record.* 90th Cong., 2nd Sess., August 1, 1968.
U.S. *Congressional Record.* 90th Cong., 2nd Sess., September 12, 1968.
U.S. *Congressional Record.* 90th Cong., 2nd Sess., October 11, 1968.
U.S. *Congressional Record.* 90th Cong., 2nd Sess., November 1, 1968.
U.S. *Congressional Record.* 91st Cong., 1st Sess., February 4, 1969.
U.S. *Congressional Record.* 91st Cong., 1st Sess., June 25, 1969.
U.S. *Congressional Record.* 91st Cong., 1st Sess., July 10, 1969.
U.S. *Congressional Record.* 91st Cong., 1st Sess., August 6, 1969.
U.S. *Congressional Record.* 91st Cong., 1st Sess., August 7, 1969.
U.S. *Congressional Record.* 91st Cong., 1st Sess., October 2, 1969.
U.S. *Congressional Record.* 91st Cong., 1st Sess., October 3, 1969.
U.S. *Congressional Record.* 91st Cong., 1st Sess., October 7, 1969.
U.S. *Congressional Record.* 91st Cong., 1st Sess., November 20, 1969.
U.S. *Congressional Record.* 91st Cong., 1st Sess., December 8, 1969.
U.S. *Congressional Record.* 91st Cong., 1st Sess., December 15, 1969.
U.S. *Congressional Record.* 91st Cong., 2nd Sess., February 4, 1970.
U.S. *Congressional Record.* 91st Cong., 2nd Sess., April 9, 1970.
U.S. *Congressional Record.* 91st Cong., 2nd Sess., April 20, 1970.
U.S. *Congressional Record.* 91st Cong., 2nd Sess., April 30, 1970.
U.S. *Congressional Record.* 91st Cong., 2nd Sess., July 31, 1970.
U.S. *Congressional Record.* 91st Cong., 2nd Sess., August 12, 1970.
U.S. Department of Defense News Release. No. 1053–57. October 28, 1957.
U.S. Department of Defense News Release. No. 868–67. *Address by Honorable Robert S. McNamara, Secretary of Defense before United Press International Editors and Publishers, San Francisco, Monday, September 18, 1967.*
U.S. Department of Defense. *Statement of Secretary of Defense Robert S. McNamara before the House Armed Services Committee on the Fiscal Year*

1964–68 Defense Program and 1964 Defense Budget. Mimeographed. January 30, 1963.

U.S. Department of Defense. *Statement of Secretary of Defense Robert S. McNamara before the House Armed Services Committee on the Fiscal Year 1965–1969 Defense Program and 1965 Defense Budget.* Mimeographed. January 27, 1964.

U.S. Department of Defense. *Statement of Secretary of Defense Robert S. McNamara before the House Armed Services Committee on the Fiscal Year 1966–70 Defense Program and 1966 Defense Budget.* Mimeographed. February 18, 1965.

U.S. Department of Defense. *Statement of Secretary of Defense Robert S. McNamara before the House Armed Services Committee on the Fiscal Year 1967–71 Defense Program and 1967 Defense Budget.* Mimeographed. March 8, 1966.

U.S. Department of Defense. *Statement of Secretary of Defense Robert S. McNamara before a Joint Session of the Senate Armed Services Committee and the Senate Subcommittee on Department of Defense Appropriations on the Fiscal Year 1968–72 Defense Program and 1968 Defense Budget.* Mimeographed. January 23, 1967.

U.S. Department of Defense. *Statement of Secretary of Defense Robert S. McNamara before the Senate Armed Services Committee on the Fiscal Year 1969–73 Defense Program and 1969 Defense Budget.* January 22, 1968.

U.S. Department of Defense. *A Statement by Secretary of Defense Clark M. Clifford on the 1970 Defense Budget and Defense Program for Fiscal Years 1970–74.* January 15, 1969.

U.S. Department of Defense. Defense Report Before a Joint Session of the Senate Armed Services and Appropriations Committee. *A Statement by Secretary of Defense Melvin R. Laird on Fiscal Year 1971 Defense Program and Budget.* February 20, 1970.

U.S. Department of State. Foreign Service Institute. *Bibliography on Science and World Affairs.* November 1964.

U.S. *Department of State Bulletin.* Vol. 46. No. 1186. March 19, 1962.

U.S. *Department of State Bulletin.* Vol. 56. No. 1437. January 9, 1967.

U.S. *Department of State Bulletin.* Vol. 56, No. 1447. March 20, 1967.

U.S. House of Representatives. Briefing before the Committee on Appropriations. *Sentinel Anti-Ballistic Missile System.* 91st Cong., 1st Sess., 1969.

U.S. House of Representatives. Committee on Armed Services. *Hearings on Investigation of National Defense Missiles, Pursuant to House Resolution 67.* 85th Cong., 2nd Sess., 1958.

U.S. House of Representatives. Committee on Armed Services. *Hearings on Military Posture and H.R. 2440.* No. 4. 88th Cong., 1st Sess., 1963.

Bibliography 253

U.S. House of Representatives. Committee on Armed Services. *Hearings on Military Posture and H.R. 9637.* No. 36. 88th Cong., 2nd Sess., 1964.

U.S. House of Representatives. Committee on Armed Services. *Hearings on Military Posture and H.R. 4016.* No. 7. 89th Cong., 1st Sess., 1965.

U.S. House of Representatives. Committee on Armed Services. *Hearings on Military Posture and H.R. 9240.* 90th Cong., 1st Sess., 1967.

U.S. House of Representatives. Committee on Armed Services. *Hearings on Military Posture and S. 3293.* No. 56. 90th Cong., 2nd Sess., 1968.

U.S. House of Representatives. Committee on Armed Services. *Hearings on Military Posture.* 2 Parts. 91st Cong., 1st Sess., 1969.

U.S. House of Representatives. Committee on Government Operations. *Organization and Management of Missile Programs.* House Report No. 1121. 86th Cong., 1st Sess., 1959.

U.S. House of Representatives. Hearings before the Subcommittee of the Committee on Appropriations. *Department of Defense Appropriations for Fiscal Year 1960.* 86th Cong., 1st Sess., 1959..

U.S. House of Representatives. Hearings before a Subcommittee of the Committee on Appropriations. *Department of Defense Appropriations for Fiscal Year 1961.* 86th Cong., 2nd Sess., 1960.

U.S. House of Representatives. Hearings before a Subcommittee of the Committee on Appropriations. *Department of Defense Appropriations for 1962.* 87th Cong., 1st Sess., 1961.

U.S. House of Representatives. Hearings before a Subcommittee of the Committee on Appropriations. *Department of Defense Appropriations for Fiscal Year 1963.* 87th Cong., 2nd Sess., 1962.

U.S. House of Representatives. Hearings before a Subcommittee of the Committee on Appropriations. *Department of Defense Appropriations for FY 1964.* 88th Cong., 1st Sess., 1963.

U.S. House of Representatives. Hearings before a Subcommittee of the Committee on Appropriations. *Department of Defense Appropriations for Fiscal Year 1966.* 89th Cong., 1st Sess., 1965.

U.S. House of Representatives. Hearings before a Subcommittee of the Committee on Appropriations. *Department of Defense Appropriations for FY 1967.* 89th Cong., 2nd Sess., 1966.

U.S. House of Representatives. Hearings before a Subcommittee of the Committee on Appropriations. *Department of Defense Appropriations for Fiscal Year 1968.* 90th Cong., 1st Sess., 1967.

U.S. House of Representatives. Hearings before a Subcommittees of the Committee on Appropriations. *Department of Defense Appropriations for 1968.* 90th Cong., 1st Sess., 1967.

U.S. House of Representatives. Hearings before a Subcommittee of the Committee on Appropriations. *Department of Defense Appropriations for 1971.* 91st Cong., 2nd Sess., 1970.

U.S. House of Representatives. Hearings before Subcommittees of the Committee on Appropriations. *Safeguard Antiballistic Missile System.* 91st Cong., 1st Sess., 1969.

U.S. House of Representatives. Hearings before the Subcommittee on National Security Policy and Scientific Development of the Committee on Foreign Affairs. *Strategy and Science: Toward a National Security Policy for the 1970's.* 91st Cong., 1st Sess., 1969.

U.S. House of Representatives. Hearings of the House Subcommittee on National Security Policy and Scientific Developments of the Committee on Foreign Affairs. *Diplomatic and Strategic Impact of Multiple Warhead Missiles.* 91st Cong., 1st Sess., 1969.

U.S. House of Representatives. *Report of the Defense Subcommittee of the House Appropriations.* Report No. 91–698. 91st Cong., 1st Sess., 1969.

U.S. Library of Congress. Legislative Reference Service. *A Compilation of Material Relating to United States Defense Policies in 1962.* House Document No. 155. 88th Cong., 1st Sess., 1963.

U.S. Library of Congress. Legislative Reference Service. *United States Defense Policies in 1958.* House Document No. 227. 86th Cong., 1st Sess., 1959.

U.S. Library of Congress. Legislative Reference Service. *United States Defense Policies in 1959.* House Document No. 432. 86th Cong., 2nd Sess., 1960.

U.S. Library of Congress. Legislative Reference Service. *United States Defense Policies in 1960.* House Document No. 207. 87th Cong., 1st Sess., 1961.

U.S. Library of Congress. Legislative Reference Service. *United States Defense Policies in 1961.* House Document No. 502. 87th Cong., 2nd Sess., 1962.

U.S. Library of Congress. Legislative Reference Service. *United States Defense Policies Since World War II.* House Document No. 100. 85th Cong., 1st Sess., 1957.

U.S. President. *United States Foreign Policy for the 1970's: A New Strategy for Peace.* Washington: GPO, February 18, 1970.

U.S. Senate. Committee on Appropriations. *Department of Defense Appropriations Bill, 1968.* Report No. 494. 90th Cong., 1st Sess., 1967.

U.S. Senate. Committee on Armed Services. *Report Together with Individual Views Authorizing Appropriations for FY 1971 for Military Procurement, Research and Development, for the Construction of Facilities for the Safeguard Anti-Ballistic Missile System, Reserve Component Strength, and for Other Purposes.* 91st Cong., 2nd Sess., 1970.

U.S. Senate. Hearings before the Committee on Armed Services. *Authorization for Military Procurement, Research and Development, FY 1971, and Reserve Strength.* 3 Parts, 91st Cong., 2nd Sess., 1970.

U.S. Senate. Hearings before the Committee on Armed Services. *Authorization for Military Procurement, Research and Development FY 1970 and Reserve Strength.* 2 Parts, 91st Cong., 1st Sess., 1969.

U.S. Senate. Hearings before the Committee on Armed Services. *Military Procurement Authorization Fiscal Year 1962.* 87th Cong., 1st Sess., 1961.

U.S. Senate. Hearings before the Committee on Armed Services. *Military Procurement Authorization Fiscal Year 1963.* 87th Cong., 2nd Sess., 1962.

U.S. Senate. Hearings before the Committee on Armed Services. *Military Procurement Authorization Fiscal Year 1964.* 88th Cong., 1st Sess., 1963.

U.S. Senate. Hearings before the Committee on Armed Services and the Subcommittee on Department of Defense of the Committee on Appropriations. *Military Procurement Authorizations for Fiscal Year 1967.* 89th Cong., 2nd Sess., 1966.

U.S. Senate. Committee on Armed Services and the Subcommittee on Department of Defense of the Committee on Appropriations. *Military Procurement Authorization for Fiscal Year 1968.* 90th Cong., 1st Sess., 1967.

U.S. Senate. Hearings before the Committee on Foreign Relations. *Briefing by Secretary of State William P. Rogers.* 91st Cong., 1st Sess., March 27, 1969.

U.S. Senate. Hearings Before the Committee on Foreign Relations. *Exchanges of U.S.-U.S.S.R. Officials.* 91st Cong., 2nd Sess., 1970.

U.S. Senate. Hearings Before the Committee on Foreign Relations. *Intelligence and the ABM.* 91st Cong., 1st Sess., Printed July 9, 1969.

U.S. Senate. Hearings Before the Committee on Foreign Relations. *Nonproliferation Treaty.* Part 1, 90th Cong., 2nd Sess.; Part 2, 91st Cong., 1st Sess., 1969.

U.S. Senate. Hearings Before the Committee on Foreign Relations. *Nuclear Test Ban Treaty.* 88th Cong., 1st Sess., 1963.

U.S. Senate. Hearings before the Preparedness Investigating Subcommittee of the Committee on Armed Services. *Status of U.S. Strategic Power.* 2 Parts, 90th Cong., 2nd Sess., 1968.

U.S. Senate. Hearings before the Subcommittee on Department of Defense of the Committee on Appropriations and the Committee on Armed Services. *Department of Defense Appropriations, 1965.* Part I, 88th Cong., 2nd Sess., 1964.

U.S. Senate. Hearings before the Subcommittee on Department of Defense of the Committee on Armed Services. *Department of Defense Appropriations, 1966.* Part I, 89th Cong., 1st Sess., 1965.

U.S. Senate. Hearings before the Subcommittee on Disarmament of the Committee on Foreign Relations. *United States Armament and Disarmament Problems.* 90th Cong., 1st Sess., 1967.

U.S. Senate. Hearings before the Subcommittee on International Organization and Disarmament Affairs of the Committee on Foreign Relations. *Strategic and Foreign Policy Implications of ABM Systems.* 3 Parts, 91st Cong., 1st Sess., 1969.

U.S. Senate. Interim Report by Preparedness Investigating Subcommittee of the Committee on Armed Services. *Military Implications of the Proposed Limited Nuclear Test Ban Treaty.* 88th Cong., 1st Sess., 1963.

U.S. Senate. Joint Hearings before the Preparedness Investigating Subcommittee of the Committee on Armed Services and the Committee on Aeronautical and Space Sciences. *Missile and Space Activities.* 86th Cong., 1st Sess., 1959.

U.S. Senate. Preparedness Investigating Subcommittee of the Committee on Armed Services. *The United States Guided Missile Program.* 86th Cong., 1st Sess., 1959.

U.S. Senate. Preparedness Subcommittee of the Committee on Armed Services. *Hearings into Satellite and Missile Programs.* Part I, 85th Cong., 2nd Sess., 1957.

U.S. Senate. Report by the Preparedness Investigating Subcommittee of the Committee on Armed Services. *Status of U.S. Strategic Power.* 90th Cong., 2nd Sess., 1968.

U.S. Senate. *Report of the Committee on Armed Services Together with Minority and Supplemental Views Authorizing Appropriations for FY 1970.* Report No. 91–920. 91st Cong., 1st Sess., July 3, 1969.

U.S. Senate. Report of the Committee on Foreign Relations. *The Nuclear Test Ban Treaty.* Executive Report No. 3. 88th Cong., 1st Sess., 1963.

U.S. Senate. Subcommittee on Disarmament of the Committee on Foreign Relations. *Status of the Development of the Anti-ballistic Missile Systems in the United States.* 90th Cong., 1st Sess., 1967.

U.S. Senate. Subcommittee to Investigate the Administration of the Internal Security Laws of the Committee on the Judiciary. *The Pugwash Conferences.* 87th Cong., 1st Sess., 1961.

U.S. Senate. Hearings before the Subcommittee on Arms Control, International Law and Organization of the Committee on Foreign Relations. *ABM, MIRV, SALT, and the Nuclear Arms Race.* 91st Cong., 2nd Sess., 1970.

Articles

"ABM Plan Challenged by Mansfield," *Washington Post.* February 1, 1970.

"ABM System Blamed on Hawks' Pressure," *Washington Post.* October 4, 1967.

Bibliography

Anderson, Raymond. "Gromyko Offers to Start Talks on Missile Curb," *The New York Times*. June 28, 1968.

"Army Unhappy on Nike-Zeus Cut," *Missiles and Rockets*. July 21, 1958.

"ARPA Studies Satellite-Borne Anti-ICBM Defense System," *Aviation Week and Space Technology*. October 31, 1960.

Astronautics. October 1960. Whole Issue Devoted to Technical Problems of Missile Defense.

Baar, James. "Painful Nike-Zeus Choice Draws Near," *Missiles and Rockets*. October 26, 1959.

Baldwin, Hanson. "Pentagon Concern on Lack of Missile Defense Grows," *The New York Times*. May 21, 1967.

Baldwin, Hanson. "Soviet Antimissile System Spurs New U.S. Weapons," *The New York Times*. February 5, 1967.

Baldwin, Hanson. "The Great Missile Debate," *The Reporter*. June 29, 1967.

Baldwin, Hanson. "U.S. Lead in ICBM's Is Said to Be Reduced by Build-up in Soviet Union," *The New York Times*. July 14, 1966.

Baldwin, Hanson. "U.S. Missile Defense," *The New York Times*. February 15, 1964.

"Ballistic Missile Defense," *Ordnance*. September-October 1964.

Beecher, William. "Air Force Plans a Giant Missile to Penetrate Enemy's Radar Defenses," *The New York Times*. June 30, 1966.

Beecher, William. "Antimissile Net at Sea Proposed," *The New York Times*. July 4, 1967.

Beecher, William. "Expansion of ABM to 3rd Missile Site Is Sought by Laird," *The New York Times*. February 25, 1970.

Beecher, William. "Fending Off Missiles," *Wall Street Journal*. December 24, 1964.

Beecher, William. "Institute's Book Upholds the ABM," *The New York Times*. July 6, 1969.

Beecher, William. "Johnson Wants Stand-by Fund for Nike-X System," *The New York Times*. January 25, 1967.

Beecher, William. "Joint Chiefs Drop Stand for Heavy Missile Shield," *The New York Times*. March 18, 1969.

Beecher, William. "Laird Says Soviet Speeds Up Threat," *The New York Times*. January 8, 1970.

Beecher, William. "Missile Killing Gains," *Wall Street Journal*. July 26, 1965.

Beecher, William. "Missile to Carry Warhead Cluster," *The New York Times*. January 20, 1967.

Beecher, William. "NIKE-X in the Balance," *Astronautics and Aeronautics.* December 1965.

Beecher, William. "Now an Anti-Anti Missile Missile?" *The New York Times.* June 26, 1966.

Beecher, William. "Pentagon Drafts Revised Proposal on Missile Shield," *The New York Times.* March 2, 1969.

Beecher, William. "President Seeks Expansion of ABM but Plans Review," *The New York Times.* January 30, 1970.

Beecher, William. "Pressure in U.S. for Defense Seen," *The New York Times.* June 18, 1967.

Beecher, William. "Soviet Arms Gain Detected by U.S.," *The New York Times.* October 28, 1969.

Beecher, William. "Soviet Criticism on Arms Dismays Top U.S. Aides," *The New York Times.* March 9, 1970.

Beecher, William. "Soviet Reported Stressing Multiple Warhead Missile," *The New York Times.* September 10, 1967.

Beecher, William. "The Antimissile Issue," *The New York Times.* November 11, 1966.

Beecher, William. "U.S. Studying Missile Defense for Western Europe and Japan," *The New York Times.* November 27, 1966.

Bell, Jack. "Revision of ABM Studied," *Washington Post.* July 14, 1969.

Bethe, Hans; Garwin, Richard L. "Anti-Ballistic-Missile Systems," *Scientific American.* Vol. 218, No. 3, 1968.

Betts, Austin W. "Stop That Missile," *Ordnance.* November-December 1960.

Binzen, Peter. "Colleges and War: Can Secret Research Be Justified in the National Interest?" *Philadelphia Sunday Bulletin.* Section 2. May 28, 1967.

Boehm, George. "Countdown for Nike-X," *Fortune.* November 1965.

Brandon, Henry. "A New Missile Race?" *Saturday Review.* January 28, 1967.

Chapman, Williams. "McCarthy Asks A-Freeze," *Washington Post.* July 11, 1968.

"Chinese Nuclear Threat Pushes Studies of Nike-X Options," *Missiles and Rockets.* May 31, 1965.

Coates, G. P. "ICBM's and Military Satellites—What Defense Is Possible?" *The Aeroplane and Astronautics.* October 12, 1961.

"Compromise on the Sentinel," Editorial. *Washington Post.* March 15, 1969.

"Containing ABM," *Commonweal.* May 27, 1966.

"Convair May Get New Pact To Work on New Anti-Missile System," *Wall Street Journal.* January 16, 1959.

Bibliography

Cousins, Norman. "ABM: President Nixon's Vietnam?" *Saturday Review.* March 8, 1969.

Daedalus, whole issue on Arms control, Fall 1960.

"Decision Time Grows Shorter for Nike-X," *Aviation Week and Space Technology.* March 15, 1965.

"Douglas Delivers A-ICBM Study," *Missiles and Rockets.* January 25, 1965.

"Dual Missile Defense Predicted," *Aviation Week and Space Technology.* March 31, 1958.

Dulberger, Leon. "Strategic Missile and Air Defense," *Space/Aeronautics.* September 1966.

Dyson, Freeman. "A Case for Missile Defense," *Bulletin of the Atomic Scientists.* April 1969.

Dyson, Freeman J. "Defense Against Ballistic Missiles," *Bulletin of the Atomic Scientists.* June 1964.

"Eisenhower Doubts 'Thin' Missile Plan Can Be Successful," *The New York Times.* January 16, 1968.

"Experts Disagree on Missile 'Role'," *The New York Times.* November 15, 1967.

Fink, Daniel J. "Strategic Warfare," *Science and Technology.* October 1968.

Finney, John W. "ABM Foes Set Back as Prouty Shifts To Support Nixon," *The New York Times.* July 15, 1969.

Finney, John W. "Army Aides Warn on Anti-ICBM Race," *The New York Times.* February 18, 1961.

Finney, John W. "Clark Urges Presidential Study of Missile Defense," *The New York Times.* July 27, 1967.

Finney, John W. "Compromise Plan Is Adopted by U.S. for Arms Parley," *The New York Times.* November 11, 1969.

Finney, John W. "Congressional Panel May Oppose Nixon if He Pushes for Sentinel Deployment," *The New York Times.* February 16, 1969.

Finney, John W. "Dispute on Soviet Missiles Hampers U.S. Arms Stand," *The New York Times.* January 1, 1970.

Finney, John W., "Halt of Sentinel Is Traced to a 10-Month Old Memo," *The New York Times.* February 9, 1969.

Finney, John W. "Johnson Backed on Missile Pact," *The New York Times.* January 18, 1967.

Finney, John W. "Kennedy Sponsored Study of ABM Upsets Pentagon," *The New York Times.* May 7, 1969.

Finney, John W. "Nike-Zeus Intercepts a Missile Fired from U.S. over Pacific," *The New York Times.* July 20, 1962.

Finney, John W. "Nixon Panel Asks Moratorium Now in Missiles Race," *The New York Times*. April 8, 1970.

Finney, John W. "Nixon Sets Goal of Broad Accord on Nuclear Arms," *The New York Times*. April 17, 1970.

Finney, John W. "Politics of ABM: A Tough Struggle that Cuts Across Party Lines," *The New York Times*. July 18, 1969.

Finney, John W. "President Warns of 'Futile' Step-Up in Nuclear Race," *The New York Times*. February 18, 1967.

Finney, John W. "Rusk Seeks Curb in Missiles Race," *The New York Times*. December 22, 1966.

Finney, John W. "Rusk Urges Speed on Missile Freeze," *The New York Times*. September 9, 1967.

Finney, John W. "Secret ABM Data Heard by Senate in Closed Session," *The New York Times*. July 18, 1969.

Finney, John W. "Senate Panel, with Film and Reports, Rests Case Against ABM," *The New York Times*. July 31, 1969.

Finney, John W. "Senators Tell of ABM Telegram from Arms Envoy," *The New York Times*. August 14, 1970.

Finney, John W. "2 Key Democrats Express Doubts on Expanded ABM," *The New York Times*. February 24, 1970.

Finney, John W. "U.S. and Russia Push Arms Talks," *The New York Times*. May 22, 1970.

Finney, John W. "U.S. and Soviet Begin a New Atomic Test Race," *The New York Times*. December 21, 1966.

Finney, John W. "U.S. Says Soviet Shows Interest in Missile Curb," *The New York Times*. January 21, 1967.

Finney, John W. "U.S. Will Suggest Missile Moratorium at Geneva," *The New York Times*. December 20, 1966.

Finney, John W. "White House Weighs Expanding Sentinel Defense," *The New York Times*. November 13, 1967.

Finney, John W. "X-Ray Missile to be Key in Defense Against China," *The New York Times*. November 16, 1967.

"Fiscal 1966 Budget," *New York Times*. January 15, 1965.

Fusca, James. "Future ICBMs Look Unstoppable," *Missiles and Rockets*. March 7, 1960.

"GE Reveals Hermes Missile Milestones," *Aviation Week and Space Technology*. March 8, 1954.

Getler, Michael. "Arms Control and the SS-9," *Space/Aeronautics*. November 1969.

Getler, Michael. "McNamara Says Soviets Err on ABM," *Missiles and Rockets*. May 2, 1966.

Getler, Michael. "Nike-X Deployment Feud Heightening," *Missiles and Rockets*. May 9, 1966.

Getler, Michael. "U.S. Opting for New Low-Cost ABM," *Technology Week*. June 20, 1966.

Gilpatric, Roswell. "Are We on the Brink of Another Arms Race?" *The New York Times Magazine*. January 15, 1967.

Gilpatric, Roswell. "Our Defense Needs," *Foreign Affairs*. April 1964.

Grose, Peter. "Clifford Exempts Missile Defense from Budget Cut," *The New York Times*. September 6, 1968.

Grose, Peter. "U.S. Intelligence Doubts Soviet Has First-Strike Goal," *The New York Times*. June 18, 1969.

Gwertzman, Bernard. "Nixon's ABM Plans Arouse Soviet Press Critics," *The New York Times*. March 28, 1969.

Gwertzman, Bernard. "Pravda Voices Soviet Displeasure with U.S. over Missile Policies and Delay on Arms Control Talks," *The New York Times*. June 11, 1969.

Gwertzman, Bernard. "Soviet Says Its ABM Can 'Reliably Hit' Attacking Missiles," *The New York Times*. February 24, 1970.

Herzfeld, Charles. "BMD and National Security." *Survival*. March 1966.

Hess, John. "NATO Is Studying Antimissile Plan," *The New York Times*. September 20, 1969.

Holahan, J. "What Have We Got to Counter the ICBM Threat?" *Space/Aeronautics*. November 1961.

Hotz, Robert. "A Vital Probe," *Aviation Week and Space Technology*. February 28, 1966.

"How Good Are the Kremlin's Weapons," *The New York Times*. March 1, 1970.

Johnson, Charles. "Ballistic Missile Defense Radars," *IEEE Spectrum*. March 1970.

Kamm, Henry. "Moscow Scores Arms-Talk Foes," *The New York Times*. April 20, 1969.

Keatley, Robert. "Laird Presents Modified ABM Expansion Requesting Only One More Site for Now," *Wall Street Journal*. February 25, 1970.

Kilpatrick, Carroll. "U.S., Russia Plan Talks on Restricting Missiles," *Washington Post*. July 2, 1968.

Klass, Phillip J. "Defense Group Evaluates Zeus Potential," *Aviation Week and Space Technology*. November 2, 1959.

Kraar, L. "Missile Defense," *Wall Street Journal.* March 20, 1959.

Lasby, Clarence G. "Operation Paperclip: German Scientists Come to America," *The Virginia Quarterly Review.* Summer 1966.

Lodge, Henry Cabot. "A Citizen Looks at the ABM," *Reader's Digest.* June 1970.

London, Michael P. "Advanced Strategic Missiles," *Space/Aeronautics.* June 1968.

London, Michael P. "Safeguard, Is There a Choice?" *Space/Aeronautics.* November 1969.

Lowenhar, Herman. "ABM Radars: Myth vs. Realty," *Space/Aeronautics.* November 1969.

Marder, Murray. "Moscow Hardens Kosygin's Remarks," *Washington Post.* June 30, 1967.

Marder, Murray. "Soviets Seen Interested in ABM Accord," *Washington Post.* February 21, 1967.

Margolis, Howard. "U.S. Plans Cheaper, Better Missile System," *Washington Post.* April 14, 1965.

Margolis, Howard. "U.S. Missile Defense Plans Pegged to Chinese Threat," *Washington Post.* May 26, 1965.

"McNamara Assays Anti-Missile Plan," *The New York Times.* May 15, 1965.

"McNamara Interview," *Life.* September 2, 1967.

Miller, Barry. "Studies of Penetration Aids Broadening," *Aviation Week and Space Technology.* October 23, 1967.

"Missile Defense Is Urged by Nixon," *The New York Times.* September 15, 1967.

Moore, Irna. "Coalition Asks ABM Hearing," *Washington Post.* April 22, 1969.

Moss, Norman. "McNamara's ABM Policy: A Failure of Communications," *The Reporter.* February 23, 1967.

Mueller, Marti. "Proposed ABM Sites Protested," *Science.* December 6, 1968.

Murphy, Charles J. V. "Khrushchev's Paper Bear," *Fortune.* December 1964.

"Nike-Zeus May Be Inadequate, Top Defense Scientist Warns," *Aviation Week and Space Technology.* November 10, 1958.

"Operation Gaslight: Anti-Missile Breakthrough," *Missiles and Rockets.* July 14, 1958.

"Opponents Cite ABM Vulnerability to High-Altitude Nuclear Bursts," *Aviation Week and Space Technology.* July 20, 1970.

Pay, Rex. "New Effort Aimed at X-Ray Protection," *Technology Week.* January 2, 1967.

"Peking Accuses U.S. on Antimissile Plan," *The New York Times*. September 22, 1967.

"Pentagon's Urgent Worry: Can U.S. Missiles Survive Russia's 'X-Ray Defenses'?" *U.S. News & World Report*. February 6, 1967.

Phelps, Robert H. "Chinese a Factor in Missile Accord," *The New York Times*. May 19, 1967.

"Plea on Missiles Is Sent to Soviet," *The New York Times*. January 15, 1967.

"Poll Finds Most Uncertain on ABM," *The New York Times*. July 27, 1969.

Rabinowitch, Eugene. "The Editor Comments: Missile Gap and Wheat Gap," *Bulletin of the Atomic Scientists*. February 1967.

Rathjens, G. W. "The Dynamics of the Arms Race," *Scientific American*. Vol. 220. No. 4, 1969.

Rathjens, G. W.; Kistiakowsky, G. B. "The Limitation of Strategic Arms," *Scientific American*. Vol. 222. No. 1, 1970.

Raymond, Jack. "Air Force Urges Joint Chiefs Bar Army Missile Bid," *The New York Times*. November 21, 1957.

Raymond, Jack. "New U.S. Delay Likely in Building Missile Defense," *The New York Times*. December 1, 1965.

Raymond, Jack. "U.S. Says Russians Plan Anti-Missile," *The New York Times*. October 15, 1960.

Raymont, Henry. "ABM Supporters Planning 2 Books," *The New York Times*. July 11, 1969.

Reston, James. "Washington: McNamara and the Anti-Ballistic Missile," *The New York Times*. July 20, 1966.

Reston, James. "Washington: The Anti-Republican Missile," *The New York Times*. September 22, 1967.

Rich, Spencer. "House Approves Funds for ABM," *Washington Post*. August 6, 1969.

Rich, Spencer. "House Unit Rejects Cut in ABM Funds," *Washington Post*. April 17, 1970.

Roberts, Chalmers. "Military Chiefs Oppose Curbs on MIRV, ABM," *Washington Post*. March 27, 1970.

Roberts, Chalmers. "Shape of Arms Pact Emerges, with 50–50 Chance of Accord," *Washington Post*. May 21, 1970.

Roberts, Chalmers. "U.S. Gave Russians Advance ABM Notice," *Washington Post*. September 20, 1967.

"Russians Say Anti-Missile System Will Protect Them from Attack," *The New York Times*. February 21, 1967.

Schmidt, Dana Adams. "Kosygin Is Cool to Missile Curb," *The New York Times*. February 10, 1967.

Schwiebert, Ernest G. "USAF's Ballistic Missiles 1954–64," *Air Force and Space Digest*. May 1964.

Semple, Robert B. "McNamara Hints Soviet Deploys Antimissile Net," *The New York Times*. November 11, 1966.

Semple, Robert B. "Nixon Staff Had Central Role in Missile Decision," *The New York Times*. March 19, 1969.

Semple, Robert B. "White House Reported to Reject ABM Opponent as Science Head," *The New York Times*. April 17, 1969.

"Senator Clark Calls Antimissile System an Expensive Toy," *The New York Times*. October 8, 1967.

"Sentinel and Beyond," *Space/Aeronautics*. September 1968.

Shabad, Theodore. "Russian Reports Solving Rocket Defense Problem," *The New York Times*. October 24, 1961.

Sheehan, Neil. "Industries Linked to an Ad for ABM," *The New York Times*. August 4, 1969.

Sheehan, Neil. "Kennedy Says Pro-ABM Book Is Aided by Pentagon," *The New York Times*. July 8, 1969.

Sheehan, Neil. "Shift of McNamara Brings Speculation of War Policy Shift," *The New York Times*. November 29, 1967.

Smith, Hedrick. "Soviet Would Widen Talks Asked by U.S. on Missiles," *The New York Times*. February 22, 1967.

Smith, Hedrick. "U.S. Makes Offer to Give Up ABM's If Soviet Does So," *The New York Times*. August 17, 1970.

Smith, Terrence. "NATO Unit Orders Atom-Mine Plan," *The New York Times*. September 30, 1967.

"Special Report on Ballistic Missile Defense," *Aviation Week and Space Technology*. October 23, 1967, Whole Issue.

"State Hits Post Story on SALT," *Washington Post*. May 22, 1970.

Stone, Jeremy. "Arms Race or Disarmament," *Bulletin of the Atomic Scientists*. September 1964.

Stone, Jeremy. "Containing The Arms Race," *Bulletin of the Atomic Scientists*. September 1965.

Sullivan, Walter. "Merits of Ballistic Missile Defenses Debated at Science Parley," *The New York Times*. December 27, 1967.

Sullivan, Walter. "Spot Check Urged on Arms Solution," *The New York Times*. January 1, 1962.

Talensky, Nicolai. "Antimissile Systems and Disarmament," *Bulletin of the Atomic Scientists*. February 1965.

"Terminal ICBM Defense," *Aviation Week and Space Technology*. April 10, 1961.

"The Useless Safeguard," Editorial. *The New York Times*. March 15, 1969.

Thurmond, Senator Strom. "The Gap in Ballistic Missile Defense," *Data; The Magazine of Research and Development Management*. June 1963.

Trainor, James. "DOD Says AICBM Is Feasible," *Missiles and Rockets*. December 24, 1962.

Trainor, James. "Missile Site Radar Paces Nike-X," *Missiles and Rockets*. May 25, 1964.

Trainor, James. "Nike-X Fate Keyed to DOD Study," *Missiles and Rockets*. May 18, 1964.

Trainor, James. "Study Aids Case of Nike-X," *Missiles and Rockets*. January 4, 1965.

Trainor, James. "U.S. Missile Defense Plans Pegged to Chinese Threat," *Washington Post*. May 26, 1965.

Trainor, James. "U.S. Plans X-Ray Defense Against Missile Warheads," *The New York Times*. May 10, 1967.

"U.S. Studies Appeal to Soviet for a Halt on Missile Defense," *The New York Times*. December 16, 1966.

Unna, Warren. "Hill Divided on Missile Plan," *Washington Post*. March 15, 1969.

Walz, Jay. "Missile Dispute Erupts in Canada," *The New York Times*. March 20, 1969.

Waring, Gerald. "Canada Won't Join U.S. in ABM System," *Washington Post*. September 23, 1967.

Weaver, Warren. "Nixon Missile Plan Wins in Senate by a 51–50 Vote," *The New York Times*. August 7, 1969.

Welles, Benjamin. "Senate Panel Adds Anti-Missile Funds," *The New York Times*. April 22, 1966.

"White House Debates Whether to Expand ABM in Budget Due in January," *The New York Times*. December 21, 1969.

Wiesner, Jerome B.; York, Herbert F. "National Security and the Nuclear-Test Ban," *Scientific American*. Vol. 211. No. 4, October 1964.

Wilson, George C. "Bell Quitting Missiles; War Protests a Factor," *Washington Post*. May 20, 1970.

Wilson, George C. "Foes Picture ABM Risk to Defended City," *Washington Post*. November 22, 1968.

Wilson, George C. "Joint Chiefs Fear Soviet Technical Coup," *Aviation Week and Space Technology*. February 28, 1966.

Wilson, George C. "President, Dr. Bethe, Differ Over Usefulness of Anti-Missile Missile," *Aviation Week and Space Technology*. February 19, 1962.

Wilson, George C. "Public Hearing Is Set on ABM Site," *Washington Post*. December 17, 1968.

Wilson, George C. "Russians Slow Work on Anti-Missile Sites," *Washington Post*. August 11, 1968.

Winston, Donald C. "U.S. May Revise Timing on ABM," *Aviation Week and Space Technology*. May 15, 1967.

York, Herbert F. "ABM, MIRV, and the Arms Race," *Science*. Vol. 169. No. 3942, July 17, 1970.

York, Herbert F. "Military Technology and National Security," *Scientific American*. Vol. 221. No. 2, 1969.

Books

Anti-Ballistic Missile: Yes or No. A Special Report from the Center for the Study of Democratic Institutions. New York: Hill and Wang, 1968.

Bar-Zohar, Michael. *The Hunt for German Scientists*. New York: Hawthorne, 1967.

Brennan, Donald (ed.). *Arms Control, Disarmament and National Security*. New York: George Braziller, 1961.

Brodie, Bernard. *Strategy in the Missile Age*. Princeton: Princeton University Press, 1959.

Brodie, Bernard. *The Absolute Weapon*. New York: Harcourt Brace, 1946.

Bush, Vannevar. *Modern Arms and Free Men*. New York: Simon and Schuster, 1949.

Chayes, Abram; Wiesner, Jerome. *ABM: An Evaluation of the Decision to Deploy an Antiballistic Missile System*. New York: Signet, 1969.

Dougherty, James and Lehman, John. *Arms Control for the Late Sixties*. Princeton: Van Nostrand, 1967.

Gantz, Kenneth F. *The United States Air Force Report on the Ballistic Missile*. New York: Doubleday, 1958.

Gatland, Kenneth. *Development of the Guided Missile*. New York: Philosophical Library, 1952.

Gilpin, Robert. *American Scientists and Nuclear Weapons Policy*. Princeton: Princeton University Press, 1961.

Goudsmit, Samuel. *ALSOS*. New York: Henry Schuman, Inc., 1947.

Goulding, Phil G. *Confirm or Deny*. New York: Harper & Row, 1970.

Holst, Johan; Schneider, William. *Why ABM: Policy Issues in the Missile Defense Controversy*. New York: Pergamon Press, 1969.

Huntington, Samuel. *The Common Defense*. New York: Columbia University Press, 1961.

Irving, David. *The Mare's Nest*. Boston: Little Brown and Co., 1964.

Kintner, William R. (ed.), *SAFEGUARD: Why the ABM Makes Sense*. New York: Hawthorne, 1969.

Klee, Ernst; Meck, Otto. *The Birth of the Missile: The Secrets of Peenemünde*. New York: E. P. Dutton, 1965.

McGovern, James. *Crossbow and Overcast*. New York: Paperback Library, 1964.

Melman, Seymour (ed.). *A Strategy for American Security: An Alternative to the 1964 Military Budget*. Lee Offset, 1964.

Proceedings from Pugwash to the World of Disarmament. McLean, Va.: Sabrepen Syndicate, 1964.

Rotblat, J. *Pugwash—The First Ten Years: History of the Conferences of Science and World Affairs*. New York: Humanities Press, 1969.

Schelling, Thomas C. *Arms and Influence*. New Haven, Conn.: Yale University Press, 1966.

Schelling, Thomas C. *The Strategy of Conflict*. New York: Oxford University Press, 1963.

Schwarz, Urs. *American Strategy: A New Perspective*. New York: Doubleday Anchor, 1967.

Shulman, Marshall D. *Stalin's Foreign Policy Reappraised*. New York: Atheneum, 1965.

Smart, Ian. *Advanced Strategic Missiles: A Short Guide*. Adelphi Paper No. 63. London: Institute for Strategic Studies, December 1969.

Stone, Jeremy. *Containing the Arms Race*. Cambridge: MIT Press, 1966.

Thorin, Duane. *The Pugwash Movement and U.S. Arms Policy*. New York: Monte Cristo Press, 1965.

The War Reports of General Marshall, General Arnold and Admiral King. Philadelphia: J. B. Lippincott Co., 1947.

Wiesner, Jerome. *Where Science and Politics Meet*. New York: McGraw-Hill, 1965.

Wolfe, Thomas W. *Soviet Strategy at the Crossroads*. Cambridge: Harvard University Press, 1964.

York, Herbert. *Race to Oblivion: A Participant's View of the Arms Race.* Simon and Schuster, 1970.

Zaehringer, Alfred. *Soviet Space Technology.* New York: Harper, 1961.

Reports, Papers, Speeches, and Transcripts

Anti-Missile Defense. Washington: Government Data Publications, 1965.

"Arms Control Issue," *Daedalus* (Fall 1960).

Betts, Austin. *Role of Ballistic Missile Defense.* Speech delivered to the Purdue University Chapter of the AIAA. Lafayette, Indiana: April 27, 1965.

The Changing Strategic Military Balance U.S.A. vs U.S.S.R. Prepared for the House Armed Services Committee by the National Strategy Committee of the American Security Council, June 1967.

Clark, Joseph S. *Anti-Ballistic Missiles and the Military Industrial Complex.* Speech Delivered before the United States Senate. Washington: August 1967.

"FAS Statement on Ballistic Missile Defense," *FAS Newsletter.* June 1964.

House Republican Policy Committee. *Statement on the Deployment of an Anti-Ballistic Missile System,* August 9, 1967.

"On an Anti-Ballistic Missile System," *Summary of Discussion at the Ninth Meeting of the European Study Commission,* January 14–15, 1966. London: Institute for Strategic Studies, 1966.

"On Anti-Ballistic Missiles and the Arms Race," A text of the *Statements of the Council for Christian Social Action of the United Church of Christ* at their 1967 Cleveland Convention. New York: Council for Christian Social Action, United Church of Christ, 1967.

Public Opinion and Ballistic Missile Defense: Report of an Exploratory Study. Santa Barbara: General Electric TEMPO, 1964.

Report of the Committee on Arms Control and Disarmament of the National Citizens' Commission prepared for the White House Conference on International Cooperation. New York: United Nations Association of the United States of America, 1966.

Republican National Committee. *The Missile Defense Question: Is LBJ Right?* Washington: February 20, 1967.

Sachs, R. G. *Atomic Explosives for Defensive and Offensive Purposes,* deleted copy, Ballistic Research Laboratory Report No. 590, 1945. Declassified with deletions by the Atomic Energy Commission, August 19, 1958.

"Scientists Group Supports McNamara's Opposition to Anti-Missile Fund Increase," Federation of American Scientists Press Release, May 8, 1966.

Bibliography

"Text of President Johnson's Budget Speech," *The New York Times.* January 15, 1965.

"Text of President Johnson's State of the Union Message," *The New York Times.* January 11, 1967.

"Text of McNamara's Statement to Platform Group," *The New York Times.* August 18, 1964.

"Text of President's Message and an Analysis of Federal Budget of $97.9 Billion," *The New York Times.* January 22, 1964.

"Text of President's Message and an Analysis of Federal Budget of $99.7 Billion," *The New York Times.* January 26, 1965.

"Text of President's News Conference on August 1, 1963," *Washington Post.* August 1, 1963.

"Text of President Nixon's Announcement on Revised Proposals for Sentinel Antiballistic Missile Program," *The New York Times.* March 15, 1969.

Toward New Horizons. A Report submitted to General of the Army H. H. Arnold. Submitted on behalf of the Army Air Force Scientific Advisory Group by Th. von Kármán. December 1945.

"Transcript of Kennedy's News Conference on Foreign and Domestic Affairs," *The New York Times.* February 8, 1962.

"Transcript of the President's News Conference on Foreign and Domestic Affairs," *The New York Times.* November 9, 1961.

"Transcript of the President's News Conference on Foreign and Domestic Affairs," *The New York Times.* April 19, 1969.

"Transcript of the President's News Conference on Foreign and Domestic Matters," *The New York Times.* January 31, 1970.

Wiesner, Jerome. *Comprehensive Arms-Limitation Systems.* Text of a paper prepared for and delivered to the Sixth Pugwash Conference, Moscow, November 29, 1960.

Index

The Absolute Weapon
  See Brodie, Bernard
Air Defense Debate, 10, 18
American Academy of Arts and Sciences Summer Study on Arms Control, 92
American Assembly, 226
Armed Services Committee (Senate)
  Preparedness Subcommittee on Test Ban, 76–77
  Preparedness Subcommittee on Soviet Threat, 184
  dispute with Foreign Relations Committee, 82, 185, 202 fn
  on SAFEGUARD-1969, 215–216
  eliminated area defense component of SAFEGUARD, 228
Arms Control and Disarmament
  U.S. program to UN for General and Complete Disarmament, 49
  Eighteen Nation Disarmament Committee (ENDC), 55, 89, 139–140, 178
  and BMD, 57, 86–89
  informal measures of, 104–106, 170–172, 180
  Moratorium on BMD, 138, 146, 154–155, 159
Arnold, General of the Army H. H.
  on missile defense, 19
ARPA
  See Department of Defense
Assured Destruction, 84–85, 169, 172, 188
Atomic Explosives for Defensive and Offensive Purposes
  See Sachs, R. G.

Baldwin, Hanson
  on Soviet BMD deployment, 87
  says Soviet destroys two ICBM in tests, 49
  on scientist's guilt feelings, 103
Ballistic Missile Defense
  systems and concepts, 3–9
  types of, 4–6
  origins of, 17–20
  early programs leading to, 17–18
  design technology, 18
  nuclear tests for, 18, 79
  future views on, 19–20, 57
  inter-service fight over, 26–29
  control over, 22, 27–28
  arguments against, 27, 100–101
  responsibilities for, 27–28
  given top priority, 28
  and penaids, 29–30

Air Force views on, 32–33
deployment policy on, 34, 230–231, 248–249
and arms control, 49, 86–89
urban (area) defense, 56–57
destabilizing, 57
and Test Ban, 76–82
blackout problem, 77–78, 88
rationale for not deploying, 101–102
effect on Soviets, 114
for allies, 137–138, 179
moratorium, 138
Service Secretaries on, 151–153
summary of effort, 239–247
Beecher, William
  on NIKE-X, 89, 119
Bell Telephone Laboratories, 20 fn
  feasibility study on BMD, 20, 24
Bethe, Hans
  chairs panel on Soviet tests, 50
  on Soviet tests, 50
  on BMD, 50, 55, 194
  opposes BMD, 55
  opposes SENTINEL, 181–182, 185
  on MIRV, 181, 194
  co-Author with Garwin of BMD article, 182
  on SAFEGUARD, 213
Betts, Austin
  questions value of ZEUS, 37
  heads threat analysis, 87
  Purdue University Speech, 121–122
Betts Report, 87–89, 112
BMD Systems
  ABMIS, 3
  ARPAT, 46
  BAMBI, 4, 39, 44
  SABMIS, 159, 188, 204 fn
  PLATO, 18
  Space based-concepts, 38–39
  HELMET, 49 fn
  DUAL ROLE MINUTEMAN, 204 fn
Brennan, Donald
  debates on SENTINEL, 187
  before Gore Subcommittee, 207–208
  at American Physical Society Meeting, 213
Brodie, Bernard
  on missile defense, 19–20
  on dynamics of offense and defense, 20
Brown, Harold
  on decision not to produce ZEUS, 53
  limitation of ZEUS, 53, 65
  BMD and fallout shelters, 65

270

Index

deployment criteria, 86
withhold deployment, 86
on arms control, 87–88
on NIKE-X, 112–113
Bulletin of the Atomic Scientists, 92, 103, 212, 246

Case for BMD Deployment, 118–119, 120–121, 148–151, 206–207
China
  detonates A-bomb, 89
  BMD deployment against, 115–117, 123, 126, 135–137
  detonates H-bomb, 130
Citizens Committee for Peace with Security, 214–215
Civil Defense
  and BMD, 52, 65, 85–86, 110–111
  G.E. Study on BMD and, 117
Clark, Joseph
  leads opposition to NIKE-X, 133–135
  amendment defeated, 135
  debate with Senator Thurmond on BMD, 157
Cohelan, Jeffrey
  opposes NIKE-X, 131–132
  amendment defeated, 133
  opposes SENTINEL, 185
Committee to Maintain a Prudent Defense Policy, 214
Commonweal
  article in opposes BMD, 100
Conclusions, 239–249
Congress
  on Zeus, 47–48
  closed session in Senate on Zeus, 67–82
  opposition to, NIKE-X, 130
  supports BMD, 159–160
  1967 debate in on BMD, 157 fn, 160 fn
  reaction to SENTINEL, 178–179
  reaction to SAFEGUARD, 200
  debates on SAFEGUARD, 217–222
Cousins, Norman, 193
  urges public debate on BMD, 187

Damage Limitation, 84–85, 108–115, 125–126, 146–148
  Studies of, 114–115
DAMP Project, 35
DDR&E
  See Department of Defense
Defense, strategic, 10, 168
  virtual attrition, 84
  McNamara on, 113
  Soviet air defense, 137 fn
Department of Defense
  Reorganization Act of 1958, 23
  Director of Defense Research and Engineering, 23
  Advanced Research Projects Agency (ARPA), 23–24
Deterrence, 1–3, 103–105
  Mutual, 2, 102–105, 108, 113, 168–169
  Stabilization and, 104

DM15X2 (Forerunner of SPARTAN ABM), 115, 119, 145
Drell, Sidney, 219 fn
Dyson, Freeman
  opposes BMD, 95–97
  changes position on BMD, 95 fn

Eighteen Nation Disarmament Committee (ENDC)
  See Arms Control and Disarmament

Fallout Shelters
  See Civil Defense
Federation of American Scientists, 103
  oppose BMD, 35, 94–95
  spokesmen of refute Teller, 157–158
  Kalkstein of calls for Public BMD debate, 187
  opposes SENTINEL, 191
Fisher, Adrian
  on BMD freeze, 139–140
  on SENTINEL at ENDC, 178
Foreign Relations Committee (Senate)
  on Test Ban, 76–78
  dispute with Armed Services Committee, 82, 158, 185, 202 fn
  Disarmament Subcommittee (Gore Committee), 145–146, 158, 193, 219, 226, 228
  on 1970 SAFEGUARD, 227, 230
Foster, John
  on BMD and Test Ban, 78
  on modular NIKE-X, 128
  on area BMD, 158
  on SAM upgrade, 116 fn
  on SAFEGUARD, 203–204, 225
Foster, William
  on BMD feasibility, 82
  on BMD and Test Ban, 82
  on BMD freeze at ENDC, 90

Gaither Committee, 26
Garwin, Richard, 181
  Co-author with Bethe of article on BMD, 182
Gatland, Kenneth
  on missile defense, 20
General Electric TEMPO Study on BMD, 117
Geneva Surprise Attack Conference, 30
Gilpatric, Roswell
  opposes BMD, 93–94
  opposes SENTINEL, 185
Goldberger Panel, 219 fn
The Great BMD Debate-1969, 203–222
Guilt feeling of Scientists, 102–103
  and Pugwash, 102 fn

Hard Point Defense, 56–57
  Wolfgang Panofsky on, 205–207
  SAFEGUARD unsuitable for, 219

Herzfeld, Charles
    case for BMD, 118–119
    reveals attempt to convince Soviets to halt BMD, 171
Holbrook, Richard
    on future offensive threat, 30
Hornig, Donald, 228
House of Representatives
    1966 debate against NIKE-X in, 131–133
    1968 debate on SENTINEL in, 184–185
    1969 debate on SAFEGUARD, 221
    1970 debate on SAFEGUARD, 226–228

ICBM
    phases of flight, 4–6
    development of, 10–12
    destruction of, 8, 49, 51–52, 116–117, 153
    MX-774, 10
    Soviets destroy 2 in tests, 49
Inglis, David
    submits questions about BMD, 186, 189

Jackson, Senator Henry, 47–177
    hearings on Soviet threat, 180
    on unilateral arms control, 180
    introduces letter from Clifford, 183
    opposes area defense component of SAFEGUARD, 224
Johnson, Lyndon
    BMD in Budget Message (1964), 84
    Message to ENDC, 89
    1965 Budget Message and BMD, 108
    seeks BMD halt, 145
    1967 Budget Message and BMD, 146
    on SALT, 183–184
Joint Chiefs of Staff
    on Zeus, 44, 47
    on BMD and Test Ban, 80–81
    favor NIKE-X deployment, 111, 128–129, 184
    favor heavy defense, 199–200

Kennan, George, 223
Kennedy, Edward
    enters SENTINEL debate, 190–191
    letter to Laird, 191
    hires private panel, 192
    attacks Hudson Institute and its BMD book, 217
Killian, James, 194, 202
Kistiakowsky, George, 78, 184–185, 194
Kosygin, Aleksey
    on BMD, 153–154, 159

Laird, Melvin
    testifies on SAFEGUARD, 202–204
    with Richard Helms before Foreign Relations Committee, 215
    1970 SAFEGUARD program 223–225
Lapp, Ralph
    opposes BMD, 158
    opposes SAFEGUARD, 210, 214

Launch-on-Warning, 204 fn
Long, Franklin, 212

Maginot Line, 27 fn
MIRV, 146 fn, 249
McElroy, Neil
    on missile organization, 23
    BMD responsibility, 27–28
    on ZEUS, 26, 29–30
    top priority for BMD, 28
    halts WIZARD, 29
McIntyre, Thomas J., 216
    amendment, 220
McMillan, William
    on SAFEGUARD, 213
McNamara, Robert S.
    oppose ZEUS, 45–46
    on decision-making, 46, 127
    and strategic defense, 52
    on civil defense, 52, 65, 85–86, 127
    on ZEUS, 52–53
    on decision not to deploy ZEUS, 63–66
    on NIKE-X, 66, 85–86, 88, 108–111
    on BMD and Test Ban, 77–79
    inconsistencies in testimony on Test Ban, 79
    assured destruction, 84–85
    damage limitation, 84–85, 108–115, 125–126, 146–148
    rationale for BMD non-deployment, 86–87, 89, 127–128, 130, 147–148, 168–172
    on Soviet BMD, 119, 136–137
    on deployment of NIKE-X, 109–110, 126–127
    SENTINEL decision, 165–172, 179, 181–182
    interview with James Mossman (BBC), 168–169
    interview in LIFE, 179

National Citizen's Commission on International Cooperation
    Report of Committee on Arms Control and Disarmament, 98–99
National Security Council Paper, 68, 10, 12
New Republic, 213
NIKE-X, 56–74, 85–90, 108–161
    description of, 63–64
    missiles for, 64
    radars for, 64
    origin of, 66
    and fallout shelters, 85–86, 110–111
    problems with, 85–86
    improved version (modular), 88, 114, 115, 128
    cost of deploying, 88, 11, 119, 135
    modular approach, 112–113, 115
    enters new phase, 145
NIKE-ZEUS, 22–58
    description of, 24–25
    missile for, 24
    radars for, 24–40

Index

limitations of, 25–53
in development, 25
Air Force opposes, 26–27
deployment decision, 29–30, 34
enters new phase, 39–40
Army defends, 34, 36–37, 44, 46–47, 53–54, 67
case for, 35–36
future of, 51
end of, 54
changes needed in, 55
alternatives to, 55
tested, 55
decision not to deploy, 53, 66
Nitze, Paul, 152, 213
Nixon, Richard
on BMD, 160
on 1970 SAFEGUARD, 222–223
announces SAFEGUARD program, 194, 198–199
Nuclear Test Ban Treaty
BMD and the, 76–82
Nuclear testing, 49
Soviets break moratorium on, 49
and BMD, 49, 51
US resumption of, 49–51
President Kennedy on, 50–51
decision to resume, 51
and BMD development, 18, 79
underground, 138 fn

Offense, the, 8–9, 33, 129
O'Neill Panel Report, 219 fn, 228
Operation Gaslight, 25 fn
Operational Requirements for Guided Missiles, 9
Opposition to BMD, 92–102, 181–182, 206–207
rationale for not deploying BMD, 101–102, 165–172
arguments against BMD, 100–101
in Congress, 130, 184–185, 217–222, 226–228
in Executive Branch, 136
by Senator Clark, 133–135, 157
at Atoms for Peace Awards, 180
at American Association for Advancement of Science, 181
from scientific/academic community, 186–187
organizations, 208–209
at American Physical Society Meeting, 213
Ordnance Technical Committee
establishes NIKE-ZEUS Project, 20
authorizes development of NIKE-ZEUS, 20

Panofsky, Wolfgang, 194, 205–207, 226, 228
PAR (Perimeter Acquisition Radar), 135, 145
Project Defender, 23–24
GLIPAR Program, 38

space based BMD concepts, 38–39
HIBEX, 126
HAPDAR, 126
Project Hermes, 17
Project NIKE, 17
Project Thumper, 17
Pugwash, 40–41, 171

Rabinowitch, Eugene
on mutual deterrence and BMD, 103
urges scientists to prevent use of nuclear weapons, 246
Rathjens, George, 197 fn, 191, 213–214, 226
Raymond, Richard
predicts new BMD, 29
Republican National Committee
Report on BMD, 160
Rogers, William
before Gore Subcommittee, 207
before Foreign Relations Committee, 192
Roles and missions controversy, 22–23, 25–29
Ruina, J. P., 37, 194, 218
Rusk, Dean
on BMD moratorium, 138

Sachs, R. G., 19
SAFEGUARD, 198–231
Nixon announces, 194
purpose of, 198–199
advantages of, 199
reaction to, 199–200
description of, 200
radars for, 200
missiles for, 200
Laird testifies on, 200–201
how decision on was made, 201–202
consultation with Canada, 202
opposition to, 208–210, 212, 216, 218
support for, 214–215, 217
and SALT, 216, 222
public opinion polls on, 218–219
unsuitable for hard point defense, 219
1970 Program, 222–223, 227–230
rationale for, 230–231
SALT (Strategic Arms Limitation Talks)
origins of, 138, 146, 154–155, 159
agreement to initiate, 184
and SAFEGUARD, 216, 222, 230–231
initiation of, 221
Chalmers Roberts on, 227
Schelling, Thomas
on arms control theory, 170
Seitz, Frederick
on SAFEGUARD, 213–214
Semple, Robert, 201–202
Senate
1966 debate on NIKE-X in, 133–135
1967 debate on NIKE-X in, 156–157, 160 fn

1968 debate on SENTINEL in, 182–183, 185
Nelson Amendment, 182–184
Cooper Amendment, 182
Cooper-Hart Amendment, 183, 218, 220, 229–230
Young Amendment, 183
1968 closed session, 185
1969 SAFEGUARD debate in, 217–222
1969 closed session, 218
Smith Amendments, 220–222
McIntyre Amendment, 221
Brooke Amendment, 228
Hughes Amendment, 228
1970 SAFEGUARD debate, 228–230
SENTINEL, 145–194
McNamara Speech on, 161, 165–172
description of, 177
forerunner of area defense, 177, 183
reaction to, 177–178
opposition to, 182, 186–187, 190–191
exempted from budget cuts, 185
public opposition to, 187–190
Clark Clifford on, 188–189
halted, 191
alternatives to, 192
Skifter Committee, 34–35
Smith, Gerard
before Gore Subcommittee, 193, 230
Sprint, 56
Soviet Union
deploys BMD, 38, 69, 79 fn, 81 fn 136–137
threat from, 44
destroys 2 ICBM's in tests, 49
officials on their BMD, 50, 155, 225
arms control talks with, 155–156, 159
Slow down in BMD, 185, 188
SS-9, 180, 210
Stone, Jeremy
opposes BMD, 97–98
Director of Federation of American Scientists, 97
Strategy
See Assured Destruction, Damage Limitation
See also McNamara, Robert S.

Talensky, Nicolai (Soviet General)
case for BMD, 120–121
Tallinn Line, 116 fn, 155–156
Taylor, Maxwell
on ZEUS, 26, 66
on BMD and Test Ban, 80–81
"Teapot" Committee, 12
Teller, Edward
opposes BMD, 40
on BMD and Test Ban, 78
changes views on BMD, 78 fn
says BMD can be developed, 157

Thurmond, Strom
on ZEUS, 47–48, 57–58
requests closed session of Senate, 67–68
on Soviet threat, 69
argues for BMD, 68–69, 74
Triumph
BMD article in, 172 fn
Trudeau, Arthur
defends ZEUS, 36, 54

United Church of Christ
Council for Christian Social Action opposes BMD, 100
Urban Defense, also area defense, 56–57
See also Ballistic missile defense

von Kármán Report, 9–10

Warnke, Paul
on SENTINEL deployment, 179–180
Weapons Development since WWII
American, 9–12
Soviet, 12–13, 11 fn
A-bomb, 10–11
H-bomb, 10–11
Wheeler, Earle
on ZEUS deployment, 67
argues for BMD, 129
case for BMD, 148–151
on deterrence, 169–170
on SAFEGUARD, 203–204
Wiesner, Jerome
opposes BMD, 40–41, 98
Pugwash paper against BMD, 40–41, 92
in article with Dr. York against BMD, 98
on mutual deterrence, 104
opposes SENTINEL, 183–185, 191
opposes SAFEGUARD, 226
co-authors book against SAFEGUARD, 217
on Cold War, 246
Wigner, Eugene, 213
Wilson, Charles
on roles and missions, 22–23
establishes Guided Missile Office, 23
Wizard, 18, 25, 33
halted, 29
Wohlstetter, Albert
attacks Lapp's and Rathjens calculations, 214, 228

X-Rays, 153

York, Herbert, 23
opposes ZEUS, 30, 37
in article with Dr. Wiesner opposes BMD, 98
on BMD, 194
opposes SAFEGUARD, 218, 226

UG
633
A6118

JAN 3 1973